The Responsibility to Protect and the International Criminal Court

This book provides an account of how the responsibility to protect (R2P) and the International Criminal Court (ICC) were applied in Kenya.

In the aftermath of the disputed presidential election on 27 December 2007, Kenya descended into its worst crisis since independence. The 2007–08 post-election crisis in Kenya was among the first cases in which there was an appeal to both the responsibility to protect and a responsibility to prosecute. Despite efforts to ensure compatibility between R2P and the ICC, the two were far from coherent in this case, as the measures designed to protect the population in Kenya undermined the efforts to prosecute perpetrators. This book will highlight how the African Union-sponsored mediation process effectively brought an end to eight weeks of bloodshed, while simultaneously entrenching those involved in orchestrating the violence. Having secured positions of power, politicians bearing responsibility for the violence set out to block prosecutions at both the domestic and international levels, eventually leading to the cases against them unravelling. As this book will reveal, by utilising the machinery of the state as a shield against prosecution, the Government of Kenya reverted to an approach to sovereignty that both R2P and the ICC were specifically designed to counteract.

This book will be of interest to students of the Responsibility to Protect, humanitarian intervention, African politics, war and conflict studies and IR/Security Studies in general.

Serena K. Sharma is a Fellow in Global Politics at the London School of Economics (LSE), UK, and a Senior Fellow of the R2P Global Scholars Network.

Global Politics and the Responsibility to Protect
Series Editors:
Alex J. Bellamy
Griffith University
Sara E. Davies
Griffith University
and
Monica Serrano
The City University of New York

The aim of this book series is to gather the best new thinking about the Responsibility to Protect into a core set of volumes that provides a definitive account of the principle, its implementation, and its role in crises, that reflects a plurality of views and regional perspectives.

Global Politics and the Responsibility to Protect
From words to deeds
Alex J. Bellamy

The Responsibility to Protect
Norms, laws and international politics
Ramesh Thakur

Humanitarian Intervention and the Responsibility to Protect
Security and human rights
Cristina G. Badescu

Sri Lanka and the Responsibility to Protect
Politics, ethnicity, genocide
Damien Kingsbury

International Responsibility and Grave Humanitarian Crises
Collective provision for human security
Hannes Peltonen

Global Justice, Kant and the Responsibility to Protect
A provisional duty
Heather M. Roff

UN Emergency Peace Service and the Responsibility to Protect
Annie Herro

International Organizations and the Implementation of the Responsibility to Protect
The humanitarian crisis in Syria
Edited by Daniel Silander and Don Wallace

Moral Responsibility, Statecraft, and Humanitarian Intervention
The US response to Rwanda, Darfur, and Libya
Cathinka Vik

Reassessing the Responsibility to Protect
Conceptual and operational challenges
Edited by Brett R. O'Bannon

The Responsibility to Protect and the International Criminal Court
Protection and prosecution in Kenya
Serena K. Sharma

The Responsibility to Protect and the International Criminal Court

Protection and prosecution in Kenya

Serena K. Sharma

LONDON AND NEW YORK

First published 2016
by Routledge
2 Park Square, Milton Park, Abingdon, Oxon OX14 4RN

and by Routledge
711 Third Avenue, New York, NY 10017

Routledge is an imprint of the Taylor & Francis Group, an informa business

© 2016 Serena K. Sharma

The right of Serena K. Sharma to be identified as author of this work has been asserted by her in accordance with sections 77 and 78 of the Copyright, Designs and Patents Act 1988.

All rights reserved. No part of this book may be reprinted or reproduced or utilised in any form or by any electronic, mechanical, or other means, now known or hereafter invented, including photocopying and recording, or in any information storage or retrieval system, without permission in writing from the publishers.

Trademark notice: Product or corporate names may be trademarks or registered trademarks, and are used only for identification and explanation without intent to infringe.

British Library Cataloguing-in-Publication Data
A catalogue record for this book is available from the British Library

Library of Congress Cataloging-in-Publication Data
Names: Sharma, Serena K., author.
Title: The responsibility to protect and the International Criminal Court : protection and prosecution in Kenya / Serena K. Sharma.
Description: New York, NY : Routledge, 2016. | Series: Global politics and the responsibility to protect | Includes bibliographical references and index.
Identifiers: LCCN 2015028343| ISBN 9780415507509 (hardback) | ISBN 9781315882130 (ebook)
Subjects: LCSH: International Criminal Court. | Jurisdiction (International law) | Responsibility to protect (International law)–Kenya. | Kenya–Politics and government–2002– | Presidents–Kenya–Election–2007. | Political violence–Kenya–History–21st century. | Impunity–Kenya–History–21st century.
Classification: LCC KZ7312 .S558 2016 | DDC 341.6/7096762–dc23
LC record available at http://lccn.loc.gov/2015028343

ISBN: 978-0-415-50750-9 (hbk)
ISBN: 978-1-315-88213-0 (ebk)

Typeset in Times New Roman
by Wearset Ltd, Boldon, Tyne and Wear

For Rick Parashar, my amazing uncle who I always looked up to. Thank you for teaching me through your extraordinary life that all things are possible. Even though your time here with us felt far too short, the impact you had on our lives was immense. It was truly a gift to have you in our family. You are deeply missed and loved beyond words.

Contents

List of abbreviations   viii

Introduction: the responsibility to protect and prosecute   1

PART I
The responsibility to protect   17

1 Kenya burning: the 2007–08 post-election crisis   19
2 The KNDR process: a model case for R2P?   45

PART II
The responsibility to prosecute   73

3 The government of national impunity   75
4 Kenya and the court of last resort: justice in the hands of the accused   101

Conclusion: from protection *and* prosecution to protection *from* prosecution   127

Bibliography   133
Index   151

Abbreviations

APRM	African Peer Review Mechanism
AU	African Union
CCP	Concerned Citizens for Peace
CIPEV	Commission of Inquiry into Post-Election Violence
CLO	Coordination and Liaison Office
ECK	Electoral Commission of Kenya
EU	European Union
ICC	International Criminal Court
ICISS	International Commission on Intervention and State Sovereignty
IDPs	Internally Displaced Persons
IEBC	Independent Electoral and Boundaries Commission
IGAD	Intergovernmental Authority on Development
IIEC	Interim Independent Electoral Commission of Kenya
IREC	Independent Review Commission
KAM	Kenyan Association of Manufacturers
KANU	Kenyan African National Unity
KEPSA	Kenyan Private Sector Alliance
KHRC	Kenyan Human Rights Commission
KICC	Kenyatta International Conference Centre
KNCHR	Kenyan National Commission for Human Rights
KNDR	Kenyan National Dialogue and Reconciliation
KPTJ	Kenyans for Peace, Truth and Justice
NARC	National Alliance Rainbow Coalition
NATO	North Atlantic Treaty Organisation
NCIC	National Cohesion and Integration Commission
OCHA	Office of the Coordination for Humanitarian Affairs
ODM	Orange Democratic Movement
OHCHR	Office of the High Commissioner for Human Rights
PNU	Party of National Unity
R2P/RtoP	Responsibility to Protect
STK	Special Tribunal for Kenya
TJRC	Truth, Justice and Reconciliation Commission
UN	United Nations

UNDP	United Nations Development Programme
UNDPA	United Nations Department of Political Affairs
UNHCR	United Nations High Commissioner for Refugees
UNICEF	United Nations Children's Fund
WFP	World Food Programme
WPA	Witness Protection Act

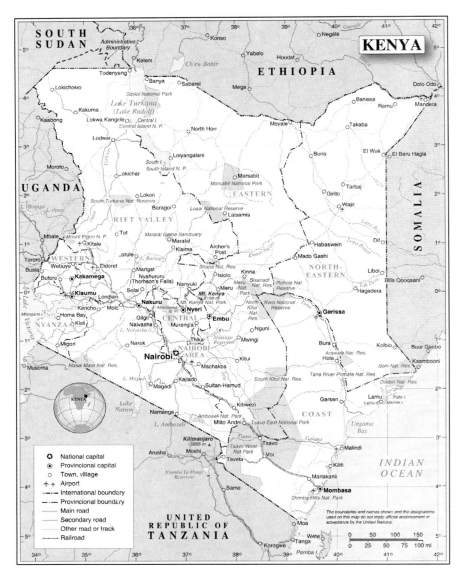

Kenya, Map No. 4187 Rev.3, December 2011, United Nations, www.un.org/Depts/Cartographic/map/profile/kenya.pdf (reproduced with the permission of the United Nations).

Introduction
The responsibility to protect and prosecute

On 30 March 2015 the Kenyan Supreme Court deliberated on a petition contesting the results of the presidential election held on 4 March 2013. In its landmark decision the judicial body upheld the victory of Uhuru Kenyatta, as declared by the Independent Electoral and Boundaries Commission (IEBC).[1] While the verdict was disappointing for Kenyatta's principal opponent in the election, Raila Odinga, the decision to contest the election through the Courts and – most crucially of all – accept its verdict, was a powerful vote of confidence in Kenya's recently reformed judiciary. These circumstances stood in sharp contrast to five years earlier during the disputed presidential election of 2007–08. At that time a lack of faith in Kenya's judiciary meant that challenges to the poll results played out in the streets, leading to widespread violence that swept across the country. With nearly 1200 killed and hundreds of thousands displaced, the 2007–08 post-election violence marked the worst political crisis in Kenya since the country's independence.

In so many ways the 2013 General Election in Kenya can be viewed as a concerted attempt to disassociate from the experience of 2007–08. In the lead-up to the polls, messages of peace flooded the airwaves and television stations across the country. On 24 February, one week prior to the election, the presidential candidates attended a peace prayer at Nairobi's Uhuru Park in what was described as a 'rare show of unity.'[2] Moreover, as part of a broader effort to deter incidences of hate speech and incitement, which were rampant in 2007–08, civil society groups embarked on media monitoring campaigns. On Election Day itself, the national newspapers, *The Daily Nation* and *The Standard,* ran the headlines 'Never Again' and 'Let Peace Prevail.'

In spite of the efforts to consciously break with the past, the shadow of the 2007–08 post-election violence was unmistakably present during the 2013 polls. The candidacy of Uhuru Kenyatta and his running mate, William Ruto, two of the suspected masterminds of the post-election violence, served as a stark reminder that justice had not been prioritised in Kenya's reform effort. In the preceding years, successive attempts to prosecute the perpetrators of the post-election violence had failed. Now that Kenyatta and Ruto had risen to the top two seats in the country, the prospect of delivering justice to the victims of the post-election violence was dealt another significant blow.

2   Introduction

The outcome of the 2013 General Election brought to light some of the challenges and internal contradictions that Kenya faces as it moves beyond the post-election violence. It also raised questions over the effectiveness of two instruments that came to be applied in the context of the crisis. The first is the responsibility to protect (R2P), an international commitment to protect populations from widespread and systemic atrocity crimes, adopted by UN Member States during the 2005 World Summit. The second is the International Criminal Court (ICC), established in 2002 as the world's first permanent Court, tasked with prosecuting perpetrators of the most serious international crimes. Despite arriving on the world stage at roughly similar moments, there are crucial differences between the two. Yet for all their differences, R2P and the ICC are united by a common purpose: reframing the way in which sovereignty is understood in the contemporary international system.

The evolution of R2P and the ICC

The responsibility to protect

The term 'Responsibility to Protect' was first coined by the International Commission on Intervention and State Sovereignty (ICISS) in 2001.[3] Under the sponsorship of the Government of Canada, ICISS was created with the aim of achieving consensus on how and when the international community should take action in emerging or actual crisis situations involving large-scale loss of life. The immediate impetus for the formation of ICISS was NATO's controversial intervention to halt the Serbian Government's campaign of ethnic cleansing against the Albanian population in Kosovo. With Russia and China threatening to veto any proposed military action, NATO resorted to force without the express authorisation of the United Nations Security Council. Notwithstanding NATO's declared humanitarian objectives, having used force in the absence of prior Security Council authorisation called into question the legality of NATO's operation.[4] The controversial intervention in Kosovo raised a host of issues and concerns over how to respond to gross and systematic violations of human rights within another country's borders.[5]

In the aftermath of the conflict, former UN Secretary-General Kofi Annan reflected on the broader consequences of the Security Council's impasse: 'If the collective conscience of humanity ... cannot find in the United Nations its greatest tribune, there is a grave danger that it will look elsewhere for peace and for justice.'[6] Equally problematic, however, were those occasions in which the international community stood by and watched as mass atrocities unfolded. Two of the most egregious examples were the 1994 genocide in Rwanda, which resulted in the slaughter of 800 000 Tutsi and moderate Hutu over a period of 100 days and the 1995 massacre of 8000 Bosniaks in the town of Srebenica during the Bosnian War. With these situations in mind, Annan provocatively posed the following question to UN Member States: 'if humanitarian intervention is, indeed, an unacceptable assault on sovereignty, how should we respond to a Rwanda, to a Srebrenica – to gross and systematic violations of human rights that offend every precept of our common humanity?'[7]

Annan's remarks highlight the challenges associated with humanitarian intervention, both in situations where it *does* occur as well as those occasions in which it *does not*. At the heart of this issue was a deep-seated tension between sovereignty on the one hand – a time honoured principle that had governed interstate relations since the inception of the modern state system – and a demand for action in the face of conscious-shocking human rights violations. It was with this tension foremost in mind that ICISS commenced its deliberations under the Chairmanship of Gareth Evans, former Australian Foreign Minister, and Mohamed Sahnoun, an Algerian diplomat.

After one year of deliberations ICISS produced its path breaking report, *The Responsibility to Protect*.[8] In its report, the Commission reframed the traditional understanding of sovereignty in order to encompass a sovereign's *responsibility* towards the population within its borders. According to the provisions of the report, the primary responsibility for protection resides, first and foremost, with the state itself. In cases where a state is 'unwilling or unable to halt or avert'[9] suffering within its own borders, the Commission agreed that the responsibility to protect must yield to the wider global community.

> Where a population is suffering serious harm, as a result of internal war, insurgency, repression or state failure, and the state in question is unwilling or unable to halt or avert it, the principle of non-intervention yields to the international responsibility to protect.[10]

There are several aspects of the Commission's findings that are noteworthy. While the report incorporated threshold criteria for military intervention, the Commissioners simultaneously endeavoured to distance R2P from the more controversial concept of humanitarian intervention. In so doing, ICISS moved beyond an exclusive focus on military measures by proposing a broadened spectrum of protection responsibilities comprising three distinct elements: the responsibility to prevent; the responsibility to react; and the responsibility to rebuild. Among the three protection responsibilities, prevention was highlighted as 'the single most important dimension of the responsibility to protect.'[11] As the report notes, 'prevention options should always be examined before intervention is contemplated and more commitment and resources must be devoted to it.'[12] Above all, the Commission endeavoured to highlight the conditional nature of sovereignty by emphasising the responsibility towards populations rather than the rights of prospective interveners.

The next crucial milestone in the evolution of R2P took place during the United Nations World Summit in 2005. In paragraphs 138 and 139 of the Outcome Document, UN member states accepted three interlinked responsibilities.[13] First, States accepted their primary responsibility to protect their own populations from genocide, crimes against humanity, war crimes, and ethnic cleansing. Second, they pledged to assist each other in fulfilling their domestic

4 *Introduction*

protection responsibilities. And finally, as members of the international community, they assumed a collective responsibility to take action in a 'timely and decisive manner:'[14]

> we are prepared to take collective action ... through the Security Council, in accordance with the Charter, including Chapter VII, on a case-by-case basis and in cooperation with relevant regional organizations as appropriate, should peaceful means be inadequate and national authorities manifestly fail to protect their populations from genocide, war crimes, ethnic cleansing and crimes against humanity.[15]

While some considered R2P's acceptance by the largest gathering of Heads of State as a 'revolution in consciousness in international affairs,'[16] others took the view that the R2P provisions in the World Summit Outcome Document represented a hollowed version of the ICISS report.[17] There were, indeed, a number of significant shifts from the ICISS Report to the 2005 World Summit's articulation of R2P.[18] First and foremost was the narrowing of R2P's scope. Whereas ICISS framed R2P's application to 'large scale loss of life, actual or apprehended,'[19] the World Summit referred to four specific crimes: genocide; crimes against humanity; war crimes; and ethnic cleansing.[20] This result of the World Summit negotiations was due in large part to a lingering concern among some states – particularly in the aftermath of the 2003 invasion of Iraq – about creating a pretext for intervention by powerful states. This manifested in a desire to transform the trigger for the application of R2P from 'large-scale loss of life'[21] into a more precise threshold. The context for intervention was also significantly raised by the shift from a state being 'unable or unwilling'[22] to protect its populations to a state 'manifestly failing.'[23] A final area in which there was a significant shift relates to the primacy of the UN within the Outcome Document. As paragraph 139 states, action is intended to take place 'through the UN Security Council, in accordance with the Charter.'[24] Some have criticised the primacy of the UN in the Summit Outcome Document, particularly given the recurrent failure of the Council to execute its protection responsibilities. The UNSC deadlock in the face of ongoing suffering in Syria is only the most recent illustration of this tendency.

In his 2009 Report, *Implementing the Responsibility to Protect*, the Secretary-General endeavoured to carry forward the consensus reached in 2005 by drawing upon paragraphs 138 and 139 as the institutional building blocks for developing R2P.[25] Since the publication of the 2009 report there has been a broader acceptance of R2P within the UN system, as witnessed by a number of institutional developments including: the annual General Assembly dialogue on R2P; the development of a joint office on the prevention of genocide and the responsibility to protect; and the appointment of a UN Special Adviser on R2P. Further to this the UN Security Council has demonstrated an increasing willingness to draw on the language of R2P within its resolutions.[26]

In recent years, there has been a deepening of the norm at the national level through the establishment of an Atrocities Prevention Board (APB)[27] in the US.

The new APB, which came into effect in April 2012, has four main functions: to provide a locus of resources, attention, and cross-agency dialogue for responding to situations of mass atrocity; to "give voice" to the executive branch's concern with atrocity issues, when in potential conflict with other competing interests; to serve as a repository for training, doctrine, and contingent planning; and to proactively develop doctrine on atrocity prevention and response, including enhancement of the range of tools (coercive and non-coercive) that the US Government may use to respond to immediate crises or situations of risk. Another notable development alongside the APB has been the creation of 'National Focal Points' for R2P within governments.[28] Focal points are senior officials explicitly earmarked and mandated to enable national efforts to improve mass atrocity prevention and response. The initiative, launched in 2010, seeks to expand the number of these officials and to embed them within a Global Focal Points Network designed to facilitate international cooperation and coordination in pursuit of protection-focused objectives. Civil society has also played a critical role in the advancement of R2P through the emergence of organisations such as the International Coalition for the Responsibility to Protect, the Global Centre for R2P and the Asia-Pacific Centre for R2P.

In addition to these activities there has been an impressive level of academic interest in the topic.[29] R2P is now a subject in its own right.[30] Books have been written, conferences convened, courses taught, and intellectual engagement continues to be fuelled by creative endeavours, such as the Australian Government's Global R2P Fund.[31] These activities are a testament to the fact that R2P has become, and will continue to be, an important field of inquiry in years to come. The vast outpouring of interest in R2P has not, however, been able to dispel some of the criticisms surrounding the principle. For many, R2P continues to be perceived as a synonym for humanitarian intervention, and at worst, a pretext for Western powers to forcibly intervene in other states. These perceptions were inflamed as a consequence of the 2011 intervention in Libya, which was justified on the basis of R2P. The fall-out from Libya has led some to make the claim 'RIP, R2P.'[32] At the same time, there have been some notable developments in the aftermath of the Libyan campaign including the Brazilian proposal of 'Responsibility While Protecting'[33] (RWP), which focuses specifically on addressing the controversies relating to the implementation of the responsibility to protect. The emergence of the RWP concept highlights the resilience and continuity of R2P even in the midst of controversy.

The International Criminal Court

As the responsibility to protect principle was being advanced, an analogous responsibility to prosecute was emerging in the international system. The process by which the International Criminal Court was established had its origins in 1998 during a diplomatic conference held in Rome. On 17 July 1998, the Heads of States that had gathered in Rome adopted a Statute establishing the International Criminal Court by a vote of 120 to 7, with 21 countries abstaining. After having achieved the requisite 60 ratifications, the Rome Statute entered into force on 1 July 2002 – one year after the publication of the ICISS report in 2001.[34] There are four principal organs of the Court: the registry, responsible for the non-judicial administration of the Court; the Judicial Branch, which hears cases brought before the Court; the Office of the President, led by a senior judge overseeing the judicial administration of the Court; and the Office of the Prosecutor, tasked with investigating alleged crimes and initiating proceedings.[35] As of 2015, there were 123 states party to the Rome Statute spread across the world. Of the 123 states, 34 are from the African continent; 19 are in the Asia-Pacific region; 27 are Latin American and Caribbean states; and 43 encompass Western European, Eastern European and other states.[36]

The adoption of the Rome Statute brought into existence the world's first permanent criminal court, responsible for prosecuting the most serious international crimes including, war crimes, genocide, crimes against humanity, and the crime of aggression. According to the provisions of the Statute: 'Acting in an official capacity as a head of state, member of government or parliament or as an elected representative or public official in no way exempts a person from prosecution or criminal responsibility.'[37] Proposals for establishing a permanent international court can be traced to the end of the nineteenth century. However, the momentum to establish a court with supranational jurisdiction continued to rapidly increase throughout the twentieth century, particularly in the aftermath of the Second World War and the consequent efforts to prosecute Nazi war criminals at Nuremberg.[38] Other crucial milestones in the path towards Rome were the ad hoc tribunals for the Former Yugoslavia and the International Criminal Tribunal for Rwanda. However, whereas these previous endeavours focused on post-war retributive justice, the creation of a permanent court opened up the possibility for criminal justice to serve in a preventive capacity. Hence, the preamble to the Rome Statute states the following as one of the key functions of the Court: 'to put an end to impunity for the perpetrators of these crimes and thus to contribute to the *prevention* of such crimes.'[39] According to Sang-Hyun Song, the President of the International Criminal Court, 'the ICC's mere existence is a deterrent to the commission of atrocities around the world.'[40]

While the deterrent function of the ICC seems to make sense intuitively, the capacity of the Court to deter perpetrators has been challenging to prove empirically.[41] Thus far only anecdotal evidence exists to back up the claims of the Court's deterrent function. For instance, the Court has been credited with catalysing national proceedings in the cases of Colombia and Guinea. Domestic proceedings in the former case are thought to have been initiated as a consequence of the Court's preliminary examination in the country,[42] while the latter is viewed as a direct response to a statement by the Chief Prosecutor.[43] Similarly, some have credited the ICC with contributing to Kenya's peaceful election in 2013.[44] Nevertheless, the ICC's deterrent function is severely hampered by the Court's inability to enforce its own decision, as Kurt Mills has observed: 'The fact that the ICC has no ability on its own to arrest suspects further undermines the deterrent prospects, since deterrence would require an expectation that the ICC could quickly and routinely transfer those with arrest warrants against them to The Hague for trial.'[45] Moreover, others contend that those who commit mass atrocity crimes are not necessarily deterred by the threat of criminal proceedings.[46]

The ICC does not have automatic universal jurisdiction, but instead, can only exercise jurisdiction in cases concerning nationals of a state party to the Court or when crimes are committed on the territory of a state party. There are three ways in which the Chief Prosecutor may open an investigation into a situation: first, a case may be referred to the Prosecutor by a state party to the Rome Statute; second, the Prosecutor may seek authorisation from the pre-trial chamber to initiate an investigation at his or her request, referred to as *proprio motu*; finally, a situation may be referred to the Prosecutor by the UN Security Council on the basis of the Council's capacity to determine threats to international peace and security. Alongside the power to refer cases to the Court, under the provisions of the Rome Statute, the Security Council is also equipped with the powers to defer Court proceedings for up to 12 months (with the possibility of indefinite renewal). To date, the Office of the Prosecutor has commenced nine formal investigations, with a further nine preliminary examinations underway. A total of 36 individuals have been indicted by the Pre-trial Chamber, including a number of high level officials such as the late Libyan leader Muammar Gaddafi; Sudanese President, Omar Bashir; and former Ivorian president, Laurent Gbagbo. However, as of 2015, the Court has convicted only two individuals.

The relatively low number of successful ICC convictions to date reflects the enormous set of challenges facing the Court. Perhaps most crucial of all are the limited funds available to the ICC, which hampers the Court's capacity to carry out its work. A related challenge, alluded to above, is the absence of a reliable enforcement mechanism, which means that the Court is utterly reliant on state cooperation.

Alongside the preceding challenges are a host of criticisms that have been directed towards the ICC. For instance, the Court has been accused of protracting conflicts, particularly in situations where an ICC investigation is initiated in the midst of an armed conflict. This criticism is based on the reality that once an investigation commences it cannot be reversed, and therein may create a disincentive to the peaceful resolution of a conflict.[47] A second criticism that has been levelled at the ICC relates specifically to the issue of UN Security Council referrals. The fact that three of the five permanent members of the Security Council are not signatories to the Rome Statute, yet retain the power to refer cases, exposes a deeply troubling double standard that threatens to undermine the legitimacy of the Court.[48] Another frequent criticism of the Court is that it has demonstrated an unfair bias towards prosecuting Africans.[49] In certain situations the narrative of the ICC as a Western court has inadvertently strengthened perpetrators. This was particularly apparent during the 2013 General Election in Kenya, as the accused portrayed themselves as victims of a neo-colonial court in order to consolidate power.

8 *Introduction*

The relationship between R2P and the ICC

Although R2P and the ICC have developed along different trajectories and were motivated by distinct concerns, there is a significant degree of commonality between the two. At their most fundamental level, both are developments of an emerging global human rights architecture, which gained momentum in the immediate aftermath of the Second World War. As Megret argues: 'R2P and the ICC, in their own ways, are part of projects to tame or civilise the power incarnated by sovereignty on the basis of a vigorous cosmopolitan outlook that emphasises the transcendent and universal character of obligations owed to human beings.'[50] Naturally, these shared features have generated considerable interest in the relationship between the R2P and the ICC For instance, as the International Coalition for R2P has noted:

> The ICC and the RtoP norm enjoy a complementary relationship; they work together towards the prevention of crimes against humanity, war crimes and genocide.... Together these components of international law and international relations produce a comprehensive foundation of deterrence and justice, and provide a basis upon which RtoP can realize the transition from concept to practice.[51]

The prospect of a complementary relationship between R2P and the ICC has also been advanced by the Responsibility to Protect Working Group:

> Individual accountability matters for reasons of justice, but it also reduces the likelihood that an aggrieved party will seek to hold its persecutors collectively responsible, thus inviting a new round of violence.... The existence of such a system at the national and international levels is central to achieving the goals of R2P.[52]

Since its inception in 2001, the principle of the responsibility to protect took notice of an associated responsibility to prosecute. Within the ICISS report, references to the ICC first appear in a chapter dedicated to responsibility to prevent. The threat of prosecution 'will concentrate the minds of potential perpetrators of crimes against humanity on the risks they run of international retribution.'[53] The chapter also highlights universal jurisdiction for international crimes, which 'void the sovereign immunity of government leaders for crimes against humanity committed while they were in office.'[54] A further reference to the role of prosecutions can be seen in the responsibility to rebuild section. Here the report highlights the need for justice and reconciliation following an intervention, noting the requirement to bring violators to justice, and the importance of making transitional arrangements where there is no functioning system.

The scope for mutual reinforcement between R2P and the ICC became even more pronounced following the ratification of the Rome Statute in 2002. For instance, the 2005 World Summit Outcome Document drew specifically on the provisions of the Rome Statute. Whether this move was fortuitous or by design, the threshold for intervention shifted from 'large scale loss of life' to four specific international crimes – genocide, ethnic cleansing, war crimes and crimes against humanity – the same crimes referred to in the Rome Statute.[55] While narrowing the applicability of R2P may have been influenced by the desire to elevate the threshold for intervention, recasting R2P through the lens of international crimes added greater specificity to the circumstances in which R2P applied, and enhanced its normative pull. As the Secretary-General has noted: 'It is significant that these well-established international crimes and the obligation to punish their perpetrators are reflected in the provisions of the Rome Statute of the International Criminal Court.'[56]

The areas of convergence continued to manifest in the next crucial phase of R2P's development. In the Secretary-General's 2009 report, *Implementing the Responsibility to Protect,* the links between the responsibility to protect and prosecute were explicitly highlighted in a number of sections. First was the acknowledgment of a joint crimes lens: 'It is now well established in international law and practice that sovereignty does not bestow impunity on those who organise, incite or commit crimes relating to the responsibility to protect.'[57] The emphasis on international crimes is reiterated in other sections of the report:

> Focusing on individuals who commit or incite such egregious acts, including the leaders of States or armed groups, the Rome Statute seeks to develop mechanisms and processes for identifying, investigating and prosecuting those most directly responsible for crimes and violations relating to the responsibility to protect, among others.[58]

The Secretary-General then urged member states to ratify the provisions of the Rome Statute. Most notable was the language used in paragraph 18:

> By seeking to end impunity, the International Criminal Court and the United Nations-assisted tribunals have added an *essential tool for implementing the responsibility to protect*, one that is already reinforcing efforts at dissuasion and deterrence.[59]

Beyond the sections of the report that explicitly highlight the linkages between the responsibility to protect and the responsibility to prosecute, as Martin Mennecke[60] has observed, the Secretary-General also drew upon a triggering mechanism for R2P that mirrored the structure of the Rome Statute. Acting on the principle of complementarity, the Rome Statute first recognises the primary responsibility of national jurisdictions to prosecute. Further to this, the Rome Statute then highlights a role for assisting states in their capacity to prosecute. Only as a last resort, if a state is either 'unable or unwilling' to initiate prosecutions, does the ICC become involved. A similar three-pillared framework is delineated in the 2009 Secretary-General's report. According to the report, the protection responsibilities associated with R2P are as follows: Pillar I encompasses the primary responsibility of states to protect their own population from genocide, crimes against humanity, war crimes, and ethnic cleansing (collectively referred to as 'atrocity crimes'). On the basis of Pillar II, states shall assist each other in fulfilling their domestic protection responsibilities. And finally, Pillar III, as members of the international community, there is a collective responsibility to react, in a timely and decisive manner, if any State were 'manifestly failing' to protect its population from atrocity crimes.[61]

What is perhaps most striking about the Secretary-General's 2009 report is the reference to the ICC serving as a tool for R2P. Gareth Evans similarly perceives the ICC 'as a relevant form of *leverage* that we ignore at a cost if we don't *use* that leverage to the fullest effect.'[62] Yet it has not only been supporters of the responsibility to protect that refer to the ICC as a tool for R2P. In 2012, the Chief Prosecutor of the ICC also advocated a connection between the Court and the principle of R2P by referring to the former as a critical tool for implementing the latter.[63]

While some encourage a close connection between R2P and the ICC, others caution against this approach. Mills has sketched out the different ways of conceiving the relationship between R2P and the ICC: 'They can be invoked individually or used together. They can be sequenced or implemented simultaneously. They might be mutually supportive, or they might undermine each other.'[64] As debates continue over how best to render the relationship between R2P and the ICC, there are still relatively few examples where both have been applied. The post-election crisis in Kenya was among the first situations in which there was an appeal to both the responsibility to protect and a responsibility to prosecute, and therefore warrants closer examination.

R2P and the ICC in Kenya

For the nascent principle of R2P and the recently established International Criminal Court, the post-election violence in Kenya seemed to be exactly the type of situation that each instrument was designed to address. From the perspective of the responsibility to protect, the crisis coincided with the appointment of Edward Luck as the first UN Special Adviser on R2P. Luck's mandate was to build consensus on R2P following the 2005 World Summit and contribute towards the conceptual and operational implementation of the norm. As the situation in Kenya worsened, a decision was made by Luck, with the full support of the Secretary-General and the other organs of the UN system, to view the situation through the prism of R2P. Unlike previous situations in which atrocity crimes were imminent or ongoing, the post-election violence in Kenya was a case where there was sufficient political will to act in a timely and decisive manner. Engaging the parties through a consensual mediation process emphasised that atrocities could be forestalled without having to resort to military force. Following the agreements that were reached through the Kenyan National Dialogue and Reconciliation (KNDR) process in 2008, the response to the crisis in Kenya was deemed a case of best practice:

As demonstrated by the successful bilateral, regional and global efforts to avoid further bloodshed in early 2008 following the disputed election in Kenya, if the international community acts early enough, the choice need not be a stark one between doing nothing or using force.[65]

To this day, the response to the post-election crisis in Kenya continues to be regarded as a success story for R2P and a model case for atrocity prevention in other contexts.

From the perspective of the ICC, the situation in Kenya appeared to offer an ideal set of circumstances in which to commence investigations. For one, the search for accountability in Kenya enjoyed widespread domestic support and, therefore, added a degree of legitimacy to the Court's actions. Second, given that the cases were initiated in the aftermath of the post-election violence, the situation in Kenya was unlikely to generate debates over the relative merits of peace versus justice. Third, the cases in Kenya were initiated through the Chief Prosecutor's *proprio motu* powers, rather than a controversial referral from the UN Security Council. Fourth, when the cases were initiated, the Prosecutor made a point of investigating both of the sides involved in the post-election violence, avoiding the frequent criticism of the Court pursuing one-sided justice. Most crucial of all, the ICC cases in Kenya benefited from following in the footsteps of a mediation process that had been widely assessed in a positive light.

Apart from presenting an ideal set of circumstances for both the responsibility to protect and the responsibility to prosecute, the situation in Kenya seemed to be a case where R2P and the ICC could be genuinely complementary. The prospects for mutual reinforcement among R2P and the ICC was enhanced by the fact that the mediation roadmap incorporated provisions for addressing the underlying causes of violence, including measures to combat the long-standing culture of impunity in Kenya. As Kofi Annan stated at the outset of the negotiations: 'We cannot accept that this sort of incident takes place every five years or so and no one is held to account ... or else we will be back here again after three or four years.'[66] As such, the prosecution of perpetrators was as an integral component of the broader R2P effort in Kenya. Moreover, when it came to initiating international prosecutions, it was Kofi Annan that was tasked with determining at what stage to involve the ICC. This added a further degree of consistency between the responsibility to protect and prosecute.

Notwithstanding the prospect for mutual reinforcement between the responsibility to protect and the responsibility to prosecute, the application of R2P and the ICC was far from coherent in this case. As this book will argue, the measures designed to protect the population in Kenya appear to have undermined the efforts to prosecute perpetrators. For instance, while the internationally–sponsored mediation process brought an end to the eight weeks of bloodshed, it simultaneously entrenched those involved in orchestrating the violence. Having secured positions of power, politicians bearing responsibility for the violence set out to block prosecutions (at both the domestic and international levels), eventually leading to the cases against them unravelling. In this respect, the situation in

12 *Introduction*

Kenya – widely regarded as a model case study for R2P – has culminated in a reversion to the use of sovereignty as a shield, which is ironically the approach to sovereignty that R2P was designed to counteract. Not only does this challenge the commonly held perception of the Kenyan case as a success story for R2P, it also illuminates some prospective tensions between the responsibility to protect and the responsibility to prosecute.

The Responsibility to Protect and the International Criminal Court: Protection and Prosecution in Kenya will explore how R2P and the ICC came to be applied in Kenya and the broader lessons that can be derived from this case. The book will be divided into two parts. Part I will examine the post-election violence and the subsequent application of the responsibility to protect. Part II will consider the efforts to apply the responsibility to prosecute in Kenya.

Outline of the book

The immediate trigger for the violence that erupted across Kenya in 2007–08 was the disputed presidential election of 27 December 2007. Chapter 1, 'Kenya burning: The 2007–08 post-election crisis,' will trace the events surrounding the election and the crisis that followed thereafter. Four distinct patterns of violence were identified during this period, leading to the deaths of approximately 1200 Kenyans and displacement levels reaching hundreds of thousands. The impact of the crisis reverberated far beyond Kenya's borders, highlighting both the vulnerability of its neighbours as well as the strategic importance of Kenya for the broader stability of the region. Although the General Election was the immediate trigger for the ensuing violence, the actual causes of the crisis were much broader and deeply rooted in a set of structural conditions that made the country particularly prone to electoral violence. While these factors had erupted into bloodshed during previous elections, the scale of violence seen in the aftermath of the 2007 General Election caught most observers off guard.

Chapter 2, 'The KNDR process: A model case for R2P?' will consider the extent to which the response to this crisis can be considered a model for future R2P situations. In contrast to previous episodes of electoral violence in Kenya's history, the 2007–08 crisis captured the gaze of concerned international actors. Following a number of failed attempts to resolve the crisis, the African Union appointed a mediation team under the leadership of former UN Secretary-General Kofi Annan. After 41 days of intense negotiations, Mwai Kibaki and Raila Odinga agreed to share power within a Grand Coalition Government. The agreement establishing the Government of National Unity effectively averted the country's descent into civil war. Shortly thereafter, commentators began to refer to the Kenyan experience as a successful illustration of atrocity prevention under the banner of R2P. As this chapter will argue, the swift designation of Kenya as a model for atrocity prevention efforts was slightly premature. Alongside the resolution of the political crisis, the mediation Agenda advocated a set of reforms, which were intended to remove the underlying causes of the violence.

Friction among the principals, and internal disputes between their respective parties, severely compromised the capacity of the Coalition Government to deliver the reforms agreed to in 2008. Chapter 3, 'The government of national impunity,' will assess the performance of the Coalition in fulfilling the Agenda items agreed to during the Kenyan National Dialogue and Reconciliation process. One exception to the otherwise dismal performance of the Government was in the area of constitutional reform. In 2010, the principals came together to support the adoption of a new Constitution, which was approved by an overwhelming majority of Kenyans during the 4 August 2010 referendum. By contrast, there was virtually no progress made on addressing the problem of impunity in Kenya. As part of the 2008 Agreement, a Commission of Inquiry (CIPEV) was mandated to investigate criminal acts committed during the post-election violence. Upon completing its work, CIPEV called on the Government to establish a Special Tribunal, which would prosecute suspected perpetrators of the violence. Three separate attempts were made to establish a Tribunal; however, forces inside the Government conspired to ensure that these efforts failed. The lack of progress in holding suspected perpetrators accountable through a domestic tribunal eventually prompted the involvement of the International Criminal Court.

Despite its rhetorical commitment to cooperate with the Court, the Government of Kenya embarked on a campaign to thwart the ICC's efforts. Chapter 4, 'Kenya and the court of last resort: Justice in the hands of the accused,' will explore the ICC cases in Kenya. Alongside attempts to pull out of the Rome Statute and the initiation of an admissibility challenge against the Court, the Government engaged in intense lobbying to have the cases deferred. In so doing, the Government argued that the ongoing cases risked destabilising the country in the run-up to the 2013 General Election. Nevertheless, the ICC factor was actually viewed as a stabilizing influence during the election, which arguably deterred incidences of hate speech and acts of violence. At the same time, there were a number of unintended consequences associated with the ICC's involvement in Kenya, most notably the 'alliance of the accused' it prompted between Uhuru Kenyatta and his running mate, William Ruto. In the aftermath of the 2013 Election, the Government of Kenya – which was now synonymous with the accused – continued to block the efforts of the Court with a new sense of urgency.

The failure to provide accountability for the crimes committed during the post-election violence significantly limits the effectiveness of Kenya's broader reform process. As the concluding chapter will argue, what is particularly striking is the manner in which impunity has been perpetuated in Kenya. The principle of R2P was developed to ensure that sovereignty could no longer serve as a shield for the commission of atrocities. By utilising the machinery of the state to shield itself from prosecution, the Government of Kenya reverted to a traditional understanding of sovereignty that R2P was specifically designed to counteract. Hence, although the Kenyan case commenced with the intention of delivering both protection and prosecution, it swiftly developed into the opposite – protection *from* prosecution for the suspected perpetrators.

Notes

1. 'Uhuru Kenyatta's election victory upheld by Supreme Court', *Guardian*, 30 March 2013, available online at www.theguardian.com/world/2013/mar/31/kenya-court-upholds-kenyatta-victory (accessed 20 May 2015).
2. 'Kenyans Unite for Peace Prayers' *All Africa*, 24 February 2013, available online at http://allafrica.com/view/group/main/main/id/00023074.html (accessed 20 June 2015).
3. *The Responsibility to Protect*, Report of the International Commission on Intervention and State Sovereignty (Ottawa: International Development Research Centre, 2001).
4. See The Independent International Commission on Kosovo, *The Kosovo Report: Conflict, International Response, Lessons Learned* (Oxford University Press, 2001).
5. Jennifer Welsh (ed.), *Humanitarian Intervention and International Relations* (Oxford University Press, 2006); Nicholas J. Wheeler, *Saving Strangers* (Oxford University Press, 2000); Deen K. Chatterjee and Don E. Scheid (eds), *Ethics and Foreign Intervention* (Cambridge University Press, 2003).
6. Cited in *The Responsibility to Protect*, p. 2.
7. Ibid.
8. Ibid.
9. Ibid., p. xi.
10. Ibid.
11. Ibid.
12. Ibid.
13. United Nations General Assembly, '2005 World Summit Outcome', A/60/L.1, 20 September 2005, paragraphs 138 and 139.
14. Ibid.
15. Ibid.
16. Todd Lindberg, 'Protect the People', *Washington Times*, 26 September 2005, available online at www.washingtontimes.com/news/2005/sep/26/20050926-092835-2083r/ (accessed 20 May 2015).
17. Michael Byers, 'High Ground Lost on UN's Responsibility to Protect', *Winnipeg Free Press*, 18 September 2005, available online at www.ligi.ubc.ca/?p2=/modules/liu/news/view.jsp&id=142 (accessed 20 May 2015).
18. For an overview of the diplomacy leading to the endorsement of R2P in 2005, see Alex J. Bellamy, *Global Politics and the Responsibility to Protect* (Routledge, 2011).
19. *The Responsibility to Protect*, p. xii.
20. For further discussion of the impact of the framing of R2P in terms of crimes, see Jennifer M. Welsh, 'Responsibility to protect and the language of crimes: collective action and individual culpability', in Don Scheid (ed.), *Armed Humanitarian Intervention* (Cambridge: Cambridge University Press, 2014).
21. *The Responsibility to Protect*, p. xii.
22. Ibid., p. xi.
23. '2005 World Summit Outcome.'
24. Ibid.
25. *Implementing the Responsibility to Protect; Report of the Secretary-General*, UN doc. A/63/677, 12 January 2009.
26. Global Centre for the Responsibility to Protect, 'UN Security Council Resolutions Referencing R2P', 23 April 2013, available online at www.globalr2p.org/resources/335 (accessed 20 June 2015).
27. The White House, Office of the Press Secretary, 'Fact Sheet: A Comprehensive Strategy and New Tools to Prevent and Respond to Atrocities', 23 April 2012, available online at www.whitehouse.gov/the-press-office/2012/04/23/fact-sheet-comprehensive-strategy-and-new-tools-prevent-and-respond-atro (accessed 20 June 2015).
28. Global Centre for the Responsibility to Protect, 'Our Work: R2P Focal Points', available online at www.globalr2p.org/our_work/r2p_focal_points (accessed 20 June 2015).

29 In recent years R2P has become firmly established as an academic field in its own right, aided in no small measure by the establishment of the journal *Global Responsibility to Protect*, and the development of the Routledge book series, *Global Politics and the Responsibility to Protect*.

30 Two seminal studies on the historical development of R2P stand out: Alex Bellamy's *The Responsibility to Protect* (Polity Press, 2009) and Gareth Evans' *The Responsibility to Protect: Ending Mass Atrocity Crimes Once and For All* (Brookings Institution, 2009). There have also been a number of edited volumes on the subject of R2P, including: Richard H. Cooper and Juliette Voïnov Kohler (eds), *Responsibility to Protect: The Global Moral Compact for the 21st Century* (Palgrave, 2008), Andy Knight and Frazer Egerton, *Routledge Handbook of the Responsibility to Protect* (Routledge, 2012), and Jared Genser and Irwin Cotler, *The Responsibility to Protect: The Promise of Stopping Mass Atrocities in Our Time* (Oxford University Press, 2011). Supplementing these works are more specialised monographs on various aspects of R2P, such as Alex Bellamy, Sara Davies, and Luke Glanville (eds), The *Responsibility to Protect and International Law* (Martinus Nijhoff/Brill, 2011) as well as more critical analyses of R2P and its potential impact on international relations, such as James Pattison, *Humanitarian Intervention and the Responsibility to Protect: Who Should Intervene?* (Oxford University Press, 2010), Anne Orford, *International Authority and the Responsibility to Protect* (Cambridge University Press, 2011), and Aidan Hehir, *The Responsibility to Protect: Rhetoric, Reality and the Future of Humanitarian Intervention* (Palgrave Macmillan, 2011).

31 Asia Pacific Centre for the Responsibility to Protect, 'Research in Focus in 2012', available online at www.r2pasiapacific.org/docs/R2P%20Fund/Research%20in%20Focus%20Booklet%202012.pdf (accessed 20 June 2015).

32 David Rieff, 'R2P, R.I.P', *New York Times*, 7 November 2011.

33 See the Brazilian concept note on 'Responsibility While Protecting', dated 9 November 2011 from the Permanent Representative of Brazil to the United Nations addressed to the Secretary-General. UN Doc. A/66/551-S/2011/701, 11 November 2011.

34 Rome Statute of the International Criminal Court, A/CONF.183/9 of 17 July 1998. The Statute entered into force on 1 July 2002.

35 Fatou Bensouda of Gambia, the current Chief Prosecutor, succeeded Luis Moreno Ocampo of Argentina, who had served as the first Chief Prosecutor from 2003–12.

36 International Criminal Court, 'State Parties to the Rome Statute', available online at www.icc-cpi.int/en_menus/asp/states%20parties/Pages/the%20states%20parties%20to%20the%20rome%20statute.aspx (accessed 20 May 2015).

37 See 'The ICC at a Glance', available online at www.icc-cpi.int/iccdocs/PIDS/publications/ICCAtAGlanceEng.pdf (accessed 20 May 2015).

38 See Antonio Cassese, *International Criminal Law*, 3rd edn (Oxford University Press, 2013); William Schabas, *Introduction to the International Criminal Court*, 4th edn (Cambridge University Press, 2011).

39 Rome Statute of the International Criminal Court, A/CONF.183/9 of 17 July 1998. The Statute entered into force on 1 July 2002.

40 Preamble to the Rome Statute.

41 Cited in Dan Saxon, 'The International Criminal Court and the Prevention of Crimes' in Serena K. Sharma and Jennifer M. Welsh (eds), *The Responsibility to Prevent: Overcoming the Challenges of Atrocity Prevention* (Oxford University Press, 2015), pp. 119–59.

42 Kirsten Ainley, 'The Responsibility to Protect and the International Criminal Court', *International Affairs*, 19.1 (2015), pp. 37–54.

43 Naomi Kikoler, ''Guinea: An Overlooked Case of the Responsibility to Prevent in Practice', in Serena K. Sharma and Jennifer M. Welsh (eds), *The Responsibility to Prevent: Overcoming the Challenges of Atrocity Prevention* (Oxford University Press, 2015), pp. 304–23.

44 Njoki Wamai, 'The International Criminal Court and the Kenyan Election', *The Huffington Post*, 7 May 2013, available online at www.huffingtonpost.co.uk/gates-cambridge-scholars/kenya-election_b_3206562.html (accessed 20 June 2015).
45 Kurt Mills, 'The Responsibility to Protect and the International Criminal Court: Competing or Complementary' *AP R2P Brief* 4.2 (2014), p. 4, available online at www.r2pasiapacific.org/docs/R2P%20Ideas%20in%20Brief/R2P%20and%20the%20ICC%20Vol%204%20No%202%202014.pdf (accessed 20 May 2015).
46 Mark Drumbl, *Atrocity, Punishment and International Law* (Cambridge University Press, 2007).
47 See, for example, Adam M. Smith, 'The Emergence of International Justice as Coercive Diplomacy: Challenges and Prospects', *HRP Research Working Paper Series* (Cambridge, MA: Harvard Law School, 2012); Jack Snyder and Leslie Vinjamuri, 'Trials and Errors: Principle and Pragmatism in Strategies of International Justice', *International Security*, 8, 3 (2003/4), pp. 5–44.
48 Louise Arbour, Address to the Stanley Foundation Conference on the Responsibility to Protect, New York, 18 January 2012, available online at www.r2p10.org (accessed 20 June 2013).
49 'African Leaders Accuse ICC of "Race Hunt"', *Al Jazeera*, 28 May 2013, available online at www.aljazeera.com/news/africa/2013/05/201352722331270466.html (accessed 20 June 2015).
50 Frederic Megret, 'ICC, R2P and the International Community's Evolving Interventionist Toolkit', 23 December 2010, pp. 7–8, available online at http://papers.ssrn.com/sol3/papers.cfm?abstract_id=1933111 (accessed 20 May 2015).
51 ICRtoP, 'The International Criminal Court and the Responsibility to Protect', available online at http://responsibilitytoprotect.org/index.php/about-rtop/related-themes/2416-icc-and-rtop (accessed 20 May 2015).
52 Madeleine K. Albright and Richard S. Williamson, 'The United States and R2P: From Words to Actions', Report of the Working Group on R2P, 2013, p. 24, available online at www.usip.org/sites/default/files/PW-UnitedStates-And-R2P-Words-To-Action.pdf (accessed 20 May 2015).
53 *The Responsibility to Protect*, p. 24.
54 Ibid., p. 25.
55 Minus ethnic cleansing, which is not an official, legal category within the Rome Statute.
56 'Implementing the Responsibility to Protect', para. 18.
57 Ibid., p. 54.
58 Ibid., p. 18.
59 Ibid.
60 For an in depth discussion of this, see Martin Mennecke, 'The International Criminal Court', in Monica Serrano and Thomas G. Weiss (eds), *The International Politics of Human Rights: Rallying to the R2P Cause?* (Routledge, 2014), pp. 87–104.
61 Ibid.
62 Gareth Evans, Address to the Stanley Foundation Conference on Responsibility to Protect, 18 January 2012, available online at www.stanleyfoundation.org/r2p.cfm (accessed 20 May 2015).
63 Fatou Bensouda, Address to the Stanley Foundation Conference on Responsibility to Protect, New York, 18 January 2012, available online at www.stanleyfoundation.org/r2p.cfm (accessed 20 May 2015).
64 Kurt Mills, 'The Responsibility to Protect', p. 4.
65 'Implementing the Responsibility to Protect', p. 9.
66 Kofi Annan Press Conference, Serena Hotel, Nairobi, 26 January 2008.

Part I
The responsibility to protect

1 Kenya burning

The 2007–08 post-election crisis

> We want to send a very, very strong message to Kibaki. Because we cannot get him, we are going to work on his ethnic group, the Kikuyu.[1]

In the aftermath of Kenya's General Election on 27 December 2007, the country descended into its worst political crisis since independence. What began as popular protests against the outcome of the presidential ballot soon escalated into violent clashes across the country. After nearly eight weeks the post-election clashes had claimed over a thousand lives, forced hundreds of thousands to flee from their homes, and brought extensive economic losses to the country and the region as a whole. As violence continued to spiral across Kenya, the country appeared to be on the brink of a civil war. The impact of the crisis reverberated far beyond Kenya's borders, highlighting both the vulnerability of its neighbours as well as the importance of Kenya's stability to the region as whole.

Although the General Election was the immediate trigger for the violence that followed thereafter, the actual causes of the crisis were deeply rooted in a set of structural conditions that made the country particularly prone to electoral violence. While these factors had erupted into bloodshed during previous elections, the sheer magnitude of the violence during the 2007–08 crisis seemed to catch most observers off guard.

This chapter will examine the 2007–08 post-election crisis in Kenya. It will begin by exploring the circumstances surrounding the 2007 General Election and the ensuing violence. After examining the different patterns of violence that emerged and the broader impact, the chapter will turn towards the underlying causes of the crisis. The final part of the chapter will consider the proximate indicators of violence and the question of whether the Government and international community could have been better prepared.

The 2007 General Election

On 27 December 2007 Kenya prepared to go to the polls in the fourth General Election since the return to multiparty politics in 1992. There was much anticipation prior to the vote, particularly in relation to the Presidential ballot, as nine candidates vied for the country's top office. In the weeks preceding the polls the race tightened between the incumbent, Mwai Kibaki of the Party of National Unity (PNU) and Raila Odinga of the Orange Democratic Movement (ODM). The final pre-election poll conducted by the Steadman Group projected a 2 per cent lead for Odinga at 45 per cent to 43 per cent for Kibaki.[2]

Although Kibaki and Odinga were bitter rivals during the 2007 General Election, the circumstances surrounding the preceding polls in 2002 could not have been more dissimilar. Five years earlier, the two presented a united front, as Odinga supported Kibaki's bid for the presidency under the National Alliance Rainbow Coalition (NARC). Through a pro-reformist platform, NARC defeated the ruling Kenyan African National Union (KANU), which had governed the country since independence. NARC's historic landslide victory led to widespread elation across the country as Kenyans from all walks of life celebrated an end to KANU's 39-year rule.[3]

Kibaki's inauguration was held at Nairobi's Uhuru Park on 30 December 2002. As jubilant crowds gathered to mark the occasion, feelings of euphoria and anticipation filled the air. The country seemed to be on the path of a new dawn. In his inaugural address, Kibaki reaffirmed his commitment to the people of Kenya:

> The era of 'anything goes' is now gone forever. Government will no longer be run on the whims of individuals.... The authority of parliament and the independence of the judiciary will be restored and enhanced as part of the democratic process.... Fellow Kenyans: I'm inheriting a country, which has been badly ravaged by years of misrule and ineptitude ... I believe that governments exist to serve the people, not the people to serve the government. Corruption will now cease to be a way of life in Kenya.[4]

Among the extensive reforms Kibaki had pledged to the Kenyan electorate in 2002 were measures to reign in the powers of the executive branch. The promise to curb presidential power was to be secured through the delivery of a new constitution and the creation of a prime ministerial post, which Kibaki had guaranteed to Odinga.

Upon his ascension to the Presidential Office central tenets of Kibaki's reformist agenda began to unravel. Apart from reneging on his promise to appoint Odinga as Prime Minister, Kibaki put forward a draft constitution that continued to vest power in an all-powerful president. Given the high expectations accompanying NARC's victory at the polls, the failure to uphold his commitment facilitated widespread disillusionment across the country. The reversal of Kibaki's reformist platform also led to internal divisions within NARC. Such divisions became increasingly pronounced during the 2005 constitutional referendum, as several Cabinet ministers, including Odinga, campaigned against the draft constitution. On 21 November 2009, the 'No' campaign carried the day with 58.1 per cent of Kenyans voting against the Government-sponsored draft.[5] For many, the defeat of the draft constitution was tantamount to a vote of non-confidence in Kibaki's leadership. Those opposed to the draft called on him to stand down and hold new elections; Kibaki's response was to dismiss his entire Cabinet in an effort to purge those who campaigned against the draft constitution.

The aftermath of the constitutional referendum became a catalyst for Odinga to launch his bid for the Presidency in 2007. Drawing on the symbol of an orange – which represented the 'No' side during the 2005 referendum – Odinga launched the Orange Democratic Movement (ODM). Hence it was in the midst of the constitutional referendum that the battle lines for 2007 were drawn. The events surrounding the 2005 constitutional referendum sowed the seeds of bitterness among the candidates and their supporters, while setting the tone for the campaign and the violence that would soon follow.

Although the 2007 General Election in Kenya has come to be associated with scenes of horror that nearly brought the country to the brink of disaster, it is worth recalling that the voting on 27 December proceeded in an atmosphere of calm. The 2007 election also witnessed the highest number of registered voters in Kenya's electoral history, with an estimated 69 per cent of those registered to vote turning out to cast their ballot.[6] In the vast majority of polling stations around the country, the vote was conducted in a peaceful fashion, without any major incidents reported. It was predominantly during the ballot counting and tabulation process at the Kenyatta International Conference Centre (KICC) in Nairobi that turmoil began to ensue.

The first sign of impending trouble was the delay in announcing the results of the Presidential ballot. When questioned on the cause of this delay, the Chair of the ECK, Samuel Kivuitu, indicated that he had lost contact with a number of returning officers who apparently had their phones switched off.[7] This set the stage for further anomalies during the vote tabulation process, including differences between results announced at the constituency level versus the KICC, the failure of returning officers to produce statutory forms, the announcement of results in the absence of required legal documentation, evidence of voter level turnout being deliberately inflated, and discrepancies between parliamentary and presidential tallies.[8] According to the report of the Kenyan Elections Observers Log, 'the discrepancies were planned systematically and were not accidental, and they involved most Commissioners who clearly organised how the tallying was to be carried out.'[9] The tallying procedures within the KICC drew concern from ECK Commissioner Kipkemoi arap Kirui, who raised these issues with a colleague: 'This is an important national exercise. I am concerned that we are not following the law and we are letting down Kenyans.'[10] Kirui subsequently resigned from his post before the presidential results were officially released.

The unexplained delay in announcing the presidential results and mounting irregularities led to mayhem at the KICC. Members of the PNU and ODM disputed the returns from a number of constituencies; party officials became embroiled in heated exchanged with members of the ECK; and the Chair of the Commission appeared increasingly beleaguered. The quarrels inside the walls of KICC were soon mirrored on the ground, as rumours of electoral fraud began to spread throughout the country. In a number of ODM strongholds including Nyanza and the Rift Valley provinces, the delay in announcing the results led to violence and widespread looting. The Chief Police Commissioner, Hussein Ali, responded by ordering the public to shun violence. Foreign observers who had earlier praised the manner in which Kenyans had cast their ballots were now expressing their concerns.

On 30 December, ODM announced its own version of the presidential poll results. According to the figures released by ODM, Odinga had garnered 49 per cent of the vote to 44 per cent for Kibaki. As Musalia Mudavadi noted: 'Honourable Raila Amolo Odinga is therefore the winner and the fourth President of the Republic of Kenya.'[11] While the initial results seemed to confirm Odinga's victory, in the final hours of the tallying process that lead 'evaporated under opaque and highly irregular proceedings'[12] and was subsequently 'transformed into a razor-thin margin of victory for Mr. Kibaki.'[13] On the same day the Chairman of the ECK announced that Kibaki had been re-elected with 4 584 721 votes to 4 352 993 for Odinga.[14] As Kivuitu stated: 'This means honourable Mwai Kibaki is the winner. The Commission therefore declares honourable Mwai Kibaki as the President of Kenya.'[15]

Less than an hour after the ECK announced its results, Kibaki was hastily sworn in at State House.[16] The ceremony, which was broadcast on the state-owned Kenya Broadcasting Corporation, took place three days ahead of schedule, absent of the grandeur of Kibaki's inauguration ceremony five years prior. Only a handful of PNU officials, the police and members of the armed forces were in attendance. By the time Kibaki completed his inaugural address, violence began to spread across the country.[17] ODM rejected the results and refused to acknowledge Kibaki as the legitimately elected President of Kenya.[18] The Government swiftly ordered a ban on live broadcasts in the middle of an ODM press conference.[19]

Election observers and monitoring groups expressed unease over the election results. In a statement released on the day of Kibaki's inauguration, Alexander Lambsdorff of the European Union monitoring group – the largest international presence during the elections – voiced concerns that the ECK 'had not succeeded in establishing the credibility of the tallying process to the satisfaction of all parties and candidates in the presidential race.'[20] Lambsdorff's remarks called into question the accuracy of the results.[21] On 31 December, the day after Kivuitu's announcement, four ECK Commissioners issued a press statement indicating that 'some of the information received from some of our returning officers now cast doubts on the veracity of the figures.'[22] Even more damning, the Chairman of the ECK conceded that he acted under pressure,[23] and that 'concerns about these situations cannot be dismissed off hand. They call for investigation.'[24]

In a post-election report, the International Crisis Group (ICG) identified two types of rigging during the 2007 General Elections. The first stage of rigging occurred on the ground at the constituency level, wherein returning officers manipulated the figures and transmitted inflated results to the KICC in Nairobi. Some of the indicators of rigging at this level included: 'the discrepancies between results and turnouts of the parliamentary and presidential elections, the reported expulsion of party agents from tallying rooms and the very high turnout (over 95 per cent) recorded in some constituencies.'[25] Interestingly, ICG found evidence of rigging at the constituency level in both PNU and ODM strongholds. A second level of rigging occurred at the KICC tallying centre, where results were deliberately doctored so as to ensure a victory for Kibaki. Officials at the tallying centre 'changed results coming from the constituency tallying centres or endorsed results which had already been changed, and instructed staff to accept and compile them without supporting documentation.'[26]

Due to the nature of the rigging it has become difficult to determine who actually won the presidential race; nevertheless, the success of ODM in the parliamentary vote – winning 99 seats to PNU's 43 – does tend to cast doubt on the authenticity of Kibaki's victory. Odinga responded to the situation by calling for countrywide 'mass action' and urging his supporters to wear black armbands in protest. He also called for a public rally to be held on 3 January; however, the police and security services blocked demonstrators following a ban on public gatherings. Over the course of the next two months, an estimated 1200 Kenyans perished, while hundreds of thousands were displaced.

How the violence unfolded

As scenes of chaos erupted across the country, the nature and dynamics of the unfolding violence tended to vary considerably from region to region. Of particular concern was the way in which the violence began to assume an ethnic dimension; supporters of the PNU, mostly Kikuyu (and to some extent the Embu and Meru communities),[27] were pitted against ODM supporters drawn primarily from members of the Luo, Luhya and Kalenjin communities. Throughout the eight-week period four distinct patterns of violence emerged. The first was spontaneous in nature and tended to involve ODM supporters exhibiting outrage over the stolen election. There were also elements of organised violence, which were largely perpetrated by Kalenjin supporters of ODM in the Rift Valley province. The third pattern of violence that emerged throughout this period were revenge attacks initiated by Kikuyus against other communities, while the fourth and final mode of violence was the result of excessive use of force by the police and security services.

Spontaneous violence: 'no Raila, no peace'

The first pattern of violence to emerge was predominantly spontaneous in nature. This type of violence was a consequence of the perceived flaws in the presidential race and the sense of outrage among ODM supporters. In some theatres, spontaneous acts of looting and violence emerged in advance of the ECK's official announcement of the presidential poll results, as rumours of electoral fraud began to spread. In its report, *On the Brink of the Precipice*, the Kenyan National Commission for Human Rights accounts for how this pattern of violence was primarily directed at Kikuyu supporters of the PNU: 'We want to send a very, very strong message to Kibaki. Because we cannot get him, we are going to work on his ethnic group, the Kikuyu.'[28] Interviews with actors on the ground corroborate this account:

> If we met a Kikuyu, we just beat him. I saw five people die that day personally. They attacked using forms [of weapons] – arrows, pangas [machetes] and even beating with any crude tool. It was mob justice. The first killing ... they approached him politely and asked him to produce his ID card. The one who got the card announced his name very loudly – it was a Kikuyu name. And the mob just attacked him. Those who produced IDs with Kalenjin or Luo names, they let them go.... 'It was an act of brutality,' he said.[29]

The general atmosphere of lawlessness was accompanied by an escalation in sexual/gender-based violence.[30]

For their part the security services tended to contribute rather than quell the growing sense of insecurity in the country. The Government's blanket ban on public gatherings was not only in contravention of international law and the Kenyan Constitution,[31] it also further inflamed the situation. Although the ban was justified as a necessary security measure, the consequence of forbidding demonstrations was that it removed a legitimate source of protest for ODM supporters to express concerns over the flawed elections, while simultaneously setting protestors up for deadly confrontations with the police.

A further factor contributing to the general atmosphere of fear was the ban on live broadcasts. As with the ban on public demonstrations, the orders prohibiting live broadcasts were justified as a necessary measure for controlling inflammatory hate speech and calming the chaos. However, these measures, which remained in place for over a month, were in clear violation of the right to freedom of expression and served only to exacerbate inter-communal tensions throughout the crisis.

Organised violence: 'according to plan'

Alongside the spontaneous outburst of protests engulfing parts of the country emerged a rather different form of violence that had been carefully orchestrated in advance. As Dan Juma, acting director of the Kenyan Human Rights Commission (KHRC) stated, 'It wasn't like people just woke up and started fighting each other.... It was organized.'[32] In the Rift Valley province in particular, meetings were allegedly held during the election campaign, urging ODM supporters to resort to violence in the event of a PNU victory. According to Human Rights Watch, in the town of Eldoret, 'ODM mobilizers and other prominent individuals called meetings ... arguing that if Kibaki was announced as the winner it must mean the polls had been rigged and the reaction should be "war" against local Kikuyu residents.'[33] During these meetings, local politicians and businessmen are alleged to have raised revenue to fund the violence, coached youth and supplied them with weapons. *New York Times* journalist, Geffrey Gettleman has recounted an interview with one of the men involved in the Rift Valley violence:

> Rono Kibet ... said elders in his community called a big meeting on December 30.... More than 2,000 young men gathered ... and the elders urged them to kill Kikuyus ... and burn down their houses.... 'The community raised the money for the gasoline.' ... He explained how the elders blessed the young men, who then split into teams of 50 to hunt down Kikuyus with bows and arrows.... 'We attack people, we burn their homes and then we take their animals,' Mr. Kibet said matter-of-factly.[34]

Those responsible for orchestrating violence also made frequent use of radio broadcasts as a vehicle for inciting ethnic hatred. Kenya's vernacular FM stations in the Rift Valley used idiomatic expressions, urging 'people of the milk' (Kalenjin) to 'cut the grass' (Kikuyu).[35] The Kalenjin language radio station – KASS FM – has been singled out for airing inflammatory messages throughout the crisis, culminating in an International Criminal Court case against its Head of Operations, Joshua Arap Sang.

In one of the most horrific episodes of violence in the Rift Valley, 30 Kikuyus were burnt to death while seeking refuge at a Church in Kiambaa on 1 January 2008. The Kiambaa massacre sent shockwaves throughout the country and around the world. One of the eyewitnesses has provided a tragic personal account of the massacre in her testimony to the Commission of Inquiry into Post-election Violence:

> On 1 January 2008 at around 10 a.m., I heard people yelling.... I saw smoke coming from some houses in our village and the houses were burning. Everyone in the village started running away to the church.... My mother who was 90 years old was with me at the time. I decided to take my mother into the church for safety.... Many people were being pushed into the Church.... The raiders threw some mattresses into the roof of the church.... They were also pouring fuel (petrol) onto the mattresses. All of a sudden I saw a fire break out.... I wanted to save my mother from the burning church, but one of the raiders prevented me. I saw the fire had reached where my mother was. I heard her cry for help as the fire burnt her, but I could not help.[36]

Reprisals attacks: 'self-defence forces'

The initial wave of violence against PNU supporters provoked counter-attacks against non-Kikuyu communities. According to a report by OHCHR, some of the first incidences of reprisal attacks occurred after the news spread about the Kiambaa church massacre. The report notes how the arrival of displaced Kikuyus fleeing from Eldoret towards the Southern Rift Valley towns and Central province facilitated a second wave of reprisals,[37] as these populations brought with them tales of the horror and destruction they had witnessed.

Revenge killings were directed primarily against the Luo, Luhya, Kalenjin and other non-Kikuyu communities. A leaflet in Central Province captured the heightened sense of discord between communities: 'No more clashes but war. Luo, Luya and Nandi we give you 24 hrs, you pack and go – failure to that we need 200 heads b4 peace hold once more.'[38] The most severe reprisal attacks, however, occurred in Molo, Naivasha and Nakuru. Subsequent interviews have revealed how PNU sympathisers and local businessmen initiated meetings in order to fundraise and mobilise youth to attack non-Kikuyus businesses and properties.[39]

> This was not done by ordinary citizens, it was arranged by people with money, they bought the jobless like me. We need something to eat each day ... they called us to a meeting around 2 p.m. They said there was a plan to push out the Luos because they were planning to attack us. They said we should be ready on Saturday. I recognised the leaders, they are owners of businesses in town, they did not hide their faces. We were paid 200 shilling for going to the meeting, and we were told we would get the rest after the job, it was like a business.[40]

Reprisal attacks tended to involve Kikuyu militia – including the notorious Mungiki. The Mungiki began as a semi-religious sect promoting traditional Kikuyu culture and values, and subsequently evolved into a network of organised crime with alleged links to Kikuyu politicians.[41] While counter-attacks were partially motivated by the desire to avenge fellow-Kikuyus, 'self-defence' was perhaps another motive for this pattern of violence. This would account for the continuation of meetings throughout the eight-week period of violence and the drawing up of contingency plans in the event that peace talks failed.[42]

Between 29 and 31 January, two ODM MPs (Mugabe Ware and David Kimutai Too) were gunned down. The opposition referred to both killings as political assassinations, designed to intimidate the party and reduce the number of ODM MPs in Parliament. The killings further stoked tensions between different communities and perpetuated the ongoing cycle of violence.

Excessive police force: shoot to kill

A fourth and final form of violence involved the excessive use of force by the police and security services. In order to crack down on looters and protesters, police used tear gas and gunfire to disperse crowds, particularly in Kisumu, a stronghold of Raila Odinga, where most of those killed were shown to have perished as a consequence of gunshot wounds. In an interview with Human Rights Watch the Provincial Police Officer for Nyanza admits 'I gave that order to shoot, things were getting out of hand.'[43] Among those shot was a 15-year-old boy after police opened fire on a group of ODM supporters without warning:

> It was evening. There was a group of boys, celebrating and carrying pictures of Raila – they thought he had been announced as the winner. As they were going up the road, I joined them, celebrating also.... We heard gunshots, so

everybody was running for his life. I was ahead of my cousin so I went back to look for him. I found myself near the police Land Rover. They had put off the headlights of the car. I realised that I was near because I heard a gunshot. I started running. Then I heard a second one. When I tried to step forward my leg had no power, I fell down.[44]

The excessive use of force by police and security services were not limited to Nyanza, as similar measures were applied against other demonstrations involving ODM supporters around the country. Instances of police brutality were most severe within the slum areas of Mathare, Kibera, Dandora and Kariobangi. Police responses drew criticism from human rights groups, as a Human Rights Watch report has observed:

The use of live rounds in Kibera and Mathare slums, some of the most densely populated areas in the world, was highly irresponsible and caused death and injury to many innocent bystanders. Slum dwellings are made of wood, sacking, and tin sheets, easily pierced by bullets. One woman was hit in the chest at 8 a.m. in the morning on December 31 as bullets came through the wall of her home.[45]

Apart from the excessive use of force, police were also criticised for demonstrating partiality in their willingness to protect citizens.[46]

During the first few weeks of 2008, each day brought increasing levels of death and destruction. Within three days, 164 people had perished; after three weeks over 500 people had been killed; and after one month, the number of fatalities had surpassed 800.[47] It was a situation that many Kenyans never imagined they would see, as Makumi Mwagiru, a Professor at the University of Nairobi observed:

[N]ew Years Day in 2008 began like no other, and the succeeding days began to resemble *pandemonium*, John Milton's description of the capital city of hell. No other experience in the Kenya of my lifetime – the political assassinations of the 1960s and 1970s, the attempted coup d'état of 1982, the infamous 1992 and subsequent land clashes, or the violence in past elections – had ever seemed so near to closing Kenya down as the post-2007 elections did.[48]

Assessing the broader impact of the violence

The continuing spiral of violence and destruction of property culminated in massive levels of displacement. A fact-finding mission led by the Office of the High Commissioner for Human Rights (OHCHR) suggests up to 300 000 people were forced to flee from their homes.[49] The Ugandan Red Cross registered more than 12 000 people who had crossed the border, while others returned to their ancestral homelands.[50] Initial figures indicate that the first wave of displacements were largely among Kikuyus in the North Rift, Western and Nyanza provinces. The evictions and displacements precipitated by the violence compounded the existing IDP crisis in the country, where hundreds of thousands were already living in IDP camps as a consequence of previous episodes of violence.

The IDP camps provided little refuge for those fleeing the violence, as the conditions were rife with poor sanitation and a general lack of security. While IDPs often fared no better after having fled, the prospect of returning to their homes was not necessarily an option. In many cases there were threats discouraging the return of IDPs;[51] in other instances there was no home to return to, as nearly 42 000 homes were destroyed during this period.

The complete breakdown of law and order put the livelihoods of many Kenyans at stake. The prices of commodities skyrocketed and became unaffordable, with several markets forced to close due to concerns over security and food shortages. Road traffic was brought to a standstill and in most towns fuel became a scarce commodity leading to long queues of people in search of cooking kerosene.

Apprehension over the deteriorating security situation in Kenya led to widespread flight cancellations. The disruption to air transport severely impacted the economy, as the country's principal exports (vegetables and flowers) lay uncollected at Kenya's airports. Travel advisories had repercussions for the tourism industry, as Kenya's resorts and safari parks experienced massive cancellations. With tourism accounting for one of the country's top foreign exchange earners, the crisis dealt a massive blow to the Kenyan economy. A Kenyan Private Sector Alliance estimate in mid-January warned of hundreds of thousands of job losses if the violence was not curbed, and estimated business losses as high as 3.4 billion dollars.[52] The value of stocks traded on the market went down by 36 billion KSH as the after-effects of the violence continued to have an impact on foreign investment.

The economic impact of the violence was by no means confined to Kenya's borders. The deteriorating situation began to demonstrate just how dependent the region had become on Kenya's stability. Kenya is a gateway to Central Africa, with 80 per cent of Uganda's and almost all of Rwanda's imported goods passing through the country.[53] As the scale of violence intensified, the road from the coastal port of Mombasa to Nairobi into the interior of Kenya and on to central Africa was impassable. Railway lines were also affected, as angry ODM supporters uprooted one kilometre of the Nairobi to Uganda rail track. Overall, the paralysis and chaos in Kenya resulted in fuel shortages in Kigali, Juba and Kampala, and was accompanied by an increase in the price of commodities throughout the region.[54] In the absence of any reprieve from the violence, fears for the stability of the region grew widespread.

The ongoing crisis also had much wider implications as a result of Kenya's strategic location. Kenya hosts one of three United Nations (UN) headquarters – the only one in the Global South – as well as large diplomatic missions, including the largest US Embassy in the region. According to Monica Juma, given Kenya's position as a logistical hub for humanitarian activities for the Horn as well as Central Africa, 'collapse of the country's infrastructure ... could have a direct negative impact on the supply chain to some of the major humanitarian theatres in Eastern Congo, Somalia and South Sudan.'[55] As the crisis continued, humanitarian organisations were forced to curb their activities in the region.

The unrelenting instability in Kenya also drew global concern, particularly from a security standpoint. Kenya had become a key ally of Western countries in relation to counter terrorism efforts in the region.[56] This has included large-scale partnerships between the United States and Kenya, with training and equipping of Kenyan police under programs such as the Anti-Terrorism Assistance programme, which helped to establish a Kenyan Anti-Terrorism Police Unit. Kenya is a key regional player in the Combined Joint Task Force-Horn of Africa, and provides a base for ongoing military operations in Somalia. The country also hosts two of the three main United Kingdom deployments on the African continent, with the British Peace Support Team and the British Army Training Unit Kenya.[57] The UK Ministry of Defence spends an average of US$6.3 million on training of Kenyan security services.[58] In their January 2008 fact-finding mission, the Regional Parliamentarians of the Great Lakes highlighted the extent to which the continuing crisis posed a threat far beyond the borders of Kenya:

> An unstable Kenya has far reaching impacts on the region.... Any animated conflicts would spiral in the region. So far, we have experienced the disruption of transport valves and humanitarian activities geared for Southern Sudan, Somalia and the Great Lakes region. Given the instability in Somalia, the ongoing US-led operations against Al Qaeda and the influx of small arms both in the region, state collapse in Kenya is likely to affect not only Kenya, but the entire African continent.... Economic resistance, especially the blocking of roads, burning of transport instruments and actions directed at the rail artery is increasingly asphyxiating not only the state but the region also.[59]

As violence continued to spiral throughout the country, the International Committee for the Red Cross and the Kenyan Red Cross launched appeals for the provision of relief supplies, including: food, water, sanitation equipment, medical kits and drugs to treat the wounded. The United Nations Office for the Coordination of Humanitarian Affairs (OCHA) provided US$7 million from its Central Emergency Relief Fund to assist victims of the post-election violence and appealed to international donors to provide additional funding for humanitarian operations.[60] In a press statement, John Holmes, UN Emergency Relief Coordinator and Under-Secretary General for Humanitarian Affairs noted, 'in many ways, this is a protection crisis as much as one of humanitarian consequences.'[61] Among the UN agencies contributing to relief efforts on the ground were the United Nations Children's Fund (UNICEF), the United Nations High Commissioner for Refugees (UNHCR), and the World Food Programme (WFP).

Humanitarian relief could, however, only provide a temporary bandage to the deteriorating situation in Kenya. Above all, a political resolution was required to restore Kenya's stability. Nobel Laureate Wangari Mathai joined the chorus of voices urging Kibaki and Odinga to come together and reach a compromise for the sake of the country.[62] Kalonzo Musyoka of ODM-Kenya,[63] also echoed the demands for dialogue and offered himself as a prospective mediator between the two sides. Nevertheless, Kibaki and Odinga remained deeply divided. ODM unequivocally demanded that a fresh election be held without the involvement of the ECK, whereas the PNU argued that the election results could only be legitimately disputed through the courts. Given the lack of faith in Kenya's judicial system, ODM vehemently rejected this option. Odinga continued to assert that he would only enter into dialogue with the PNU if Kibaki agreed to stand down.

With each passing day the situation seemed increasingly more intractable. Kenya appeared to be on the brink of civil war, as George Wachira observed, 'a country with a record for brokering peace in the region was now headed for total collapse.'[64] Reflecting on the tragic experience of his own country 13 years prior, the Rwandan President, Paul Kagame, called for military intervention in Kenya to forestall the crisis:

> It starts with five deaths, then 10, then 50, shortly it grows to 100, then it goes to thousands.... By the time you realise, it has a dimension that is wiping out life in villages and communities and is getting out of control and the whole political situation is in a mess.... This is a case of emergency where certain things have to be done very quickly to stop the killings that are going on. There's no time to go into niceties and debates when the killings are taking place.[65]

Kagame conceded that his suggestion may be unpopular, but he continued to argue that it may be necessary given the gravity of the situation and the potential for escalation: 'I know that it is not fashionable and right for the armies to get involved in such a political situation. But in situations where institutions have lost control, I wouldn't mind such a solution.'[66]

The underlying causes of the violence

The disputed outcome of the 2007 General Election in Kenya was not, on its own, a sufficient cause for the crisis that erupted thereafter. While the election may have sparked the eight-week period of violence that followed in its wake, the causes of the crisis were much broader and more deeply rooted. Underneath the immediate trigger of the fraudulent presidential election observers have identified Kenya's crisis of governance as a fundamental root cause of the violence. This principal underlying cause has been sustained by two further factors: the privatisation of violence and the politicisation of ethnicity. In essence these are the means through which politicians have retained power. A final root cause, which serves to reinforce all others, is Kenya's long-standing culture of impunity. The fact that political leaders have been able to resort to any means without being held to account invariably perpetuates the cycle of violence in Kenya.

Crisis of governance

The violent protests following the 2007 General Election were symptomatic of a larger crisis of governance facing the country. While Kenya had come to be regarded as a democratic model for the rest of the continent, it was a version of democracy that tended to exist more on paper than in practice. Behind the facade of a strong and stable democracy was a system whereby political power was vested in the hands of an all-powerful president. Since the time of independence in 1963, the Kenyan constitution had been subject to 32 amendments, which collectively had the impact of watering down any meaningful checks and balances on presidential power. These amendments included measures to weaken judicial independence and parliamentary scrutiny, thereby ensuring that political power remained in the hands of the president. The power of the executive branch in Kenyan politics fundamentally shaped the approach to elections, as the electoral process became infused with a winner-take-all mentality.

For over two decades, the reform of Kenya's constitution had come to be regarded as the main antidote to the country's crisis of governance. Despite the urgent need for constitutional reform, several failed attempts to launch the process had reduced the issue to a mere talking point in Kenyan politics. As has been noted, the promise of a new constitution was a crucial component of NARC's platform of change, in which a pledge was made to deliver a new constitution within 100 days. Had the 2005 draft actually been adopted its provisions would have done very little to alter the structure of governance in Kenya and therefore, it is not particularly surprising that it was rejected by an overwhelming majority of Kenyans. In the absence of any substantive governance reforms, a zero-sum calculus has continued to frame the mind-set of the political class in Kenya.

Privatisation of violence

In their efforts to consolidate power politicians in Kenya have frequently demonstrated a willingness to resort to political violence. The first two Presidents of Kenya, Jomo Kenyatta[67] and Daniel Arap Moi,[68] commonly resorted to a range of violent and criminal practices including torture, detention without trial and political assassinations. According to Suzanne Mueller, the use of violence as means to retain power had led the Kenyan state to lose its monopoly on the legitimate use of force.[69] Whereas Jomo Kenyatta had used the machinery of the state to consolidate his power base and eliminate opponents, Moi had a profound mistrust for the state security apparatus, which led him to outsource political violence. Under Moi's leadership, Kenya's political class began to hire their own bodyguards and enlist youth to carry out acts of violence against their rivals. The upshot of this outsourcing of political violence has been the rise of armed militia in Kenya, the most notorious being the Kikuyu led Mungiki sect. Armed militia have become a fixture of daily life in Kenya, contributing to the country's escalating crime rates. As noted, these groups were key participants in the 2007–08 post-election violence, as businessmen and politicians recruited youths and criminal gangs to carry out acts of violence on their behalf.[70]

Politicisation of ethnicity

The tendency for the electorate to vote along ethnic lines has become a well-established pattern in Kenyan elections. While attempts have been made to encourage the electorate to overcome tribal divisions – particularly through the activities of the National Cohesion and Integration Commission (NCIC) – voting patterns in the 2013 Elections reveal that this trend persists.[71] Rather than being indicative of an inherent discord among Kenya's different ethnic groups, the importance attributed to ethnicity derives from the way in which politics is organised in the country. It is also worth noting that the political class in Kenya persistently transcends ethnic divides when it comes to forming political alliances, adding further weight to argument that it is not ethnicity itself that has generated cycles of violence in Kenya, but rather, the *politicisation* of ethnicity.

The inclination to vote along tribal lines derives from the historical favouritism that Kenya's presidents have exhibited towards their ethnic kin, and the ensuing belief that the presidency will yield advantages for those of the same ethnic group.[72] During Kenyatta's presidency Kikuyu were awarded patronage with top civil service jobs and the redistribution of land that had been bequeathed from the former colonial administration. Under Moi's leadership, it was his Kalenjin brethren that stood to benefit from top civil service appointments and the redistribution of state resources.

The redistribution of land in particular has facilitated grievances between different ethnic communities. To this day, land continues to be a flashpoint for violent conflict, particularly in the fertile Rift Valley, which was the locus of the Government's various 'land grabbing' schemes.[73] In their efforts to consolidate power, politicians have effectively mobilised support on the basis of historical grievance narratives.[74] For instance, during the 1990s President Moi managed to secure his power base in the Rift Valley by provoking anti-Kikuyu sentiment among his fellow Kalenjin.[75] According to OHCHR: 'As a result of the 1990s politically instigated communal clashes, some 380 000 Kenyans were still internally displaced in 2007.'[76]

Evidently the capacity to mobilise on the basis of ethnicity relies upon tapping into genuine grievances and an actual sense of disenfranchisement. With one of the largest income inequality gaps in the world, and 60 per cent of the population surviving on less than US$1 a day, it is certainly not a coincidence that the vast majority of violence during the post-election period was concentrated in some of the poorest parts of the country where daily life is a constant struggle for survival.

Impunity: 'the order of the day in Kenya'

A final underlying cause of the post-election violence, that serves to reinforce the above-mentioned factors, is Kenya's long-standing culture of impunity.

According to the United Nations Human Rights Council impunity can be defined as:

> the impossibility, de jure or de facto, of bringing the perpetrators of violations to account – whether in criminal, civil, administrative or disciplinary proceedings – since they are not subject to any inquiry that might lead to their being accused, arrested, tried and, if found guilty, sentenced to appropriate penalties, and to making reparations to their victims.[77]

As this definition highlights, impunity has a systemic dimension that permeates all aspects of the prosecutorial process. This definition would certainly apply to the situation in Kenya prior to the 2007 General Election, as the culture of impunity was embedded within all levels of the prosecutorial process, ranging from: limited investigative capacity, police corruption, a corrupt judiciary, the propensity for intimidation of witnesses, a lack of protection for victims, and the absence of reparations or financial compensation for victims. Kenya's culture of impunity can be traced to the previous colonial administration, under which no British national was investigated for actions taken to curb the Mau Mau uprising.[78] Therefore, the Kenyan state inherited 'a demoralised judiciary, a violent, oppressive and corrupt police force, and a contemptuous and venal bureaucracy.'[79]

Following previous episodes of electoral conflict in 1992 and 1997, no efforts were made to prosecute perpetrators who participated in and organised these clashes. Investigations were, however, conducted under the remit of the Government sponsored Kiliku[80] and Akiwumi judicial inquiries.[81] The findings of the Akiwumi Commission, in particular, implicated several high level politicians for their role in financing, organising and inciting the clashes.[82] The report made a series of recommendations, including a demand for accountability. In the first instance the findings of the report were concealed; when they were eventually made public the recommendations were ignored.

Other notable instances of violence in Kenya's history that have eluded prosecution include the Wagalla massacre of 1984.[83] During this episode, 5000 Somali men were stripped and confined to the Wagalla airstrip for five days without food and water, and eventually executed by Kenyan Security Forces. In the aftermath of this horrific episode there were no attempts to prosecute those responsible and no compensation offered to the victims. In 1998, a further incident took place in North Eastern Kenya, in Mbalambala, when security forces rounded up and tortured 38 local residents.[84] The Government eventually yielded to pressure to conduct an inquiry into this incident; however, the findings of the inquiry were not made public and to date no one has been held accountable.

A similar failure to hold Kenya's leadership accountable can be seen in the Government's approach to grand-scale corruption. Major corruption scandals, such as the infamous Goldenberg[85] and Anglo-leasing[86] scandals have emboldened Kenyan politicians by facilitating the impression that they can engage in criminal behaviour without fear of prosecution. As the Commission of Inquiry investigating the post-election violence remarked: 'Impunity has become the order of the day in Kenya.'[87]

Was the post-election violence predictable (and preventable)?

Even though the structural preconditions for violent conflict were readily apparent in Kenya, there continued to be a genuine sense of shock, and to a certain extent, disbelief among observers. These sentiments are captured in the preface of Makumi Mwagiru's study, *The Water's Edge: Mediation of Violent Electoral Conflict in Kenya*:

> This is a book about Kenya that I hoped I would never write.... I had always believed that my concerns with international and comparative conflict analysis would forever be restricted to conflict in other countries, and their experiences as victims and perpetrators and the like.... I believed that Kenya was made for those escaping from conflicts at home, and a place where other people came to negotiate and sue for peace in their countries. The events following the general elections in Kenya in December 2007 disabused me of these intellectual comforts.[88]

As Mwagiru's remarks reflect, there was a widely held perception of Kenya as being an oasis of peace before the 2007 polls. Not only was Kenya a popular destination for tourists, as host to one of three UN headquarters, diplomatic missions, media outlets and international organisations, the country was often perceived as a hub for government officials, aid workers, and journalists. Although there had been episodes of violence surrounding previous elections – with casualty and displacement figures roughly paralleling those reached in 2007 – these prior incidences were largely confined to particular pockets of the country and therefore, neglected to capture widespread media attention.

The conventional perception of Kenya has also been nurtured by the General Election in 2002 and the referendum in 2005. Viewing the peaceful transfer of power in 2002 as an indication of Kenya's democratic maturation puts more stock in the rhetoric of change rather than its substance. As noted earlier in this chapter, key planks of NARC's reform agenda began to unravel as soon as Kibaki achieved victory. Moreover, while the defeat of the government's constitutional bill in 2005 may have been perceived as a further marker of Kenya's democratic embrace, the rejection of the draft constitution actually provided Kibaki with an opportunity to consolidate his power base in advance of the 2007 General Election.

A more accurate assessment of Kenya's democracy was provided in the African Peer Review Mechanism (APRM) in 2006:

> In spite of Kenya's many strengths that have succeeded in containing outbreaks of mass violence, the country still exhibits many of the factors that have been markers of civil strife elsewhere, such as strong ethnic divisions,

polarized political issues, political manipulation, rampant violence, socio-economic disparities, deepening levels of poverty and endemic corruption.[89]

Alongside some of the structural preconditions for violent conflict highlighted in the APRM Kenya report were more proximate crisis indicators that manifested prior to the polls. These included: Kibaki's efforts to tamper with the composition of the Electoral Commission; incidences of hate speech throughout the campaign period; and increasing levels of pre-poll violence.

The Electoral Commission of Kenya

Having presided over a peaceful General Election in 2002 and the constitutional referendum in 2005, there was a high degree of faith placed in the ECK and its Chairman to deliver free and fair elections in 2007. The international donor community also exhibited confidence in the capacity of the Chairman by lobbying the Kenyan Government to re-appoint Kivuitu in November 2007. This was in spite of a series of decisions that severely compromised the capacity of the ECK to conduct the General Election in a fair and impartial manner. In his 6 February testimony to the US House of Representatives, Maina Kiai, Chairman of the Kenyan National Commission for Human Rights, highlighted some of these measures:

(i) President Kibaki's decision to abrogate the agreement of 1997 on the formula for appointments to the Electoral Commission ensuring that all the Commissioners were appointed by him alone;
(ii) an administrative decision within the ECK to give responsibility to Commissioners for their home regions, something that had never been done before, meaning that they appointed all the election officials in the constituencies in their home regions, in a manner that created conflicts of interest;
(iii) the rejection of an offer from IFES to install a computer program that would enable election officials in the constituencies to submit results electronically to Nairobi and then on to a giant screen available to the public making it virtually impossible to change results;
(iv) a decision to abandon the use of ECK staff in the Verification and Tallying Centre in favour of causal staff provided by the Commsioners directly; and
(v) a refusal to ensure that election officials in areas with large predictable majorities for any of the candidates came from different areas so as to reduce the likelihood of ballot stuffing.[90]

Taken together, these measures signify a 'well-orchestrated plan to ensure a predetermined result.'[91] Although there had been some concern over the partiality of the ECK in the lead-up to the 2007 polls, the extent of manipulation appeared to be lost on most observers. The level of confidence invested in Kivuitu is perhaps most clearly reflected in the decision of the Kenyan branch of the International Commission of Jurists (ICJ), in the two weeks preceding the General

Election, to name him 'Jurist of the Year.' The award was in recognition of Kivuitu's exemplary human rights record. The ICJ outlined Kivuitu's role in overseeing the 2002 General Election and 2005 referendum, as well as his 'determination to uphold the rule of law in this year's General Election.'[92] Through his work, Kivuitu was regarded as having been 'fearless in the face of political intimidation.'[93] In accepting this honour, Kivuitu promised to 'uphold the expectations that came with the award.'[94]

Relatively early on in the electoral process, the capacity of the ECK was put to the test. With the date for the General Election set, party primaries were to be held in November 2007. In order to prevent those who lost their seats in the primaries from defecting to other parties, the ECK originally set 19 November 2007 as the deadline for submitting the finalised list of candidates. This decision was, however, subsequently retracted, which allowed candidates to affiliate themselves with multiple parties depending on the outcome. This invariably led to confusion during the nomination process. It also facilitated grievances and provided grounds for challenging the outcome of parliamentary and local elections. In some locations MPs were injured as the results were announced and police used tear gas to disperse groups of angry supporters.[95] The scenes of chaos that marred the party primaries were an ominous sign of what was to come during the General Election.

The tone of the electoral campaign

As the election drew nearer, the tone of the campaign became a source of concern for some observers. For instance, the European Union Observer Mission noted with apprehension that the electoral campaign had become dominated by 'a strong ethno-political polarisation between the two main contenders in the presidential election and their alliances, leading to a generally tense atmosphere in their respective regional strong hold towards the other side.'[96] During election rallies, politicians frequently characterised their opponents in a derogatory manner, relating to their ethnicity. Whereas ODM candidates framed the election as a contest involving all 41 tribes in Kenya against one tribe (the Kikuyu) and frequently made reference to devolution using the emotive language of *majimboism*,[97] the PNU 'made Luo cultural traditions a target, claiming that an uncircumcised man could not rule Kenya.'[98]

Throughout the campaign period incidences of incitement became rampant. Further to the broadcasting of dangerous speech across radio stations, inflammatory messages directed towards particular candidates and ethnic communities were also disseminated through SMS and over email. The rising incidences of hate speech prior to the election became a source of alarm and a precursor to the violence that would soon follow. In an effort to curb these incidences, the ECK set up a tribunal for investigating those engaging in incitement. However, only two individuals were charged and issued with relatively inconsequential fines.

Pre-poll violence

Following the clashes that broke out during the party nomination process there were other incidences of violence in the pre-election period.[99] In its campaign-monitoring project the Kenyan National Commission for Human Rights documented nearly 30 examples of pre-electoral clashes.[100] Most incidents tended to occur in and around campaign rallies, with the scale of violence escalating in particular regions, including Kuresoi, Molo and Mount Elgon.[101] There were also deliberate efforts to intimidate female candidates.[102]

As incidences of violence increased throughout the pre-election period, there were many complaints about the lack of security before the polls. Incidences of violence and intimidation were reported to the police in advance. As the EU Observer Mission noted, 'in most cases, abuses did not receive an appropriate response from the police.'[103] On the eve of the election, Police Commissioner, Mohammed Hussein Ali, spoke directly to this issue at a news conference in Nairobi: 'Everything is under control and people in those areas, who will vote, will be assured by the presence of the police.'[104] In contrast to Ali's assurances, the police and security services actually did more to aggravate rather than calm the situation. As noted earlier in this chapter, the police and security services were directly implicated in some of the worst episodes of violence throughout post-election period.

Pre-poll preparedness

The prior occurrence of electoral related violence in Kenya, along with the mounting levels of hate speech and incidences of pre-poll violence in 2007, do raise questions over why the Government was not better prepared. Even more damning is the accusation that the Government's response to the violence was uneven and deliberately biased. According to OHCHR, the discrepancy between levels of preparedness and 'the means dedicated by the State to address one type of violence rather than the others strongly suggests that the Government failed to take appropriate measures.'[105]

> The failure of the State to take preventive measures to address signs of ethnic radicalisation and early occurrences of ethnic violence must be looked at in correlation with the decision of the State to ensure heavy police presence at all polling stations on election day and to deploy strong police contingents to the slums and opposition strong holds as early as 29 December.[106]

A lack of preparedness has also been levelled against international actors, who appeared similarly caught off guard by the violence. Beyond the failure to anticipate the full extent of the violence, some have gone a step further in assigning international actors with responsibility for consistently overlooking conflict indicators in Kenya. The response of donor governments to political instability in Kenya has been described as 'woefully inadequate.'[107] According to Stephen Brown, 'One of the biggest handicaps to an international role in conflict prevention in Kenya is its strategic and economic importance to Western countries and their concomitant reluctance to compromise their relationship with the ... government.'[108] The desire to maintain good relations with the Kenyan Government has arguably encouraged international actors to turn a blind eye, not only to ongoing violence and instability, but systemic corruption.[109] On the basis of this perspective, the actions of international actors intensified the problem of impunity in Kenya. As John Githongo, the former Permanent Secretary for Governance and Ethics has argued, the donor community, in particular, has 'blood on their hands' for neglecting to act earlier and 'imparting the view that leaders could get away with anything.'[110] Ben Sihanya and Duncan Okello have similarly attributed the absence of earlier action to the 'taxonomy of interests' in Kenya:

> the taxonomy of interests in Kenya is internal, regional, and international: Internationally, because of Kenya's strategic location, the US, UK, and the EU had an interest in a functional and orderly country. The quest for stability in Kenya was desperate and it explains why the US State Department hastily released a statement congratulating President Kibaki only to withdraw it immediately when it realized that Kibaki could neither guarantee US interests nor govern.[111]

Notwithstanding the tepid response of external actors to prior episodes of violence in Kenya's history, as the next chapter will demonstrate, the 2007–08 crisis captured the attention of the international community. The concern of international actors culminated in a decisive and multi-layered engagement to halt the spiralling violence in Kenya.

Conclusion

This chapter has examined the 2007 General Election in Kenya and the crisis that erupted in its aftermath. The polling on 27 December 2007 proceeded in a relatively peaceful atmosphere, as the tensions began to emerge predominantly during the ballot counting and tabulation process. Although Raila Odinga initially appeared to be in the lead, the Electoral Commission of Kenya announced, under opaque circumstances, the re-election of the incumbent Mwai Kibaki. By the time Kibaki had completed his inaugural address violence began to engulf parts of the country.

The nature and dynamics of the unfolding violence tended to vary considerably from region to region. Of particular concern was the way in which the violence began to assume an ethnic dimension; supporters of the PNU, mostly Kikuyu, were pitted against ODM supporters drawn primarily from members of the Luo, Luhya and Kalenjin communities. Throughout the eight-week period, four distinct patterns of violence emerged. The first was spontaneous in nature and tended to involve ODM supporters exhibiting outrage over the stolen election. There were also elements of organised violence, which were largely perpetrated by Kalenjin supporters of ODM in the Rift Valley province. A third pattern of violence that emerged throughout this period was the revenge attacks initiated by Kikuyus against other communities, while the fourth and final mode of violence was the result of excessive use of force by the police and security services.

Given Kenya's strategic importance, the violence was felt far beyond its borders. Kenya's neighbours were severely impacted by the crisis, politically and economically. Recalling the tragic experience of his own country, the President of Rwanda, Paul Kagame, called for military action to forestall the crisis. While neighbouring countries made urgent appeals to the Kenyan leadership to work together to end the violence, the two sides remained deadlocked.

Although the General Election in Kenya was the immediate trigger for the violence, the roots of the crisis were much broader and more deeply rooted. Several underlying causes have been highlighted, which made Kenya particularly prone to electoral related violence. Underneath the immediate trigger of the fraudulent presidential election observers have identified Kenya's crisis of governance as a fundamental root cause of the violence. This principal underlying cause was sustained by two further factors: the privatisation of violence and the politicisation of ethnicity. A final root cause, which served to reinforce all others, was Kenya's long-standing culture of impunity. The fact that political leaders have been able to resort to any means without being held to account invariably perpetuated the cycle of violence in Kenya.

Aside from the structural factors contributing to the crisis were more proximate indicators that signalled a looming threat of violence. These included Kibaki's efforts to tamper with the composition of the Electoral Commission, alarming levels of hate speech throughout the campaign, and incidences of pre-election violence. Criticism has also been levelled at international actors for overlooking emerging crisis signals and failing to act earlier. However, as the next chapter will argue, the post-election crisis in Kenya did eventually elicit a robust response from external actors, not seen before and arguably not replicated since.

Notes

1 Kenya National Commission on Human Rights, *On the Brink of the Precipice: A Human Rights Account of Kenya's Post-Election Violence*, Kenyan National Commission on Human Rights, August 2008, p. 67, available online at http://fidakenya.org/sites/default/files/khrc-report ... on-the-blink.pdf (accessed 20 May 2015).
2 'Steadman releases its last poll before election', *The East African Standard*, 19 December 2007.
3 'New Kenya leader promises reform', *BBC News*, 30 December 2002, available online at http://news.bbc.co.uk/1/hi/world/africa/2614963.stm (accessed 20 May 2015).
4 'Kibaki and Moi Speech Excerpts', *BBC News*, 30 December 2007, available online at http://news.bbc.co.uk/1/hi/not_in_website/syndication/monitoring/media_reports/2615369.stm (accessed 20 May 2015).

40 *The responsibility to protect*

5 'Kenyans reject new constitution', *BBC News*, 22 November 2005, available online at http://news.bbc.co.uk/1/hi/world/africa/4455538.stm (accessed 20 May 2015).
6 The International Republican Institute, 'Kenya Presidential, Parliamentary and Local Elections, December 2007: Election Observation Mission Final Report', p. 7, available online at www.iri.org/sites/default/files/Kenya%27s%202007%20Presidental,%20Parliamentary%20and%20Local%20Elections.pdf (accessed 20 May 2015).
7 Kenyans for Peace, Truth and Justice, 'Countdown to Deception: 30 Hours that Destroyed Kenya', 18 January 2008, available online at www.africog.org/reports/KPTJ-%20Countdown%20to%20Deception.pdf (accessed 20 May 2015).
8 Ibid.
9 Ibid.
10 Ibid.
11 Xan Rice, 'Riots and vote-rigging claims as Kenyan polls go to the wire', *Guardian*, 30 December 2007, available online at www.theguardian.com/world/2007/dec/30/kenya.xanrice (accessed 20 May 2015).
12 Human Rights Watch, *Ballots to Bullets. Organized Political Violence and Kenya's Crisis of Governance*, 2.1(A), March 2008, p. 22, available online at www.hrw.org/sites/default/files/reports/kenya0308web.pdf (accessed on 20 May 2015).
13 Ibid.
14 'Kenya's dubious election', *BBC News*, 8 January 2008, available online at http://news.bbc.co.uk/1/hi/world/africa/7175694.stm (accessed 20 May 2015).
15 'Kibaki named victor in Kenya vote', *BBC News*, 30 December 2007, available online at http://news.bbc.co.uk/1/hi/world/africa/7164890.stm (accessed 20 May 2015).
16 Juliet Njeri, 'Kibaki: Dream or Nightmare', *BBC News*, 2 January 2008, available online at http://news.bbc.co.uk/1/hi/world/africa/7079210.stm (accessed 20 May 2015).
17 Jeffrey Gettleman, 'Disputed Vote Plunges Kenya into Bloodshed', *New York Times*, 31 December 2007, available online at www.nytimes.com/2007/12/31/world/africa/31kenya.html?pagewanted=all&_r=0 (accessed 20 May 2015).
18 'Odinga rejects Kenya poll result', *BBC News*, 31 December 2007, available online at http://news.bbc.co.uk/1/hi/7165406.stm accessed 20 May 2015).
19 Committee to Protect Journalists, 'Attacks on the Press in Kenya: 2008', available online at https://cpj.org/2009/02/attacks-on-the-press-in-2008-kenya.php (accessed 20 May 2015).
20 'Kibaki named victor in Kenya vote', *BBC News*, 30 December 2007, available online at http://news.bbc.co.uk/1/hi/world/africa/7164890.stm (accessed 20 May 2015); See also: European Union Election Observation Mission, *Kenya. Final Report. General Election 27 December 2007*, 3 April 2008
21 'Kibaki re-elected as President of Kenya', *Financial Times*, 30 December 2007, available online at www.ft.com/cms/s/0/7aacfdd6-b6f1–11dc-aa38–0000779fd2ac.html#axzz3awmaGFXo (accessed 20 May 2015).
22 'Press Statement by Ambassador Jack Tumwa, D.A. Ndambiri, S.K. arap Ngeny and J. Matagaro, 31 December 2007', cited in International Crisis Group, 'Kenya in Crisis', *Africa Report* 137, 21 February 2008, p. 8, available online at www.crisisgroup.org/~/media/Files/africa/horn-of-africa/kenya/137_kenya_in_crisis_web.pdf (accessed 20 May 2015).
23 Human Rights House, 'I acted under pressure – says Electoral Commission Chairman, Kivuitu', 2 January 2008, available online at http://humanrightshouse.org/noop/page.php?p=Articles/8420.html&d=1 (accessed 20 May 2015).
24 'Press Statement by S.M. Kivuitu, Chairman, Electoral Commission of Kenya, Parliamentary election result, 1 January 2008', cited in International Crisis Group, 'Kenya in Crisis', p. 8.
25 Ibid.

26 Ibid.
27 PNU drew most of its support from Central and Eastern Provinces, with some following in Nairobi, Coast and in the Rift. ODM drew support from Nyanza, Western, Rift Valley, with some following in Coast and North Eastern.
28 Kenya National Commission on Human Rights, *On the Brink of the Precipice*, p. 67.
29 Human Rights Watch, *Ballots to Bullets*, p. 41.
30 The Waki report has highlighted the challenges associated with collecting reliable evidence on sexual violence in the context of the post-election period. Given the extent to which such crimes tend to be underreported in conflict theatres, the actual number of sexual crimes committed throughout the crisis is thought to be much higher. See, in particular, Chapter 6 of the report.
31 Ibid., p. 24.
32 Jeffrey Gettleman, 'Signs in Kenya that the killings were planned', *New York Times*, 21 January 2008, available online at www.nytimes.com/2008/01/21/world/africa/21kenya.html?pagewanted=all&_r=0 (accessed 20 May 2015).
33 Human Rights Watch, *Ballots to Bullets*, p. 5.
34 Jeffrey Gettleman, 'Signs in Kenya that the killings were planned.'
35 'Kenya: Spreading the word of hate', *IRIN News*, 22 January 2008, available online at www.irinnews.org/report/76346/kenya-spreading-the-word-of-hate (accessed 20 May 2015).
36 Final Report from Kenya's Commission of Inquiry into Post-election Violence, 15 October 2008 (The Waki Report), pp. 46–7.
37 Report from OHCHR Fact-Finding Mission to Kenya, 6–28 February 2008, p. 10, available online at http://responsibilitytoprotect.org/OHCHR%20Kenya%20Report.pdf (accessed 20 May 2010).
38 Human Rights Watch, *Ballots to Bullets*, p. 55.
39 Ibid., p. 5.
40 Ibid., p. 46.
41 International Crisis Group, 'Kenya in Crisis', p. 13.
42 'Raising Funds to arm gangs for revenge poison delicate peace', *Daily Nation*, 27 February 2008.
43 Human Rights Watch, *Ballots to Bullets*, p. 28.
44 Ibid., p. 30.
45 Ibid., p. 33.
46 As noted in the Human Rights Watch report:

> The police responded in an uneven fashion to the political, ethnic-based violence. While willing to shoot to kill without justification in Kisumu, when lives were not at stake, police officers in other areas markedly did not use lethal force in circumstances when they might have been justified in doing so to protect lives.
>
> p. 60

47 Makumi Mwagiru, *The Water's Edge: Mediation of Violent Electoral Conflict in Kenya* (Institute of Diplomacy and International Studies, 2008), p. 3.
48 Ibid., p. vi.
49 Ibid., p. 12.
50 Report from OHCHR Fact-Finding Mission to Kenya, p. 14.
51 Human Rights Watch, *Ballots to Bullets*, p. 57.
52 Tom Maliti Kenya: 'The Long Dark Night for Business', *Africa Report*, 21 November 2008, available online at www.theafricareport.com/archives2/business/3278865-kenya-the-long-dark-night-for-business.html (accessed 20 May 2015). See also Africa Review of Business and Technology, 'Post-election Violence Causes Regional Fallout: Post-election Violence in Kenya Has Already Left its Mark on East African Business', April 2008, available online at www.entrepreneur.com/tradejournals/article/179048794.html (accessed 20 May 2015).

53 Mary Kimani, 'East Africa Feels Blows of Kenyan Crisis', *Africa Renewal* 22.1, 1 April 2008, p. 3, available online at www.un.org/ecosocdev/geninfo/afrec/vol.22no1/221-kenyan-crisis.html (accessed 20 May 2015).
54 Katie Hunt, 'Violence threatens Kenya's Economy', *BBC News*, 2 January 2008, available online at http://news.bbc.co.uk/2/hi/business/7168060.stm (accessed 20 May 2015); 'Kenyan Violence Hits Fuel Supply', *BBC News*, 4 January 2008, available online at http://news.bbc.co.uk/2/hi/7171439.stm (accessed 20 May 2015).
55 Monica Kathina Juma, 'African Mediation of the Kenyan post-2007 election crisis', *Journal of Contemporary African Studies*, 27.3 (2009), p. 423.
56 Daniel Volman, 'U.S. Military Activities in Kenya, African Security Research Project', January 2008, available online at http://concernedafricascholars.org/african-security-research-project/?p=3 (accessed 20 May 2015).
57 The British Army Overseas Deployments, 'The British Army in Africa', available online at www.army.mod.uk/operations-deployments/22724.aspx (accessed 20 May 2015).
58 Xan Rice, 'MoD Threatens to Halt Training of Kenyan Military over Claims of Rights Abuses', *Guardian*, 29 July 2008, available online at www.guardian.co.uk/world/2008/jul/29/kenya.military (accessed 20 May 2015).
59 Regional Parliamentarians Fact Finding Mission to Kenya on the Post Election Violence, 13–21 January 2008, p. 22, The Amani Forum, The Great Lakes Parliamentary Forum on Peace, available online at www.responsibilitytoprotect.org/files/Fact-Finding%20Mission%20Report%20by%20Great%20Lakes%20Parliamentarians%20on%20Kenyan%20Post-Election%20Violence.pdf (accessed 20 May 2015).
60 'Press conference to seek flash appeal seeking more than $40 million in humanitarian, early recovery aid for 500 000 Kenyans', *United Nations Meetings Coverage and Press Releases*, 16 January 2008, available online at www.un.org/press/en/2008/080116_Holmes.doc.htm (accessed 20 May 2015).
61 'Press conference by United Nations Emergency Relief Coordinator to update humanitarian situation in Kenya, 9 January 2008', available online at www.un.org/press/en/2008/030109_Holmes.doc.htm (accessed 20 May 2015).
62 Statement by Professor Wangari Maathai on the Unrest and Violence in Kenya, 1 January 2008 available online at http://greenbeltmovement.org.s126284.gridserver.com/a.php?id=270 (accessed 20 May 2015).
63 ODM-Kenya was a splinter group of ODM that formed prior to the 2007 General Election led by Kalonzo Musyoka. During the 2007 Presidential Election Musyoka captured 879 903 votes.
64 George Wachira, *Citizens in Action: Making Peace in the Post-Election Crisis in Kenya – 2008* (NPI-Africa, January 2010), p. 4.
65 'Kagame calls for military intervention in Kenya crisis', *Panapress*, 31 January 2008, available online at www.panapress.com/Kagame-calls-for-military-intervention-in-Kenyan-crisis--13-511451-17-lang1-index.html (accessed 20 May 2015).
66 Ibid.
67 Jomo Kenyatta served as President of Kenya from 1964 to 1978.
68 Daniel Arap Moi served as President of Kenya from 1978 to 2002.
69 Suzanne Mueller, 'The Political Economy of Kenya's Crisis', *Journal of Eastern African Studies*, 2.2 (2008), pp. 185–210.
70 'Profile: Kenya's Secretive Mungiki Sect', *BBC News*, 24 May 2007, available online at http://news.bbc.co.uk/1/hi/world/africa/6685393.stm (accessed 30 June 2015).
71 The Carter Centre, *Observing Kenya's March 2013 National Elections*, Final Report, available online at www.cartercenter.org/resources/pdfs/news/peace_publications/election_reports/kenya-final-101613.pdf (accessed 30 June 2015).

72 See in particular Michaela Wrong, *It's Our Turn to Eat: The Story of a Kenyan Whistleblower* (Harper Collins, 2009).
73 See Jacqueline M. Klopp, 'Pilfering the Public: The Problem of Land Grabbing in Contemporary Kenya', *Africa Today*, 47.1 (2000), pp. 7–26.
74 See David K Leonard *et al.*, The Political and Institutional Context of the 2007 Kenyan Elections and Reforms Needed for the Future, *Journal of African Elections*, 8.1 (2009), pp. 71–107.
75 Human Rights Watch, *Ballots to Bullets*, p. 17.
76 Report from OHCHR Fact-Finding Mission to Kenya, p. 6.
77 Commission of Human Rights, Report of the Independent Expert to Update the Set of Principles to Combat Impunity, 8 February 2005, E/CN.4/2005/102/Add.1.
78 See Daniel Branch, *Defeating Mau Mau, Creating Kenya: Counterinsurgency, Civil War and Decolonization* (Cambridge University Press, 2009); David Anderson, *Histories of the Hanged: Britain's Dirty War in Kenya and the End of Empire* (Weidenfeld and Nicolson, 2005).
79 Kim Mathews and William H. Coogan, 'Kenya and the Rule of Law: The Perspective of Two Volunteers', *Maine Law Review* 60 (2008), p. 561.
80 The Report by the Parliamentary Select Committee to Investigate Ethnic Clashes in Western and other parts of Kenya 1992 (Kiliku Report), (National Assembly, 1992).
81 Report of the Judicial Commission Appointed to Inquire into Tribal Clashes in Kenya (The Akiwumi Report), (The Commission, 1999).
82 Human Rights Watch, *Ballots to Bullets*, p. 18.
83 'Kenya: Wagalla Massacre Survivors Testify', *BBC News*, 18 April 2011, available online at www.bbc.co.uk/news/world-africa-13123813 (accessed 20 June 2015).
84 Lucy Hannon, 'Minister Forces Kenya to Hold Torture Inquiry', *Mail and Guardian*, 17 April 1998, available online at http://mg.co.za/article/1998-04-17-minister-forces-kenya-to-hold-torture-inquiry (accessed 20 June 2015).
85 Paul Ogemba, 'Pattni Cleared in Goldenberg Scam', *Daily Nation*, 19 April 2013, available online at www.nation.co.ke/News/politics/Pattni-cleared-in-Goldenberg-scam/-/1064/1753240/-/146dhe5z/-/index.html (accessed 20 June 2015).
86 David Pallister, 'Scandals Cast Shadow Over Kenya's Government', *Guardian*, 6 July 2004, available online at www.theguardian.com/world/2004/jul/06/kenya.davidpallister (accessed 20 June 2015).
87 The Waki Report, p. 16.
88 Makumi Mwagiru, *The Water's Edge*, p. vi.
89 'Country Review Report of the Republic of Kenya', Africa Peer Review Mechanism Country Report for Kenya, 2006, p. 14; See Also, Bronwen Manby, 'Was the APRM Process in Kenya a Waste of Time: Lessons that Should be Learned for the Future', *Open Society Institute*, April 2008, available online at www.afrimap.org/english/images/paper/Manby_APRM-Kenya.pdf (accessed 20 May 2015).
90 'Maina Kiai statement to US House of Representatives', 6 February 2008, available online at https://kenyanemergency.wordpress.com/2008/02/06/maina-kiais-statement-to-us-house-of-representatives/ (accessed 20 May 2015).
91 Ibid.
92 Peter Opiyo, 'Kivuitu Wins Jurist Award', *All Africa Stories*, 13 December 2007.
93 Ibid.
94 Ibid.
95 'Chaos Mars Kenya Party Primaries', *BBC News*, 20 November 2007, available online at http://news.bbc.co.uk/1/hi/world/africa/7103746.stm (accessed 20 May 2015).
96 Human Rights Watch, *Ballots to Bullets*, p. 20.
97 See David Anderson, 'Majimboism: The Troubled History of an Idea', in Daniel Branch, Nic Cheeseman, and Leigh Gardner (eds), *Our Turn to Eat: Politics in Kenya Since 1950*, (Lit Verlag, 2010), pp. 23–52.

98 Ibid., 4.
99 Peter Kagwanja and Roger Southall, 'Introduction: Kenya – A Democracy in Retreat?' *Journal of Contemporary African Studies*, 27.3 (2009), pp. 259–77.
100 Kenyan National Commission for Human Rights, 'Still Behaving Badly', Second Periodic Report of the Election Monitoring Project, December 2007, available online at www.rwi.lu se/NHRIDB/Africa/Kenya/Kenya_KNCHR_Election_Report_2007.pdf (accessed 20 May 2015).
101 Human Rights Watch, *Ballots to Bullets*, p. 20.
102 In their report, KNCHR noted that 30 female Parliamentary and Civic Aspirants were threatened or attacked prior to the election. On 1 December 2007, Ms Alice Onduto, a parliamentary aspirant for Lugari Constituency, was killed.
103 European Union Election Observation Mission (EUEOM), Kenya 2007, 'Preliminary Statement'. Nairobi, 1 January 2008.
104 'EU Condemns Pre-election Violence in Kenya', *Reuters*, 21 December 2007, available online at www.reuters.com/article/2007/12/21/us-kenya-election-idUSL2120 415120071221 (accessed 20 May 2015).
105 Ibid.
106 Report from OHCHR Fact-Finding Mission to Kenya, p. 12.
107 Stephen Brown. 'Donor Responses to the 2008 Crisis in Kenya: Finally Getting it Right? *Journal of Contemporary African Studies*, 27.3 (2009), pp. 289–406.
108 Stephen Brown. 'Quiet Diplomacy and Recurring "Ethnic Clashes" in Kenya', in Chandra Lekha Sriram and Karin Wermester (eds), *From Promise to Practice: Strengthening UN Capacities for the Prevention of Violent Conflict* (Lynne Rienner, 2003), pp. 69–100.
109 Interview with Michaela Wrong, UK, 19 March 2010.
110 Interview with John Githongo, Inuka Trust, Nairobi, 13 August 2010.
111 Ben Sihanya and Duncan Okello, 'Mediating Kenya's Post-Election Crisis: The Politics and Limits of Power Sharing Agreement', in Karuti Kanyinga and Duncan Okello (eds), *Tensions and Reversals in Democratic Transitions: The Kenya 2007 General Elections* (Society for International Development: Nairobi, 2010), p. 672.

2 The KNDR process
A model case for R2P?

> I saw the crisis in the R2P prism with a Kenyan government unable to contain the situation or protect its people.... I knew that if the international community did not intervene, things would go hopelessly wrong.... Kenya is a successful example of R2P at work.[1]
>
> (Kofi Annan)

As Kenya burned, the nature of the killings evoked memories of Rwanda, where 13 years earlier the international community stood by and watched the slaughter of hundreds of thousands. Yet, the responses to these two situations could not have been more dissimilar. Almost immediately the crisis in Kenya captured the attention of concerned international actors, united in their determination to halt the spiralling violence. The international response centred on an African Union-sponsored mediation process led by the former UN Secretary-General, Kofi Annan. Support for the mediation process became 'the embodiment of a battle for the protection of democracy in Kenya, seen by many as a model for the continent.'[2] After 41 days of intense negotiations, a compromise was reached between President Mwai Kibaki and Raila Odinga.

The global interest that the crisis in Kenya generated can be attributed to several factors. As seen in the previous chapter, Kenya was viewed as an important stabiliser in the region and therefore, the prospect of any turmoil in the country had far-reaching consequences. Further to this, one might argue that there had been a shift in consciousness since the adoption of R2P two years prior during the United Nations World Summit in 2005. During this meeting, the largest gathering of heads of state endorsed their responsibility to protect populations from atrocity crimes (genocide, crimes against humanity, war crimes and ethnic cleansing) in situations where state authorities are manifestly failing to do so. The crisis in Kenya became the first 'test case' for the principle of R2P since its endorsement at the World Summit.

In contrast to previous situations wherein atrocity crimes have been ongoing or imminent, the post-election violence in Kenya was a situation where there was sufficient political will to act in a timely and decisive manner. Engaging the parties through a consensual mediation process underscored that atrocities could be forestalled without having to resort to military force. Moreover, the fact that the global response could be channelled through the African Union added legitimacy to these efforts. The response to the post-election crisis in Kenya continues to be regarded as a success story for R2P and an example of best practice for atrocity prevention in other contexts.

This chapter will trace the international response to the crisis in Kenya and its framing as a success story for R2P. It will begin with the initial attempts to resolve the crisis, leading to the appointment of the High Level Panel of Eminent African Personalities. After exploring the key stages of the mediation process the chapter will critically assess this case from the perspective of R2P. Although the Kenyan situation is often referred to as a model case for R2P, as this chapter will argue, the factors that contributed to success in this situation may prove difficult to replicate in other contexts. Moreover, the notion of this case constituting a success story may have been slightly premature. Alongside the resolution of the political crisis, the mediation agenda advocated a set of longer-term reforms, which were intended to address the underlying causes of the violence. In this regard the signing of the accords on 28 February not only signified the culmination of an intense mediation effort, the agreements also marked the commencement of Kenya's reform process.

The world watching Kenya

During the first two months of 2008, the eyes of the world were firmly transfixed on the deteriorating situation in Kenya. From Pope Benedict II to UN Secretary-General Ban Ki-Moon,[3] impassioned appeals were made to restore peace and calm to the country.[4] The situation also drew the attention of the International Criminal Court's Chief Prosecutor, who subsequently issued a statement advising that his office was carefully considering information pertaining to alleged crimes that may have been committed.[5] Through these expressions of concern the international community conveyed that it was not prepared to stand by and watch as Kenya fell apart.

Rather fortuitously, the crisis in Kenya coincided with the appointment of the first UN Special Adviser on R2P in late 2007. Having solidified support for R2P two years prior during the 2005 UN World Summit, Ban Ki-Moon appointed Columbia University Professor, Edward Luck, to the post. Through this role, Luck was tasked with the conceptual development of R2P and building normative consensus following the World Summit. In this capacity, Luck was not only mandated to work closely with the UN Special Adviser on the Prevention of Genocide, the two would eventually form a joint office in order to facilitate a coordinated UN approach to the prevention of genocide and mass atrocities.

As these bureaucratic developments were taking place within the UN system, the violence in Kenya began to unfold. The crisis in Kenya therefore, became the 'first instance in which the United Nations employed a responsibility to protect (R2P) lens in shaping its response to an ongoing crisis.'[6] Luck has since recalled how the situation developed:

We were not set up in any way, shape, or manner.... But the situation there looked like an R2P contingency in terms of the risk of growing violence.... So it just seemed important to me to flag this one early, and to say it's an R2P situation. Now we had no mechanism set up or anything. So it was a little premature, but other high-level UN officials agreed.[7]

As early as 31 December 2007, UN Secretary-General Ban Ki-moon issued a statement expressing concern with the ongoing violence.[8] He called on the population to remain calm and urged the Kenyan security forces to practice restraint. On the same day, then UN High Commissioner for Human Rights, Louise Arbour, called on the Kenyan Government to abide by its international human rights obligations.[9] A few days later, on 2 January 2008, the Office of the Secretary General released a further statement that made explicit reference to the principle of R2P:

> The Secretary-General reminds the Government, as well as the political and religious leaders of Kenya of their legal and moral responsibility to protect the lives of innocent people, regardless of their racial, religious or ethnic origin and he strongly urges them to do everything within their capacity to prevent any further violence.[10]

Throughout the crisis, R2P was similarly invoked by Francis Deng, the UN Special Adviser on the Prevention of Genocide[11] and Desmond Tutu,[12] who visited Kenya under the umbrella of the All Africa Conference of Churches (AACC). The French Foreign Minister, Bernard Kouchner, also called for action on the basis of R2P: 'In the name of the responsibility to protect ... the United Nations Security Council must take up this question and act.'[13]

The Security Council convened on 6 February 2008 to consider the escalation of violence in Kenya and thereafter issued a Presidential Statement expressing concern with the situation.[14] Interestingly, references to the norm were 'not explicitly part of the debate in the Council,'[15] as the association between the Kenya case and R2P became much more pronounced in the aftermath of the crisis. On the one hand, this may reflect continuing reluctance among Council Members to use the language of R2P; as US Ambassador to the UN Susan Rice has observed, 'raising the R2P flag may be morally satisfying, but it can be politically fraught.'[16] However, the relatively muted role of R2P may also reflect the principally *supporting* role of the United Nations throughout the crisis. As Luck has observed, 'rather than competing for glory or headlines,' the United Nations 'provided quiet but essential political support and capacity building for the AU-led effort,'[17] which swiftly became the focal point of the regional and international response.

While the response to the crisis in Kenya has come to be regarded as an exemplary case of well-coordinated and timely action, preliminary efforts to resolve the crisis were diffuse and disorganised. With a plethora of prospective mediators flooding into Nairobi, a series of diverging – and often competing – attempts were made to initiate talks between Kibaki and Odinga. These ranged from bilateral efforts to regional and international initiatives. Among the first efforts were those of Bishop Desmund Tutu, operating under the aegis of the African Conference of Churches. This was followed by a visit from Jendayi Frazer, US Secretary of State for African Affairs. A further attempt to launch a dialogue between the two sides was initiated by the Forum of Former African Heads of States, through Benjamin Mkapa (Tanzania), Joachim Chissano (Mozambique), Kenneth Kaunda (Zambia) and Ketumile Masire (Botswana). Alongside these efforts were additional attempts to resolve the crisis through the World Bank Country Director, Colin Bruce, who endeavoured to get the two sides to sign an agreement. Finally, President Yoweri Museveni of Uganda also attempted to push through a peace plan of his own. The sheer volume of early interventions in the crisis contributed to their collective failure, as the multiplicity of mediation channels tacitly encouraged both sides to engage in 'mediator shopping.' Kibaki, in particular, seized upon an initially fragmented international response to evade talks, as the plethora of options increased 'both the channels of communication and the possibilities for stalling any real efforts toward peace.'[18]

As the situation became more intractable, President John Kufour of Ghana, Chair of the African Union at the time, called for an emergency meeting of the AU's Peace and Security Council. Shortly thereafter, Kufour flew to Nairobi on 8 January in order to persuade the parties to consent to an African Union mediation process. Kufour experienced considerable difficulty, however, as his arrival coincided with Kibaki's controversial appointment of a new cabinet.[19] The appointment of 16 Ministers, along with Kalonzo Musyoka of ODM-Kenya as Vice President, appeared to be a direct attempt to undermine Kufour's efforts to resolve the crisis.

At this point there remained crucial differences between the two sides, which severely hampered the prospects for mediation. Odinga continued to demand Kibaki's resignation and a re-run of the presidential election; whereas, the PNU were not particularly keen on international mediation. They insisted that Kibaki was the legitimate President and that those disputing the results should bring their concerns before a court of law. Given their lack of faith in the Kenyan judiciary, which they argued would be partial to the Government, ODM ruled out this option relatively early on in the crisis. In this regard the only matter both parties could agree on was an unwillingness to negotiate.

Unable to reach a breakthrough, Kufour put forward the suggestion of a Panel of Eminent Africans to lead negotiations, which would consist of Kofi Annan (former UN Secretary General) Graça Machel (Mozambican politician and humanitarian) and Benjamin Mkapa (former President of Tanzania). As Kufour has subsequently explained: 'I phoned Kofi Annan ... from here and prevailed on him. [The] situation was so dire it needed someone like him – otherwise, there may be a continuation of the situation and no end to it.'[20] According to a report by the Panel of Eminent African Personalities:

> The African Union's willingness to engage, through the Panel, owed a good deal to growing support in Africa for the responsibility to protect doctrine,

as well as Article 4(h) of the African Union's Constitutive Act ... which affirmed the right to intervene in the affairs of Member States under certain conditions.[21]

The African Union was therefore, well placed to act in a timely and decisive manner. Not only did the organisation swiftly respond to the crisis, it selected the esteemed former UN Secretary-General to Chair the negotiations. Through his authority and professional stature Kofi Annan brought considerable influence to the mediation process in Kenya.

The AU Panel of Eminent African Personalities

Although the Panel's efforts benefited tremendously from Annan's highly regarded record in peacemaking, the negotiations would prove to be far from straightforward. The road to a resolution encountered a number of stumbling blocks, the first of which occurred prior to Annan's arrival in Kenya. Annan was meant to travel to Nairobi on 16 January, but his journey was delayed until 22 January due to illness. The time in between his intended and actual departure date was, however, put to good use, as Annan was able to build a strong base of political support for the Panel's work. Before arriving in Kenya, he had the backing of the AU, UN, EU and a number of key allies. Along with securing the essential support of the international community, Annan's approach assured that external actors spoke with one voice. Building cohesion among international actors proved to be an essential component of the Panel's success, effectively putting an end to the multiple and competing channels of negotiation that arose at the outset of the crisis. In the lead-up to formal negotiations Annan also began to assemble a Secretariat, tasked with providing administrative and logistical support for the Panel's efforts. The Secretariat was staffed with officials from UNDP in Nairobi, UNDPA in New York, the African Union and the Centre for Humanitarian Dialogue. The Panel would also draw upon the advice of technical experts throughout different stages of the negotiations.

By the time the Panel arrived in Nairobi on 22 January 2008, Kibaki made a last ditch effort to avoid external mediation by cancelling a meeting with Annan in order to engage in talks with the Ugandan President Museveni. When Museveni's peace plan failed to bear fruit, Kibaki and Odinga agreed to a preliminary meeting with Annan on 24 January 2008. While there was some resistance, particularly from Odinga who expressed concern that a meeting at State House would legitimatise Kibaki's presidency, the option of Harambee house was proposed as an alternate location. In his initial meeting with Kibaki and Odinga, Annan came to realise the level of mistrust between the two, given their acrimonious history. He nevertheless impressed upon them the gravity of the situation and urged them to appear in public together to calm the rising tensions and dissuade the growing violence on the ground.

On the same day, Kibaki and Odinga appeared on the steps of Harambee House in front of the media. While this appearance and the subsequent handshake between Kibaki and Odinga, was intended to build trust and pave the way towards dialogue, the event had the reverse effect. To the dismay of Odinga, Kibaki was not only accompanied to the meeting by his entire cabinet, he used the occasion as an opportunity to convey that he was the 'duly elected President of Kenya.' As a member of the ODM stated: 'True to his fraudulent character, Mr. Mwai Kibaki abused the occasion by attempting to legitimize his usurpation of the presidency.'[22] He continued: 'This was supposed to be an event to build good faith. Kibaki politicized it.'[23] Notwithstanding the controversy generated by the 24 January meeting, in bringing Odinga and Kibaki together and encouraging them to shake hands in public, Annan accomplished more during his first two days in Kenya than any other negotiator had achieved during the preceding three weeks.

On 26 January the Panel visited some of the areas most adversely affected by the violence. Accompanied by the Chair of Kenyan Red Cross, the delegation travelled to IDP camps around the country and witnessed first-hand the level of violence and devastation. In reflecting on this trip, Annan has stated: 'It was when I got on the ground and saw the ethnic nature of the killings and the conflict that the responsibility to protect, and the Rwandan and Yugoslavian stories came to mind.'[24] Upon his return from this trip Annan emphasised the severity of the crisis: 'What we saw was rather tragic ... and I think it is important that all Kenyans respond with sympathy and understanding and not try to [seek] revenge.'[25]

The next few days were spent preparing the groundwork for negotiations. Given the intensely acrimonious relationship between Kibaki and Odinga, Annan invited the two principals to elect three representatives to negotiate on their behalf. After deliberations, the size of the negotiating teams were increased to four members per party. For the PNU side, Kibaki nominated Martha Karua, Sam Ongeri, Mutula Kilonzo, and Moses Wetangula. The ODM side included Musalia Mudavadi, William Ruto, Sally Kosgei, and James Orengo. Along with agreeing on the terms of reference and specific modalities for negotiations, the two sides had to agree on what to call the negotiating process. The PNU strongly favoured the term 'dialogue' over mediation – as the former sounded more conciliatory and played down the level of external involvement. From that point forward, the process came to be referred to as the Kenyan National Dialogue and Reconciliation (KNDR).

Formal negotiations begin

The KNDR process was formally launched on 29 January 2008 at the Serena Hotel in Nairobi. In order to bring a sense of unity and shared purpose to the process, Annan encouraged the teams to commence the KNDR sessions with a prayer, with each of the members alternating as the lead. Throughout the duration of the negotiating process, the practice of starting each session with a prayer continued.[26]

In order to keep the negotiations inclusive and give Kenyans a sense of ownership over the process, regular press briefings were held after each session and translated into Swahili. At the same time, members of the negotiating teams were discouraged from making statements to the media. Given the sensitive nature of the negotiations, unauthorised statements to the media could potentially undermine the process and further inflame tensions throughout the country.

The first order of business was to agree on a road map for negotiations. During this part of the process the Panel elicited input from Kenyan civil society. Two organisations that emerged during the post-election crisis, and continued to play an important role in consultations with the Panel, were the Kenyans for Peace, Truth and Justice (KPTJ) and Concerned Citizens for Peace (CCP). The Panel also held consultations with humanitarian organisations, most notably the Kenyan Red Cross (KRC) as well as established private sector organisations including the Kenyan Private Sector Alliance (KEPSA) and the Kenyan Association of Manufacturers (KAM). Through its consultations with civil society organisations, the Panel asserted its autonomy and therein indicated to the Kenyan public 'that it was mediating a negotiation for the benefit of the entire country, not only the political class and that every stakeholder who had something to say would be heard.'[27]

The Road Map that was subsequently agreed to included four agenda items:

(1) Immediate actions to stop the violence and restore fundamental liberties.
(2) Immediate measures to address the humanitarian crisis, and promoting reconciliation, healing and restoration.
(3) Overcoming the political crisis.
(4) Long-term issues and solutions.

The specific ordering of the Agenda items was by no means arbitrary, but reflected both the urgency of certain issues and the ease with which agreement could be reached on particular points. In this respect, the structure of the Agenda was intended to build confidence among the negotiating teams by progressing on the less contentious items before moving on to some of the more divisive areas.[28] Between 1 February and 4 February the negotiating team reached agreement on the first two Agenda items – ending the violence and addressing the humanitarian situation on the ground. Following briefings from the Kenyan Red Cross and UNDP, a series of actions were agreed to, including: 'concrete measures to hold joint meetings to promote peace, ensure freedom of expression and the right to peaceful assembly; investigations into crime and police brutality; assisting the safe return of internally displaced persons; and the establishment of a truth and reconciliation commission.'[29]

Although negotiations appeared to be off to a promising start, a minor setback occurred on 1 February during Kibaki's attendance at the Intergovernmental Authority on Development (IGAD) summit. During this meeting, Kibaki blamed ODM for the ongoing political crisis in Kenya by suggesting that their supporters had unleashed a campaign of civil unrest following the election. As if to pre-empt the negotiations, he also said that the situation could be resolved amicably through the Courts.[30] Many perceived these actions as part of the PNU's strategy to buy time 'and wear down both the opposition and the international community's resolve.'[31] Annan, therefore, took the opportunity to reiterate that there was one process and one process only[32] – a sentiment that was reinforced by a well-timed visit of the Secretary-General. Ban held talks with the PNU and ODM and impressed upon them the gravity of the situation: 'The killing must stop, the violence must end for the sake of the Kenyan people and for the sake of Kenya.... I call on the negotiation teams to persevere and show the courage, vision and leadership to expeditiously find a just and peaceful solution.'[33]

Some further progress was made following the Secretary-General's visit, as the Government announced a lifting of the prohibition on live broadcasts on 4 February 2008.[34] This was followed by a decision to revoke the ban on public gatherings.[35] Both of these controversial bans – which had been instituted over a month earlier – had drawn widespread criticism from human rights groups.

Overcoming the political crisis

Having reached agreement on the first two issues of the Road Map, the negotiating team now turned to what would prove to be the most contentious issue on the Agenda – overcoming the political crisis. Making progress on Agenda Item 3 could not be disentangled from the controversy surrounding the outcome of the 2007 Presidential Elections. On this point, both sides remained firmly deadlocked. The PNU continued to insist that it had won freely and fairly; ODM reiterated that attempts to rig the election were apparent well in advance of the 2007 polls.

While the EU had initially called for a forensic audit, there was no reliable way to determine who actually won the election. In his testimony to the US Congress on 7 February 2008, Joel Barkan argued the following: 'it does not really matter at this juncture in fact who won the election if in fact it can ever be determined.... Neither side can govern Kenya by itself.'[36] Annan had come to a similar conclusion: 'when looking at the election results, it was clear to me that there was no way that either party could run the government effectively without the other. So some type of partnership/coalition was going to be necessary.'[37] He subsequently described how he had to go through various options 'and let them come to the conclusion that they had no option but to share power.'[38] For this part of the process, Annan relied on technical experts from the UN Department of Political Affairs, Electoral Assistance Division to brief the parties on the feasibility of various options. In so doing, the Panel took the negotiating teams on a deductive process of elimination:

> I put all the items on the table and let them run ... through what each option means. For example, if you are going to do a rerun, it's almost like full elections. And they knew the situation on the ground; 'Given the environment, do you think we can have a rerun? ... Counting 11 million votes and sending people to all the constituencies – it's another election, and it's going to get people killed. Is that what you want? Retallying gives you bits and pieces of

paper, but it doesn't give you anything else. The so-called forensic audit doesn't really make sense. If this is the case, we don't want to sweep the election issue under the carpet. We have to find some way of dealing with it.' And ... I thought the Independent Review would be the way.[39]

Once it became apparent to the negotiating team that there was no quick and reliable way to arrive at the truth of the results, the parties agreed to conduct an Independent Review to investigate all aspects of the elections and make recommendations to ensure the mistakes of the 2007 polls were never repeated. The decision to hold an Independent Review was a necessary step in getting the parties to refrain from revisiting the past and to focus on forward-looking solutions to the crisis. Speaking at a press conference, the Panel summarised its perspective on the issue:

> I think everyone realises that we have a serious problem in the country. They also accept that we have to find a way of uniting and reconciling the nation. In the negotiations we have agreed that what is needed is a political solution. We are actively discussing the terms of that solution and I sincerely hope that we will conclude our work on Item 3 – the settlement of the political issues by early next week.[40]

Precisely what type of political solution would be required to resolve the stalemate remained undefined until the informal briefing to Parliament (*Kamakunji*) on 12 February. During the *Kamkunji,* Annan made explicit reference to the constitution of a 'grand coalition.' For Annan it was a foregone conclusion that 'the resolution of the crisis would require some form of power-sharing arrangement, however, the term "grand coalition" implied a level of agreement which had not yet been reached'[41] and therefore elicited a strong level of condemnation from the negotiating teams. In a sternly worded letter to Annan, Martha Karua argued, 'as Chair of the Panel, you are expected to be impartial and to take every care not to misrepresent or compromise the position of either party.'[42] In a subsequent press statement, Annan insisted that 'a grand coalition was an option often chosen when a country was in deadlock and that this represented "his perspective on the discussions", rather than any formal agreement.'[43] Despite the strong reaction to Annan's statement, as Lindemayer and Kaye have argued, his remarks helped 'plant the seeds' for a possible resolution of Agenda 3.[44]

With the most divisive aspects of Agenda 3 yet to be resolved, Annan transferred the talks to Kilaguni Lodge in Tsavo National Park. The retreat outside of Nairobi was intended to provide a calmer and more relaxed atmosphere to deliberate on the more polarising aspects of Agenda 3, with the added benefit of being outside the glare of the national and international media. The location of the retreat was initially undisclosed so as to allow the parties space to focus on the important business at hand. During this phase of the negotiations, the Panel was joined by Hans Corell, former Under-Secretary-General for Legal Affairs and Legal Counsel of the UN and Gernot Erler, German Minister of State. While

Corell provided the negotiators with advice on legal issues, particularly in relation to a constitutional amendment that would allow for power sharing, Erler engaged the parties in discussions concerning coalition governments.

The Kilaguni retreat failed to yield a significant breakthrough; however, it did facilitate the signing of an agreement on 14 February for establishing an Independent Review as well as agreement on the need for a political settlement to deal with longer-term issues. By the time the parties departed from Kilaguni, there was still continued disagreement on a number of issues including: representation of each party in a possible coalition government; prime ministerial power within a coalition; the process for appointing ministers; and the appropriate course of action to take should the coalition dissolve. Each side was instructed to engage with the principals and come back to the negotiating table with solutions during their next meeting on 19 February.

Although not much progress had been made, Annan was keen to convey that the parties were moving closer to a resolution.

> Let me assure you that there is real momentum. We are at the water's edge and the last difficult and frightening step will be taken. I am confident that, in the interests of Kenya and its people, the parties will show wisdom, flexibility and foresight to conclude an agreement.[45]

Annan also signalled that he would remain in Kenya until a resolution to the crisis could be found, which as Lindenmayer and Kaye have noted, emphasised his commitment to the process. 'To the people of Kenya for whom he had come to epitomize hope, this was a message that he was as invested in the future of Kenya as they were and had no intention of abandoning the process.'[46]

What followed was a particularly intense period of negotiations. Remarking on this part of the process, Annan emphasised the urgency of the situation and the task before him: 'time was running out, and I really thought they were wasting time, and that's why I pushed them the way I did. If I had sat back and waited for them, we would probably still be there.'[47] Both sides agreed to set up a committee of four negotiators to explore the legal implications of power sharing and begin drafting the National Accord and Reconciliation Act. There was, however, continuing disagreement over whether a coalition arrangement could be incorporated within the scope of the existing constitution, which provided for a powerful president. The PNU rejected the creation of a prime ministerial post on the grounds that it would facilitate two centres of power. On 25 February ODM threatened to return to the streets with 'mass action' should the parties fail to come to a resolution by the end of the week. As the negotiating teams bickered amongst themselves, violence continued to spiral across the country.

The 'prisoner of peace'

It soon became apparent to Annan that the negotiating team had personal stakes in a prospective cabinet reshuffle and were therefore unlikely to arrive at an agreement themselves.[48] As the negotiations dragged on, Annan began to view himself as '"a prisoner of peace," unable to leave and unable to broker a deal.'[49] At that point he took a decision to suspend the peace talks and engage with the leaders directly. In explaining his decision, he stated:

> The talks have not broken down, but I am taking steps to make sure we accelerate the process and give peace to the people as soon as possible. The leaders have to assume their responsibilities and become directly engaged in these talks.[50]

Annan was keen to convey that the peace talks had not broken down, but rather reflected the urgency of the situation and the resultant need for a breakthrough.

The pressure would continue to mount as George W. Bush[51] sent his Secretary of State, Condaleeza Rice to Kenya on 18 February. During her visit Rice held meetings with both Kibaki and Odinga, and reiterated the call for a power sharing agreement:

> I want to emphasise that the future of our relationship with both sides and their legitimacy hinges on their cooperation to achieve this political solution. In that regard, we are exploring a wide range of possible actions. We will also exert leadership with the UN, Africa Union, European Union, and others to ensure that the political solution the Kenyan people deserve is achieved. It is extremely important that this country be able to move forward.[52]

In the hopes of accelerating the negotiations, Annan requested that the President of Tanzania, Jakaya Kikwete, join the Panel for discussions with the principals. Apart from Tanzania having a direct interest in its neighbour's stability, the Tanzanian model of governance, which included both a Prime Minister and a President, served as a useful model for Kenya to draw upon.[53] After a five-hour marathon session on 28 February 2008, Mwai Kibaki and Raila Odinga signed the National Accord and Reconciliation Act and The Principles of Partnership of the Coalition Government.[54] At the core of these agreements was the creation of a prime ministerial post 'with the authority to coordinate and supervise the execution of the functions and affairs of the Government of Kenya.'[55] Through the 2008 agreements the principals agreed to 'work together in good faith as true partners, through constant consultation and willingness to compromise.[56]

Interestingly, as Lindenmayer and Kaye have observed: 'The agreement met neither of the parties' initial demands' and in that sense was 'nothing less than a compromise.'[57] Nevertheless, this degree of compromise was necessary given the severity of the crisis facing Kenya, as the preamble to the Principles of Partnership highlights:

> The crisis triggered by the 2007 disputed presidential elections has brought to the surface deep-seated and long-standing divisions within Kenyan

society. If left unaddressed, these divisions threaten the very existence of Kenya as a unified country. The Kenyan people are now looking to their leaders to ensure that their country will not be lost. Given the current situation, neither side can realistically govern the country without the other. There must be real power-sharing to move the country forward and begin the healing and reconciliation process.[58]

Kenya as a model for R2P

Throughout the 41 days of mediation in Kenya, references to R2P are nowhere to be found in the official minutes of the dialogue process. Yet, Kofi Annan has intimated that the principle of R2P shaped his understanding and approach to the crisis:

> I saw the crisis in the R2P prism with a Kenyan government unable to contain the situation or protect its people.... I knew that if the international community did not intervene, things would go hopelessly wrong.... Kenya is a successful example of R2P at work.[59]

Shortly after the National Accord and Reconciliation Act and Principles of Partnership were signed, the linkages between the Kenya case and R2P became much more pronounced. Given that 'the violence did subside markedly as the mediation gained momentum,'[60] Kenya became the 'first realization of the international community's "responsibility to protect" (RtoP).'[61] As ICISS Commissioner and advocate of R2P Gareth Evans has observed:

> Kenya in early 2008 is probably the best example we have so far of the responsibility to protect appearing to play an important energising role in stimulating an effective response – here diplomatic rather than military, be it noted – to a rapidly emerging large-scale atrocity situation.[62]

No other case to date has received as much recognition as a successful illustration of R2P in practice.[63] In the years following the resolution of the crisis, Kenya has come to be viewed as the quintessential success story for R2P. What is most notable, however, is not simply the perception of the Kenyan case as a success story, but the suggestion that it might serve as a model for other impending atrocity situations. The President of Human Rights Watch has used language to that effect, noting the case as a '*model* of diplomatic action under the responsibility to protect.'[64] Roger Cohen has similarly stated that while 'R2P ... has had a rough start ... on a *Kenyan model* ... it might have a brighter future.'[65]

Part of the allure of the Kenya case resides in the extent to which it counters some of the criticisms most commonly associated with R2P. First, the development of R2P is beset with instances where critics have dubbed it a tool of Western imperialism. Post-colonial countries have been particularly weary of endorsing the principle given the concerns that it could lead to an infringement on their sovereignty. This has led to fractured debates and significant push back in the normative development of R2P.[66] Having the AU take the lead role sets the Kenyan case apart from others and offers an illustration of regional action as envisaged in the UN Charter.

A second factor that sets this case apart is the fact that it was resolved in the absence of military force. In a debate that has become overly focused on use of force, an external response involving non-coercive and consensual mediation has furthered the perception of the Kenyan case as 'the purest version of R2P.'[67] Kenya is one of the few effective examples of atrocity *prevention* in practice. Each of these factors will be considered in turn.

African Union led mediation

The outcome of the African Union mediation process in Kenya has been considered 'a triumph of African Diplomacy.'[68] By acting through a regional body and confirming a mandate to mediate on the basis of the AU's Peace and Security Council, the High Level Panel was able to assemble in a timely and decisive manner. Whereas attempting to garner a UN mandate may have also been an option, it would have inevitably slowed down the process.[69] Instead, the UN provided essential background support to the AU's efforts. In the words of Edward Luck, the Kenya case became an illustration of 'what the founders had in mind when they drafted Chapter VIII of the Charter on regional arrangements.'[70] According to Article 52(2), efforts should be made 'to achieve pacific settlement of local disputes through such regional arrangements or by such regional agencies before referring them to the Security Council.'[71]

The effective resolution of the crisis in Kenya has led to considerable interest in mediation as an atrocity prevention tool.[72] The Centre for International Conflict Resolution (CICR) at Columbia University has, for instance, prepared an in-depth best practice analysis of the case. In its report 'A Choice for Peace: The Story of Forty-One Days of Mediation in Kenya' the authors have identified the following as crucial to the peaceful resolution of Kenya's post-electoral crisis: a single mediation process fully supported by the international community, strong engagement by civil society, division of issues into short-term and long-term categories, a carefully orchestrated media strategy, emphasis on pragmatism over politics, understanding of peace as a process rather than an event, a high level of creativity and flexibility on the part of mediators.[73]

Much of the effectiveness of this case came down to the individual personalities involved and, most notably, Annan – who brought considerable weight and authority to the process. There are few international mediators that could have rivalled Annan in terms of his ability to effectively navigate through the trickier parts of the mediation. As Annan has acknowledged, 'I came with unique skills and attributes and also the ability to pick up the phone and speak to anyone around the world.... It gave me a leverage that other mediators wouldn't have had.'[74] Annan used this leverage extremely effectively, demonstrating remarkable resourcefulness in his capacity to orchestrate measures from behind the scenes. Most notably, he consolidated international support for the mediation process by encouraging external actors to apply pressure to the negotiating teams and the principals at decisive moments during the crisis.

Among the main tools for applying pressure to the parties were carefully timed public statements. One of the aims of these statements was to signal that there could be 'no business as usual' with the Government of Kenya. This was evident in statements by both the European Union[75] and was echoed by the US Secretary of State.[75] Australia indicated that it would limit contact with Kibaki's cabinet ministers; while the Canadian government suggested that it would be difficult to envisage maintenance of prior methods of direct Government-to-Government cooperation with the Kenyan Government. The UK went a step beyond its counterparts when the Deputy Minister of State asserted in the House of Commons that Britain did not recognise the Kibaki government.[77]

As the crisis continued, external actors backed up their statements with more coercive measures. On 18 January 2008, the EU 'asked for a freezing of all further budgetary support to the Government of Kenya until a political resolution to the ... crisis has been found.'[78] Further to this, 14 key donors issued a statement threatening to cut aid to the government if the political crisis was not resolved.[79] In view of the fact that Kenya relies on aid for only 5 per cent of its overall budget, the impact of these threats may have been largely symbolic.[80] Nevertheless, the unrelenting pressure from external actors did demonstrate the cohesion and determination of the international community, particularly when collective statements were issued.[81]

While threats to cut aid may not have been felt directly by Kenyan leaders, external actors did resort to measures that were more targeted. In early February, Canada and the US threatened to ban specific individuals who they accused of 'subverting democracy' from travelling to their countries.[82] These actions were followed up by a powerful statement by US Ambassador, Michael Ranneberger, that those instigating and supporting violence, along with their family members, would not be issued visas to travel to the US.[83] When the talks appeared to stall, a US Congressional Sub-Committee on Africa hinted at the possibility of more forceful action: 'Kenya was too important in the region and the world to be allowed to go the way of Rwanda and Somalia.'[84] Therefore, '[i]f the warring parties are not ready to compromise to stop the country from sliding into tribal anarchy, the international community should move in to help.'[85] This coded threat to use force was also evident in statements by the US Secretary of State: 'The future of our relationship with both sides and their legitimacy hinges on their cooperation to achieve a political solution. In that regard, we are exploring a wide range of possible actions.'[86]

The level of pressure exerted on the parties evoked a considerable degree of hostility among the negotiating team, particularly the Government/PNU side, as Moses Wetangula noted: 'We will not be led, guided or given conditions by foreign States on how to reach a solution to solve the political impasse in Kenya.

They will not tell us to do this or that. Holding a gun to our heads is something we will not take.'[87] Similarly, Martha Karua remarked,

> It is unfortunate to note that some diplomats are abusing Kenya's hospitality by giving their unsolicited views on the mediation talks.... I would like to remind them we are not a colony.... I urge them to refrain from such behaviour and adhere to the diplomatic convention of not interfering with sovereign states.[88]

The extensive level of external pressure in this case has been read in different ways. At one end of the spectrum are those that the view the case as a positive illustration of collaboration between a regional body and the international community. As a report by the International Peace Institute has noted: 'In a uniquely successful exception, the early 2008 international response to the post-election violence in Kenya ... was a combination of regionally backed mediation with UN support deployed from DPA's newly established Mediation Support Unit.'[89] As the report emphasises, the Kenya situation provides a successful illustration of the 'two levels working together to avert crisis.'[90] At the other end of the spectrum are those, such as Makumi Mwagiru, who are more sceptical about the role of external actors during the crisis: 'What had originally began as an internal Kenyan conflict had rapidly become internationalised.... Although the mediator(s) were African, the West exerted unprecedented pressure on the parties to reach an outcome that would leave Western interests in Kenya intact.'[91]

The prospect of Western interests does raise questions over the extent to which R2P concerns actually compelled external involvement in the crisis. Commentary on the case tends to suggest that the decisiveness of external actors emanated from their global commitment to prevent and protect populations from atrocity crimes. Indeed, even among those who concede that references to R2P were more implicit throughout the crisis, there remains an inclination to describe the response as taking place 'in the shadow of R2P,'[92] or with R2P serving as the 'background music' to the crisis.[93] However, as Edward Luck has argued: 'Operationally, did it [R2P] change the way the UN went about its work in Kenya? I don't know. I'm not sure that it did in really observable ways. So whether one can show cause and effect, I'm not sure.'[94]

While the determination to act in Kenya came down to a host of factors, the international commitment to upholding the R2P norm was but a small piece of a larger puzzle. Alongside the specific concern with halting atrocity crimes in Kenya were an array of economic, political, and security interests. As the Former UN Special Adviser on the Prevention of Genocide has noted: 'Kenya was too important to too many actors to just stand by and watch.'[95] The presence of these strategic interests ensured the necessary support of external actors insofar as the prospect of continuing violence threatened these interests. Strategic considerations, therefore, proved to be a necessary enabling condition for action. While this does not diminish the fact that international action was essential in this situation, the crisis in Kenya wasn't so much a 'test case' for R2P, but, rather, an ideal case where interests aligned with the effort to halt atrocities. In this regard, many of the aspects that contributed to the KNDR process's effectiveness may prove to be difficult to replicate in other contexts.

A successful example of preventive action?

A second factor that sets this case apart from others is the fact that it was resolved in the absence of military force. The Kenyan case has been perceived as an effective illustration of atrocity prevention in practice. According to ICISS Co-Chair Mohamed Sahnoun, 'preventive action will often be peaceful and consensual, as it was in Kenya.'[96] Similarly, in his 2009 report *Implementing the Responsibility to Protect*, the Secretary-General draws upon the Kenya case in a discussion of Pillar III (timely and decisive response) – a section, which might otherwise be understood as encompassing Chapter VII measures:

> Pillar three is generally understood too narrowly. As demonstrated by the successful bilateral, regional and global efforts to avoid further bloodshed in early 2008 following the disputed election in Kenya, if the international community acts early enough, the choice need not be a stark one between doing nothing or using force.[97]

Viewing the Kenya crisis as an effective illustration of atrocity prevention is by no means straightforward. A death toll exceeding 1000 and displacement figures in the level of hundreds of thousands seems to defy the definition of preventive action. Reflecting on the case of Kenya, Edward Luck has observed: 'It clearly was a case for prevention ... the possibility of escalation seemed very real.'[98] However, 'the goal could be no more than preventing the bad from becoming even worse' and therefore, Luck acknowledges, 'Yes, it was prevention, but hardly of an ideal sort.'[99] Human Rights Watch has similarly cautioned against international actors taking a self-congratulatory approach in their assessments of the Kenya case given that 'decades of turning a blind eye to corruption, impunity, and mismanagement by Kenya's governments had contributed to the recent crisis.'[100]

Taking into consideration the stage at which international actors became actively involved, the case of Kenya could be more accurately described as an illustration of 'late stage escalatory prevention.' The notion of escalation prevention accounts for the fact that while international actors neglected to become engaged at an earlier stage and prevent the 2007–08 crisis itself, their actions did effectively prevent the crisis from further worsening. To the extent that preventive action was applied in Kenya, it was primarily directed towards preventing a recurrence of the violence in the future.

Agenda item 4: preventing a recurrence of violence

While international actors had consistently overlooked the systemic risk factors of violence, in the wake of the 2007–08 post-election crisis these underlying issues could no longer be ignored, as Kofi Annan stated at the outset of the negotiation process: 'Let's not kid ourselves and say that this is an electoral problem. It's much broader and much deeper.'[101] With that in mind, the KNDR process went beyond the cessation of violence by advocating a comprehensive reform package directed at addressing the underlying causes of instability in the country. As the Preamble to the Principles of Partnership of the Coalition Government noted: 'This agreement is designed to create an environment conducive to ... build mutual trust and confidence.... It provides the means to implement a coherent and far-reaching reform agenda, to address the fundamental root causes of recurrent conflict.'[102] Likewise, the last paragraph of the preamble noted: 'A coalition must be a partnership with a commitment on both sides to govern together and push through a reform agenda for the benefit of all Kenyans.' The preamble emphasised that 'the coalition had not been created as an end in itself, or to resolve a short-term political crisis.'[103] In seeking to address the root causes of the crisis, the primary purpose of the coalition was, therefore, to prevent a recurrence of violence.

On 29 February 2008, Annan nominated Oluyemi Adeniji, former Foreign Minister of Nigeria, as Session Chair to oversee the agreements on long-term issues and solutions (otherwise referred to as Agenda 4) and ensure the effective implementation of Agenda Items 1 to 3. Within the context of Agenda 4, a broad spectrum of issues were identified such as, constitutional, institutional and legal reform; land reform; poverty, inequity and regional imbalances; unemployment, particularly among the youth; consolidation of national cohesion and unity; transparency, accountability and impunity. In order to facilitate reform in these areas, a number of commissions were created, including: (A) The Independent Review Commission; (B) The Commission of Inquiry into Post-Election Violence; (C) The Truth Justice and Reconciliation Commission; and (D) The Constitutional Review Committee.

(A) Independent Review Commission (IREC)

The Independent Review Commission was established to investigate all aspects of the 2007 Presidential Election.[104] The decision to establish IREC was an essential prerequisite for resolving the political crisis in Kenya, as it allowed the parties to focus on forward looking solutions. IREC's mandate included surveying all stages of the electoral process from civic and voter education and registration through to logistical preparedness, security provisions during the election, and the tabulation process – this also entailed an analysis into the integrity of the results. A further component of IREC's mandate involved examining the structure, composition and management of the ECK, including an assessment relating to its independence, efficiency and general conduct preceding the election and during the election itself. On the basis of this analysis, the Commission was tasked with making recommendations to improve the electoral process in Kenya.

(B) Commission of Inquiry on Post-Election Violence (CIPEV)

The Commission of Inquiry was established with a view to eradicating impunity in Kenya and promoting reconciliation across the country. The importance of combating impunity and ensuring accountability was highlighted by Kofi Annan early on in the negotiation process:

> The Crisis has ... a high potential for recurrence. We cannot accept that this sort of incident takes place every five years or so and no one is held to account ... or else we will be back here again after three or four years.[105]

With this objective in mind, CIPEV was tasked with the following: (1) to investigate the facts and circumstances relating to incidences of violence committed in the aftermath of the 2007 General Election; (2) to investigate the actions of State security agencies (including the police); and (3) to provide legal, political, or administrative recommendations, as relevant, in accordance with the Commission's findings, including measures for bringing persons bearing responsibility for criminal acts to justice.

(C) Truth, Justice and Reconciliation Commission (TJRC)

Alongside the retributive measures for justice that would be explored through CIPEV, a Truth, Justice and Reconciliation Commission (TJRC) was also established. The mandate of the Commission was, however, much broader than the 2007–08 post-election violence. In conjunction with inquiring into the post-election period, the TJRC had a mandate to examine a wider spectrum of human rights violations committed by individuals, groups and the state. This encompassed politically motivated violence, economic crimes (including grand corruption), historical land injustices, and the illegal acquisition of land. Given this broadened mandate, the Commission's inquiry was focused on events ranging from independence through to the post-election period (12 December 1963 to 28 February 2008). Statements from victims, witnesses, and other relevant parties would be gathered with the option of retaining confidentiality. The Commission was to complete its work and release a final report within two years. According to the TJRC Act, blanket amnesty was not an option for the crimes under investigation; however, individual amnesty could be recommended in certain cases (apart from those involving international crimes). Further to this, the TJRC Act underscored that the Commission's work should, at all times, be guided by independence, fairness and balance.

(D) Constitutional Review Committee

As noted in the previous chapter, constitutional reform had been a major discussion point in Kenya for decades. The 2007–08 post-election crisis brought the issue to the fore once again, though in a much more urgent and compelling way. Throughout the deliberations relating to Agenda 4, the negotiating team agreed to initiate a constitutional review process, which would involve five key stages. First, provisions for initiating a statutory constitutional review were to be completed in 12 months. The second step entailed the enactment of a constitutional referendum law by parliament, followed by the preparation of a draft constitution. A fourth stage provided for parliamentary consideration of the proposed constitution, while the fifth and the final stage would involve holding a national referendum. In recognition that any new constitution should be seen as belonging to the people of Kenya, the Committee urged for public and stakeholder consultations throughout each stage of the process.

As the negotiations over Agenda 4 continued, the negotiating team established a number of additional Commissions including the National Cohesion and Integration Commission (NCIC); the Interim Independent Constitutional Dispute Resolution Court (IICDRC); the Interim Independent Electoral Commission (IIEC); and the Interim Independent Boundaries Review Commission (IIBRC). The latter two Commissions were eventually merged into one and replaced by the Independent Electoral and Boundaries Commission (IEBC). Taken together the Agenda 4 Commissions provided the institutional framework for a complete overhaul of the Kenyan state. In this regard, the initial agreement reached between the principals on 28 February 2008 should by no means be viewed (as it so often is) as the culmination of successful preventive action. As the agreements pertaining to Agenda 4 reveal, genuine preventive action in Kenya had only just begun.

Tensions between Agenda 3 and Agenda 4

The formal end of the mediation process in no way implied the disengagement of the High Level Panel. Over the next few years, the Panel continued to play an active role in supporting Kenya's reform efforts. The Panel's continuing involvement in Kenya was facilitated through the Coordination and Liaison Office (CLO) in Nairobi. The CLO was established in 2008 under the sponsorship of the UN Development Programme. While the overarching aim was to support the Coalition Government in implementing the KNDR agreements, the CLO's terms of reference also included the following:

- To maintain the political dialogue between the coalition partners and the Panel.
- To put in place a comprehensive and coordinated system to monitor and evaluate implementation of the KNDR agreements and ensure that its findings were processed and analysed.
- To ensure that knowledge and information generated by the KNDR process is preserved for posterity, and made available to improve national understanding of and expertise in conflict prevention and mediation, in Kenya and beyond.[106]

In effect, the CLO served as the institutional home for the Panel's evolving role in Kenya. Through the CLO, the Panel observed the implementation of the

KNDR agenda, issued public statements relating to the reform process, and made periodic visits to Kenya. Implementation of the agreements was also to be monitored by an independent research firm, South Consulting,[107] which was tasked with producing periodic status reports. These reports were initially presented to the Panel and the Coalition Government, and then subsequently made available to the general public.

Whereas reforms of a political, legal, and institutional nature had long been discussed and recognised as necessary, the chaos of 2007–08 provided an impetus for putting the rhetoric of reform into reality. The far-reaching reform agenda that was put in place in Kenya was one of the most valuable elements of the KNDR process. The agreements relating to Agenda 4 were undeniably comprehensive and impressive on paper. Although the requisite ingredients for addressing long-term issues were now firmly in place, the actual success of Kenya's reform process would ultimately depend upon the extent to which Agenda 4 was pursued in good faith. Very early on in the process, however, signs of trouble began to emerge as it quickly became apparent that the negotiating teams did not approach Agenda 4 with the same sense of urgency. The primary focus for political leaders, both during and after the initial phase of negotiations, was securing and maintaining their own positions of power. John Githongo has argued:

> The elections were merely a trigger for the crisis, with the subsequent mayhem simply symptomatic of a wider leadership failure.... This will not change and we should not pretend it will. Putting all the belligerents into one government merely buys time. We need to be prepared to think outside of the box.[108]

While the power-sharing agreement was perhaps a necessary measure that spared the country from further bloodshed, at the same time, there are a number of drawbacks associated with power-sharing arrangements. Power-sharing solutions tend to send a signal to politicians that they may stir up violence as a means to retain power.[109] In the context of a fraudulent election, power-sharing arrangements appear as a reward for rigging and a further subversion of the democratic process. On this note, it is striking that neither IREC nor CIPEV had a mandate for investigating electoral offenses and seeking prosecutions of those responsible for rigging. The failure to investigate and charge those bearing responsibility for electoral fraud was a fundamental oversight of the Agenda 4 Commissions.[110]

Although external actors seemed to agree that power-sharing was the preferred path for Kenya, alternative options were discussed. In his testimony before the US Senate Foreign Relations Committee, Maina Kiai recommended, 'an interim transitional government to be formed with limited powers of governance and for a limited time – between one and two years – with Kibaki and Odinga exercising equal powers.'[111] While it is impossible to predict whether a transitional government might have been more effective, it could be argued that the entrenchment of the Coalition Government for a full five-year term served as a disincentive for reform.

Apart from the apparent lack of political will to pursue reform, certain elements of Agenda 4 were doomed to fail because of an inherent tension between Agenda Items 3 and 4. For instance, by addressing the underlying causes of the violence, one of the principal aims of Agenda 4 was to end impunity and ensure accountability for the crimes committed during the post-election period. While this was certainly a logical and worthy objective, the vehicle entrusted with achieving it was the Coalition Government. In this regard, the composition of the Coalition Government was key, as a Human Rights Watch report noted at the time: 'One of the first priorities for the Coalition Government must be to ensure that no one suspected of inciting or organising political violence is rewarded with cabinet positions.'[112] The rationale for this was rather simple, as the report explained: 'If the new regime is to address impunity it needs to be above suspicion itself.'[113] Nevertheless, those who were suspected of involvement in the post-election violence were incorporated in the Government of National Unity. As Part II of this book will demonstrate, the outcome of Agenda Item 3 therefore, significantly compromised the capacity to pursue one of the key tenets of Agenda Item 4 – prosecuting perpetrators of the post-election violence.

Conclusion

In the years following the resolution of the post-election crisis, the Kenyan case has come to be viewed as the quintessential success story for R2P. As has been noted, part of the allure of the Kenya case resides in the extent to which it counters some of the criticisms most commonly associated with R2P. First, R2P has been commonly referred to as a tool of Western powers that may be used to infringe upon the sovereignty of non-Western states. Having the AU take the lead role helped counter this criticism, and added to the legitimacy of the mediation process in Kenya. A second factor that sets this case apart is the fact that it was resolved in the absence of military force. In a debate that has become overly focused on the use of force, an external response involving non-coercive and consensual mediation has furthered the perception of the Kenyan case as 'the purest version of R2P.'

While the determination to act in Kenya came down to a host of factors, the commitment to upholding the R2P norm was but a small piece of a larger puzzle. Alongside the specific concern with halting atrocity crimes in Kenya were an array of economic, political, and security interests. The presence of these strategic interests ensured the necessary support of external actors insofar as the prospect of continuing violence threatened these interests. Strategic considerations, therefore, proved to be a necessary enabling condition for action. While this does not diminish the fact that international action was essential to save lives, the crisis in Kenya wasn't so much a 'test case' for R2P, but rather, an ideal case where interests aligned with the effort to halt atrocities. In this regard, many of the aspects that contributed to the KNDR process's effectiveness may prove to be difficult to replicate in other contexts.

Taking into consideration the stage at which international actors became actively involved, the case of Kenya could be more accurately described as an illustration of 'late stage escalatory prevention.' The notion of escalation prevention accounts for the fact that while international actors neglected to become engaged at an earlier stage and prevent the 2007–08 crisis itself, their actions did effectively prevent the crisis from further worsening. To the extent that preventive action was applied in Kenya, it was primarily directed towards preventing a recurrence of the violence in the future.

The far-reaching reform agenda that was put in place in Kenya was one of the most valuable elements of the KNDR process. Whereas reforms of a political, legal, and institutional nature had long been discussed and recognised as necessary, the chaos of 2007–08 provided an opportunity for putting the rhetoric of reform into reality. The agreements relating to Agenda 4 are undeniably comprehensive and impressive on paper. Although the requisite ingredients for addressing long-term issues were now firmly in place, the actual success of Kenya's reform process would ultimately depend upon the extent to which Agenda 4 was pursued in good faith. Very early on in the process, however, signs of trouble began to emerge as it became apparent that the negotiating teams did not approach Agenda 4 with the same sense of urgency.

Apart from the apparent lack of political will to pursue reform, certain elements of Agenda 4 were doomed to fail because of an inherent tension between Agenda Items 3 and 4. In addressing the underlying causes of the violence, one of the principal aims of Agenda 4 was to end impunity and ensure accountability for the crimes committed during the post-election period. While this was certainly a logical and worthy objective, the vehicle entrusted with achieving it was the Coalition Government. The next chapter will assess the Government of National Unity's efforts to prosecute the perpetrators of the post-election violence.

Notes

1 Kofi Annan, cited in Roger Cohen, 'How Kofi Annan Rescued Kenya', *New York Review of Books* 55.2, 14 August 2008, available online at www.nybooks.com/articles/archives/2008/aug/14/how-kofi-annan-rescued-kenya/ (accessed 20 May 2015).
2 Monica Kathina Juma, 'African Mediation of the Kenyan post-2007 election crisis', *Journal of Contemporary African Studies*, 27.3 (2009), p. 423.
3 'Secretary-General calls for restraint from all Kenyans in post-election violence', *UN News Centre*, 31 December 2007, available online at www.un.org/apps/news/story.asp?NewsID=25189&Cr=kenya&Cr1#.VWB6OqZ95FU (accessed 20 May 2015).
4 John Thavis, 'Pope appeals for immediate end to ethnic violence in Kenya', Catholic News Service, 7 January 2008, available online at www.catholicnews.com/data/stories/cns/0800088.htm (accessed 20 May 2015).
5 'OTP Statement in relation to events in Kenya', 5 February 2008, available online at http://www.icc-cpi.int/nr/rdonlyres/1bb89202-16ae-4d95-abbb-4597c416045d/0/iccotpst20080205eng.pdf (accessed on 20 May 2015).
6 Edward Luck cited in Elisabeth Lindenmayer and Josie Lianna Kaye, 'A Choice for Peace: The Story of 41-days of Mediation in Kenya', *International Peace Institute*, August 2009, p. iii, available online at http://responsibilitytoprotect.org/kenyamediation_epub.pdf (accessed 20 May 2015).

7 Interview with Edward Luck, International Peace Institute, New York, 14 July 2010.
8 'Secretary-General calls for restraint from all Kenyans in post-election violence' *UN News Centre*, 31 December 2007, available online at www.un.org/apps/news/story.asp?NewsID=25189&Cr=kenya&Cr1#.VWB6OqZ95FU (accessed 20 May 2015).
9 Ibid.
10 UN, Department of Public Information, 'Secretary-General Troubled by Escalating Kenyan Tensions, Violence', SG/SM/11356-AFR/1641, 2 January 2008, available online at www.un.org/press/en/2008/sgsm11356.doc.htm (accessed 20 May 2015).
11 'UN Genocide Adviser Urges End to Violence, Sends Staffers There', *UN News Centre*, 28 January 2008, available online at www.un.org/apps/news/story.asp?NewsID=25425&Cr=kenya&Cr1 (accessed 25 March 2010).
12 Desmond Tutu, 'Responsibility to Protect', *International Herald Tribune*, 20 February 2008.
13 Statement by Bernard Kouchner, Violence in Kenya, 31 January 2008, available online at www.ambafrance-ke.org/Statement-by-Bernard-Kouchner-on (accessed 20 October 2014).
14 UNSC, 'Statement by the President of the Security Council', S/PRST/2008/4, 6 February 2008.
15 Remarks by Ambassador Susan E. Rice, US Permanent Representative to the United Nations, on the UN Security Council and the Responsibility to Protect, at the International Peace Institute Vienna Seminar (15 June 2009). See also the statement by Jean Ping speaking at the Round-table High Level Meeting of Experts on 'The Responsibility to Protect in Africa', Addis Ababa, 23 October 2008, available online at www.responsibilitytoprotect.org/index.php/component/content/article/129-africa/1910-african-unions-commission-on-r2pkeynote-speech-by-chairperson-jean-ping (accessed 20 June 2015). Ping highlights significant grey areas in applying R2P to the Kenyan case.
16 Ibid.
17 Edward Luck in Elisabeth Lindenmayer and Josie Lianna Kaye, 'A Choice for Peace', p. iii.
18 Elisabeth Lindenmayer and Josie Lianna Kaye, 'A Choice for Peace', p. 5.
19 Xan Rice, 'Fury as Kenyan leader names ministers', *Guardian*, 8 January 2008, available online at www.theguardian.com/world/2008/jan/08/kenya.xanrice (accessed 20 May 2015).
20 Office of the AU Panel of Eminent African Personalities, *Back from the Brink: The 2008 Mediation Process and Reforms in Kenya*, African Union Commission, p. 21, available online at www.knchr.org/Portals/0/GeneralReports/backFromBrink_web.pdf (accessed 20 May 2015).
21 Ibid., p. 22.
22 Jeffrey Gettleman, 'Kenya's Political Rivals Meet', *New York Times*, 25 January 2008, available online at www.nytimes.com/2008/01/25/world/africa/25kenya.html?_r=0 (accessed 20 May 2015).
23 Ibid.
24 Martin Griffiths, 'The Prisoner of Peace: An Interview with Kofi A. Annan', Geneva: Centre for Humanitarian Dialogue, 9 May 2008, 18, available online at http://reliefweb.int/sites/reliefweb.int/files/resources/6F9DC0AD3921DFA7C12575890033E862-Full_Report.pdf (accessed 20 May 2015).
25 Annan hits out at Kenya abuses', *BBC News*, 26 January 2008, available online at http://news.bbc.co.uk/1/hi/world/africa/7210419.stm (accessed 20 May 2015).
26 Office of the AU Panel of Eminent African Personalities, *Back from the Brink*, p. 28.
27 Office of the AU Panel of Eminent African Personalities, *Back from the Brink*, p. 31. Among the key civil society groups was the Concerned Citizens for Peace (CCP), which was formed spontaneously in response to the post-election violence. Based at Nairobi's Serena Hotel, the CCP had the advantage of proximity to the negotiations,

68   *The responsibility to protect*

and met with Kofi Annan's team throughout the process. For an account of the CCP initiative see George Wachira, *Citizens in Action: Making Peace in the Post-Election Crisis in Kenya – 2008*, NPI-Africa, January 2010.
28 Martin Griffiths, 'The Prisoner of Peace', p. 9.
29 Elisabeth Lindenmayer and Josie Lianna Kaye, 'A Choice for Peace', p. 11.
30 ODM objected to Kibaki's statements, as well as the plan to host an IGAD Heads of State summit in Nairobi given that the very legitimacy of Kibaki's position was in question. Following this incident, it was decided that the IGAD meeting would proceed at ministerial level only.
31 International Crisis Group, 'Kenya in Crisis', *Africa Report* 137, 21 February 2008, p. i, available online at www.crisisgroup.org/~/media/Files/africa/horn-of-africa/kenya/137_kenya_in_crisis_web.pdf (accessed 20 May 2015).
32 Elisabeth Lindenmayer and Josie Lianna Kaye, 'A Choice for Peace', p. 12.
33 'Ban Ki-moon calls on Kenyans to "wake up" and halt the violence', *UN News Centre*, 1 February 2008, available online at www.un.org/apps/news/story.asp?NewsID=25477#.VWFdraZ95FU (accessed May 2015).
34 Human Rights House Network, 'Kenyan Government Lifts Ban on Live Broadcasts', 5 February 2008, available online at http://humanrightshouse.org/Articles/892.html (accessed 20 June 2015).
35 'Progress at Kenya Peace Talks', *BBC News*, 8 February 2008, available online at http://news.bbc.co.uk/1/hi/world/africa/7235038.stm (accessed 20 June 2015).
36 Joel Barkan, 'Hearing on the immediate and underlying causes and consequences of flawed democracy in Africa', prepared for the Senate Foreign Relations Committee's Subcommittee on African Affairs, 7 February 2008, p. 4., available online at http://csis.org/files/media/csis/congress/ts080212barkan.pdf (accessed 20 May 2015).
37 Martin Griffiths, 'The Prisoner of Peace', p. 4. The first reference to power-sharing was made rather early on in the crisis by British Prime Minister, Gordon Brown. See also Paul Reynolds, 'Diplomacy Falters as Kenya Burns', *BBC News*, 4 January 2008, http://news.bbc.co.uk/1/hi/world/africa/7170600.stm (accessed 20 May 2015).
38 Martin Griffiths, 'The Prisoner of Peace', p. 10.
39 Martin Griffiths, 'The Prisoner of Peace', p. 10.
40 'Annan Hopes for Kenyan Deal Next Week', *Sydney Morning Herald*, 9 February 2008, available online at www.smh.com.au/world/annan-hopes-for-kenyan-deal-next-week-20080208-1r5z.html (accessed 20 June 2015).
41 Elisabeth Lindenmayer and Josie Lianna Kaye, 'A Choice for Peace', p. 15. See also 'Your Role is Vital and We Can't Afford to Fail, Annan Tells MPs', *Daily Nation*, 13 February 2008, available online at www.ogiek.org/news-4/news-post-08–02–417.htm (accessed 20 May 2015).
42 Katie Nguyen and C. Bryson Hull, 'Kenyan minister criticizes crisis mediator Annan', *Reuters*, 12 February 2008, available online at http://uk.reuters.com/article/2008/02/12/uk-kenya-crisis-idUKL1264995120080212 (accessed 20 May 2015).
43 Elisabeth Lindenmayer and Josie Lianna Kaye, 'A Choice for Peace', p. 15.
44 Ibid.
45 Office of the AU Panel of Eminent African Personalities, *Back from the Brink*, p. 39.
46 Elisabeth Lindenmayer and Josie Lianna Kaye, 'A Choice for Peace', p. 17.
47 Martin Griffiths, 'The Prisoner of Peace', p. 14
48 Elisabeth Lindenmayer and Josie Lianna Kaye, 'A Choice for Peace', p. 20.
49 Ibid.
50 'Kenya Poll Crisis Talks Suspended', *BBC News*, 26 February 2008, available online at http://news.bbc.co.uk/1/hi/world/africa/7265234.stm (accessed 20 June 2015).
51 'Bush urges Kenya power-sharing', *BBC News*, 16 February 2008, available online at http://news.bbc.co.uk/1/hi/world/americas/7248271.stm (accessed 20 May 2015).

52 'Talks Suspended as US Threatens to Act', *Daily Nation*, 27 February 2008.
53 Elisabeth Lindenmayer and Josie Lianna Kaye, 'A Choice for Peace', p. 21,
54 The PNU rejected the suggestion of Cyril Ramaphosa to lead negotiations on Agenda 4 on this basis of his alleged proximity to ODM. Ambassador Adeniji of Nigeria was therefore, selected to assume the role of Session Chair, and presided over a further four agreements pertaining to Agenda Item 4 – developing longer-term strategies for a durable peace.
55 Agreement on the Principles of Partnership of the Coalition Government, 28 February 2008.
56 Ibid.
57 Elisabeth Lindenmayer and Josie Lianna Kaye, 'A Choice for Peace', p. 22.
58 Agreement on the Principles of Partnership.
59 Kofi Annan, cited in Roger Cohen, 'How Kofi Annan Rescued Kenya', *New York Review of Books* 55.2, 14 August 2008, available online at www.nybooks.com/articles/archives/2008/aug/14/how-kofi-annan-rescued-kenya/ (accessed 20 May 2015).
60 Edward Luck in Elisabeth Lindenmayer and Josie Lianna Kaye, 'A Choice for Peace', p. iii.
61 Elisabeth Lindenmayer and Josie Lianna Kaye, 'A Choice for Peace', p. 2.
62 Gareth Evans, 'Response to Reviews by Michael Barnett, Chris Brown and Robert Jackson', *Global Responsibility to Protect* 2.3 (2010), p. 327.
63 See, for example, Naomi Kikoler, 'Responsibility to Protect', Keynote paper at the International Conference 'Protecting People in Conflict and Crisis: Responding to the Challenges of a Changing World', Oxford, September 2009, available online at www.rsc.ox.ac.uk/publications/responsibility-to-protect (accessed 20 October 2014); Gareth Evans, 'The Responsibility to Protect: Meeting the Challenges', lecture to the 10th Asia Pacific Programme for Senior Military Officers, S. Rajaratnam School of International Studies, Singapore, 5 August 2008, available online at www.crisisgroup.org/en/publication-type/speeches/2008/the-responsibility-to-protect-meeting-the-challenges.aspx (Accessed 20 October 2014); Alexander Stubb, 'Keynote address at Hanforum', 28 August 2009, available online at http://formin.finland.fi/public/default.aspx?contentid=169644&nodeid=15149&contentlan=2&culture=en-US (accessed 22 April 2010); Mark Sneider, 'Implementing the Responsibility to Protect in Kenya and Beyond', address to the World Affairs Council of Oregon, Portland State University, Portland, Oregon, 5 March 2010, available online at www.crisisgroup.org/en/publication-type/speeches/2010/implementing-the-responsibility-to-protect-in-kenya-and-beyond.aspx (accessed 20 October 2014); Public Radio International, 'America Abroad', reported and hosted by Deborah Amos, 7 March 2009; 'International Community Coming to Realize "The Responsibility to Protect"', *UCLA Today*, 15 April 2009, available online at http://today.ucla.edu/portal/ut/international-community-coming-88897.aspx (accessed 22 April 2010).
64 Human Rights Watch, *Ballots to Bullets*, p. 67.
65 Kofi Annan cited in Roger Cohen, 'How Kofi Annan Rescued Kenya.'
66 'The Responsibility to Protect: An Idea Whose Time Has Come – And Gone?' *The Economist*, 23 July 2009, available online at www.economist.com/node/14087788 (accessed 20 June 2015).
67 Donald Steinberg, 'Responsibility to Protect: Coming of Age?' *Global Responsibility to Protect*, 1.4 (2009), p. 435.
68 Elisabeth Lindenmayer and Josie Lianna Kaye, 'A Choice for Peace', p. 2.
69 Martin Griffiths, 'The Prisoner of Peace', p. 16.
70 Edward Luck in Elisabeth Lindenmayer and Josie Lianna Kaye, 'A Choice for Peace?' p. iii.
71 Ibid.

72 See Eileen Babbitt, 'Mediation and the Prevention of Mass Atrocities', in Monica Serrano and Thomas G. Weiss (eds), *The International Politics of Human Rights: Rallying to the R2P Cause?* (Routledge, 2014), pp. 29–47.
73 Elisabeth Lindenmayer and Josie Lianna Kaye, 'A Choice for Peace', p. 1.
74 Martin Griffiths, 'The Prisoner of Peace', p. 17.
75 'EU Might Cut Aid Over Poll Results Crisis' *Daily Nation*, 16 January 2008.
76 'EU Adds Pressure on Leaders', *The Standard*, 14 January 2008.
77 'Britain Does Not Recognise Kibaki', *Sunday Nation*, 20 January 2008.
78 'Europeans Vote to Freeze Aid', *Daily Nation*, 18 January 2008.
79 'Solve Crisis or Suffer Aid Cuts, Warn Donors', *Daily Nation*, 17 January 2008.
80 'Kenya Donors Have Few Options in Crisis', *Nairobi Star*, 19 January 2008.
81 At one point in the crisis 20 Diplomatic Missions issued a statement raising concerns that negotiations were not making progress, 'Pressure Mounts to End Crisis', *Daily Nation*, 28 February 2008.
82 'US, Canada Ban Threat as Talks Register Gains', *The Standard*, 5 February 2008.
83 'Ranneberger Explains US Stance on Crisis', *The Standard*, 5 February 2008.
84 'The Political Crisis in Kenya: A Call for Justice and Peaceful Resolution', US Sub-Committee on Africa and Global Health, 6 February 2008.
85 'Agree or Else . ', *The Standard*, 8 February 2008.
86 'Talks Suspended as US Threatens to Act', *Daily Nation*, 27 February 2008.
87 Caroline Mango and Ayub Savula, 'Kenya: Foreign Powers Will Not Dictate to the Government', *CCM*, 17 February 2008, available online at https://chamachamwananchi.wordpress.com/2008/02/17/kenya-foreign-powers-will-not-dictate-to-the-government-warns-government/ (accessed 10 April 2013).
88 'Annan's Team Strikes Half-Way Deal in Talks', *Daily Nation*, 14 February 2008.
89 International Peace Institute, 'Conflict Prevention and the Responsibility to Protect', *IPI Blue Paper* No. 7, Task Forces on Strengthening Multilateral Security Capacity, (New York, 2009).
90 Ibid.
91 Makumi Mwagiru, *The Water's Edge: Mediation of Violent Electoral Conflict in Kenya* (Institute of Diplomacy and International Studies, 2008), p. 18.
92 Michael Doyle, Human Rights, Sovereignty and Military Intervention: A Dialogue with JS Mill Institute for Ethics Law and Armed Conflict Seminar Series, 9 February 2010.
93 Thomas Weiss, 'Halting Atrocities in Kenya', Great Decisions 2010, p. 24 available online at www.globalr2p.org/media/files/kenya-fpa-weiss.pdf (accessed 20 May 2015).
94 As Luck reiterated, 'although Kenya is a notable success for RtoP, it is not clear that RtoP itself caused the intense international engagement.' Edward Luck Interview, International Peace Institute, New York, 14 July 2010; see Alex Bellamy, 'The Responsibility to Protect: Five Years On', *Ethics and International Affairs*, 24.2 (2010), p. 165.
95 Francis Deng Interview, United Nations, New York, 13 July 2010.
96 Mohamed Sahncun, 'Uphold Continent's Contribution to Human Rights, Urges Top Diplomat', *All Africa*, 21 July 2009, available online at http://allafrica.com/stories/200907210549.html (accessed 20 May 2015).
97 *Implementing the Responsibility to Protect; Report of the Secretary-General*, UN doc. A/63/677, 12 Jan. 2009, p. 9.
98 Edward Luck Interview, International Peace Institute, New York, 14 July 2010.
99 Edward Luck, 'The Responsibility to Protect: Growing Pains or Early Promise', *Ethics and International Affairs*, 24.2 (2010), pp. 349–65.
100 Human Rights Watch, *Ballots to Bullets, p.* 68.
101 Tracy McVeigh, 'Dozens Die in Kenyan Riots', *Guardian*, 27 January 2008, available online at www.theguardian.com/world/2008/jan/27/kenya.tracymcveigh (20 June 2015).

102 Preamble to the Agreement on the Principles of Partnership of the Coalition Government, 28 February 2008.
103 Office of the AU Panel of Eminent African Personalities, *Back from the Brink*, p. 70.
104 For the full report see 'Report of the Independent Review Commission on the General Elections Held in Kenya on 27 December 2007', 17 September 2008, available online at http://aceproject.org/regions-en/countries-and-territories/KE/reports/independent-review-commission-on-the-general (accessed 20 June 2015).
105 Kofi Annan Press Conference Serena Hotel Nairobi, 26 January 2008.
106 Office of the AU Panel of Eminent African Personalities, *Back from the Brink*, p. 53.
107 To view the KNDR review reports, see South Consulting Kenya, 'KNDR Review Reports' available online at www.south.co.ke/index.php/projects-and-reports/kndr-project/2-uncategorised/11-review-reports (accessed 20 June 2015).
108 'Rice in Kenya to press talks to end crisis', *New York Times*, 18 February 2008, available online at www.nytimes.com/2008/02/18/world/africa/18iht-kenya.1.10135967.html?_r=0 (accessed 20 May 2015).
109 See Stephen Brown, 'Donor Responses to the 2008 Kenyan Crisis: Finally Getting it Right', *Journal of Contemporary African Studies*, 27.3 (2009), pp. 389–406.
110 Human Rights Watch, *Ballots to Bullets. Organized Political Violence and Kenya's Crisis of Governance*, 2.1(A), March 2008, p. 65, available online at www.hrw.org/sites/default/files/reports/kenya0308web.pdf (accessed on 20 May 2015).
111 'Maina Kiai statement to US House of Representatives', 6 February 2008, available online at https://kenyanemergency.wordpress.com/2008/02/06/maina-kiais-statement-to-us-house-of-representatives/ (accessed 20 May 2015).
112 Human Rights Watch, *Ballots to Bullets*, p. 65.
113 Ibid.

Part II
The responsibility to prosecute

3 The government of national impunity

> I am aware that many Kenyans require justice for past injustices, but let us also keep in mind that ... justice must be tempered with forgiveness for reconciliation to take root.[1]
>
> (Mwai Kibaki, 20 October 2008)

> We, therefore, commend the efforts of the international community and, particularly, the International Criminal Court (ICC) for recognizing early enough that there was absolutely no political will on the part of this Government to get a local tribunal established and, therefore, begin the process of bringing justice to those who bear the greatest responsibility for the post election violence well before the next elections are held.[2]
>
> (Gitobu Imanyara, 2 December 2009)

The peace agreement that was brokered by Kofi Annan during the Kenyan National Dialogue and Reconciliation process helped facilitate stability in Kenya following the 2007–08 post-election crisis. As extremely difficult as it was to get the principals to reach an agreement, the task ahead for the Government of National Unity made the mediation process appear relatively straightforward. The Coalition Government was not an end in itself, but rather, a vehicle for facilitating much needed reforms in Kenya – reforms that would address the underlying causes of the violence. The ultimate aim of the KNDR process was, therefore, to ensure that the violence experienced in 2007–08 was never again repeated in the future. As the Government of National Unity embarked on implementing the KNDR agreements, the High Level Panel remained engaged. Kofi Annan, in particular, continued to be closely connected to the implementation of the KNDR agreements. Through his support for the reform agenda, which included periodic visits to the country, Annan assumed an almost custodial role of the country during the implementation phase of the agreements.

Despite the promise of the reform agenda, wrangling within the Coalition Government stifled progress in crucial areas. Friction among the principals and disputes between – and eventually within – their respective parties, severely compromised the capacity of the Government to deliver the reforms agreed to in 2008. One exception to the otherwise dismal performance of the Government was in the area of constitutional reform. In 2010, the principals came together to support the adoption of a new Constitution, which was approved by an overwhelming majority of Kenyans during the 4 August 2010 referendum.

The long-awaited adoption of a new constitutional dispensation was a moment of euphoria for Kenya and a key step forward for the reform agenda. Nevertheless, other key aspects of Agenda 4, which were crucial to Kenya's future, proceeded rather slowly. For instance, there was virtually no progress made on addressing the problem of impunity in Kenya. As part of the 2008 Agreement, a Commission of Inquiry (CIPEV) was mandated to investigate criminal acts committed during the post-election period. Upon completing its work, CIPEV called on the Government to establish a Special Tribunal, which would prosecute suspected perpetrators of the violence. Three separate attempts were made to establish a Tribunal, however, forces inside the Government conspired to ensure that these efforts failed. The lack of progress in holding suspected perpetrators accountable through a domestic tribunal eventually prompted the involvement of the International Criminal Court.

This chapter will assess the performance of the Coalition in fulfilling the Agenda items agreed to during the Kenyan National Dialogue and Reconciliation process. It will begin by highlighting some of the key areas of discord between the coalition members and the unfinished business from the KNDR process. After exploring the progress made in the arena of constitutional reform, the chapter will turn towards the efforts of the Government of National Unity to tackle the problem of impunity. In particular, the final part of the chapter will consider the attempts of the Coalition Government to frustrate the search for accountability in Kenya.

Discord after the accord

When Kibaki and Odinga met on the steps of Harambee House on 28 February 2008 the country breathed a collective sigh of relief. The National Accord and Reconciliation Act and the Principles of Partnership for Coalition Government represented the culmination of an intense negotiation process, which effectively brought an end to the darkest chapter in Kenya's history. Yet, difficulties within the newly constituted Government of National Unity began to emerge even before the ink had begun to dry on these Agreements. Therefore, the celebrations that followed the 28 February Agreements were short-lived, as the realities of coalition politics began to set in. Major disagreements would eventually surface in relation to both substantive and procedural matters. With countless disagreements frequently resulting in deadlock, the governance of the country often took a back seat to divisions within the Government.

Among the early issues that became a source of discord between Kibaki and Odinga was the unveiling of the Grand Coalition Cabinet. Disagreement over the allocation of key portfolios and the size of the cabinet became sources of friction. When the two sides had still failed to come to an agreement by April 2008, Kofi Annan issued a statement in which he encouraged the Principals to resolve the matter swiftly. Annan also utilised the moment as an opportunity to remind the parties that the agreement was not and end in itself.

> When I sat with the parties on 1 February, they agreed to a list of issues under Agenda Item 4 that must be addressed within one year from the beginning of the dialogue process. There is just a little more than nine months left to do that and, even if the tasks ahead seem daunting, the new government must seize the day and take advantage of this unique opportunity to get it right for Kenya.[3]

The Grand Coalition cabinet was finally unveiled on 12 April 2008. With an unprecedented number of 40 ministers and 52 deputies, Kenya's newly constituted cabinet was one of the largest in the world. The size of the cabinet generated controversy given the sheer costs of maintaining the government. Each cabinet member was entitled to US$18 000 per month, two cars, security personnel and an allowance. These immense costs were to be carried by the Kenyan tax-payer. As Adam Mynott has argued: 'In a country with an annual per capita income of less than US$400, the bill for the bloated unity cabinet is huge.'[4] While some viewed the costs of the cabinet as 'a price worth paying for reconciliation'[5] it could also be viewed as 'another example of the political class enriching itself on the backs of ordinary Kenyans.'[6] In reference to the size of the cabinet, the Panel of Eminent African Personalities has acknowledged: 'With the wisdom of hindsight, it would probably have been sensible to have imposed a ceiling on the cabinet's size. So large a cabinet created a patronage opportunity and hindered efficient and effective implementation of the reform agenda.'[7] The size of the cabinet further contributed to the impression that there were two governments operating side by side. Power struggles would continue to characterise the tenure of the Coalition, as 'running the government remained fraught with difficulties throughout its five-year term.'[8] The most high profile disputes tended to gravitate around the issue of appointments and dismissals. There were two disputes in particular that captured widespread attention.

On 14 February 2010, Prime Minister Odinga issued a three-month suspension of William Ruto, Minister for Agriculture and Samuel Ongeri, Minister for Education, for their alleged involvement in corruption scandals.[9] Large-scale corruption scandals continued throughout the duration of the Coalition Government. According to David Anderson, the Government of National Unity constituted 'a gangster state run by criminals who extract from the state for themselves.'[10] With respect to the two scandals in question, an independent audit into a maize scandal indicated that US$26 million had been diverted, therein implicating William Ruto.[11] Whereas, in the case of Ongeri, over US$1 million was reportedly stolen in a scam relating to free primary education.[12] Despite Odinga's suspension of the two Ministers, President Kibaki argued that the Prime Minister had overstepped his powers and immediately overturned the decisions. On 15 February 2009, Attorney General, Amos Wako, issued a press statement in support of the President's position.[13] Wako noted that the authority vested in Odinga 'to coordinate and supervise'[14] through the National Accord, 'does not of itself confer a power to suspend.'[15] ODM subsequently called on the Panel to intervene in the dispute and announced that it would boycott Cabinet meetings until the matter was resolved. The Panel released a statement on 18 February 2009 highlighting their concern with the impasse and calling on the parties to resolve their differences.[16]

A further high profile rupture in the Coalition arose in 2011 following the unilateral nominations put forward by President Kibaki for the posts of Chief Justice, Director of Public Prosecutions, Attorney General and Controller of the Budget. Prime Minister Odinga objected to the nominations on the grounds that he had not been consulted. The appointments were also heavily criticised by the Judicial Service Commission and the Commission for the Implementation of the Constitution. On 31 January 2011, Kofi Annan issued a statement calling on the two sides to work together to overcome the impasse.[17] The issue was eventually resolved by the Speaker of the National Assembly and the High Court, both of which ruled that the nominations did not abide by the requirements of the Constitution.

The impact of recurring disputes within the Coalition Government could be most immediately felt in relation to Agenda Item 4. As the Government of National Unity was pre-occupied with internal disputes and various controversies surrounding power sharing, this left little scope for addressing the underlying causes of the 2007–08 violence. One key indicator of the tepid level of support for Agenda 4 could be seen in the fact that the negotiating team met only eight times between 4 March and 29 July (in contrast to 19 times during 29 January and 3 March). While this could be indicative of other factors, including the fact that members of the negotiating team were also engaged in Cabinet business, there was also a sense in which it signalled a lack of commitment to reform.[18] In an opinion poll conducted one year after the power-sharing agreement had been established, 70 per cent of respondents indicated that Kibaki and Raila had achieved nothing during their first year in office.[19] Hence there was a high degree of public frustration regarding the performance of the Coalition Government. In this regard, the reality of the Government of National Unity marked a sharp contrast to the high ideals of the National Accord.

Many have attributed the 'dysfunctional behaviour' of the coalition to the absence of a more detailed power-sharing agreement, specifying 'goals, objectives and procedures that are vital to the successful operation of a coalition.'[20] However, as the Panel has since argued, 'the coalition that emerged represented a cease-fire arrangement;'[21] anything beyond this, including a more detailed agreement, would have been too onerous to work out during the height of the post-election violence. Nevertheless, one notable omission that was highlighted with each recurring dispute was the lack of an effective dispute resolution mechanism. In the absence of a developed mechanism for resolving disputes, the Coalition continued to rely on the Panel to intervene at critical junctures to assist in the resolution of disputes. While the Coalition Government moved at an exceptionally slow pace in addressing Agenda 4, it is also worth noting that there was a break in momentum in relation to some of the earlier Agenda Items. In particular, 'the Coalition's inability to fully address Agenda Items 1 and 2 meant that the country continued to struggle with insecurity and IDPs, even after five years.'[22]

Continuing insecurity

Although the post-election violence had ended, the problem of insecurity in Kenya continued. This issue was urgently highlighted in an investigation led by the UN Special Rapporteur on Extra-judicial Killings, Philip Alston. Alston visited Kenya from 16–25 February 2009 with a three-part mandate: first, to investigate the nature and causes of unlawful killings; second, to investigate whether those deemed responsible were held to account; and, finally, to propose measures to reduce unlawful killings and impunity. The central focus of his investigation was on police killings, violence in the Mount Elgon region and killings during the post-election violence. When presenting his final report[23] to the Human Rights Council in Geneva, Alston noted that 'for all its strengths, Kenya has a major problem of extra judicial executions and it is one that has not been adequately acknowledged and addressed.'[24] Alston's investigations identified four specific areas of concern:

1   post-election violence, and in particular the immunity of politicians and police officers 18 months later;
2   police shootings, which occured regularly without being recorded publicly or accounted for;
3   the Mount Elgon region, where approximately 200 people either disappeared or were killed by the security services in 2008; and
4   the systematic harassment and intimidation of human rights groups.

Of particular concern for Alston were the human rights defenders testifying during his mission that they were repeatedly threatened and harassed by Government officials and security forces. Two activists were murdered after the Special Rapporteur's mission ended, which only corroborated Alston's finding of 'a systematic attempt to silence criticism of Kenyan security forces.'[25]

During his visit to Kenya, Alston called for the resignation[26] of the two officials he viewed as responsible for the current state of affairs: Attorney General Amos Wako, the 'embodiment of the phenomenon of impunity'[27] and Police Commissioner, Mohammed Hussein Ali, described as an obstacle to police reform. In relation to Ali, Alston argued, 'there is abundant evidence linking him to a central role in devising and overseeing the policy of extra-judicially executing large numbers of "suspected criminals."[28] He accused Ali of having 'utterly failed to devise any law enforcement strategy worthy of the name for dealing with the Mungiki and other forms of criminality.'[29] He was also critical of the witness protection programme in Kenya which he argued had 'yet to protect a single witness.'[30]

80 *The responsibility to prosecute*

The Government accused Alston of going beyond his mandate and took particular exception with his recommendation to sack officials:

> The Government expresses grave concern regarding the allegations contained in the report by the Special Rapporteur. His questioning of the very basis of the Kenyan state and in particular its institutions is totally unacceptable, and impinges on Kenya's sovereign rights.[31]

Notwithstanding their dissatisfaction with the Alston report, the Government eventually conceded to its recommendation for implementing police reform. Ali was replaced in September 2009.[32] In January 2010, a National Task Force was appointed under Justice Philip Ransley to implement the report's recommendations.[33] However, the pressure to reform the security sector in Kenya was not generated from the Alston report alone. As will be discussed further on in this chapter, the eyes of the international community were increasingly on Kenya as the Chief Prosecutor of the ICC continued to step up his involvement in the country.

The IDP situation in Kenya

As noted in Chapter 1, the 2007 General Elections resulted in massive levels of displacement. Whereas internal displacement had already been a persistent problem before the 2007 polls, the most recent pattern of displacement exacerbated the extent of Kenya's IDP crisis.[34] The majority of those displaced remained within Kenya, while a smaller proportion fled across the border to Uganda. As the Kenyan Red Cross observed, the conditions within Kenya's displacement communities fell well below accepted international standards. Displacement camps were overcrowded, had poor sanitation and were rampant with disease. Compounding these issues were frequent attacks by criminal gangs and an over-extended police force that proved unable to provide for the protection of displaced communities.

During the Kenyan National Dialogue and Reconciliation process, the displacement crisis was identified as the principal task relating to Agenda Item 2 (Addressing the Humanitarian Crisis). Once the Coalition Government was formed, both principals assured that they were committed to resolving the IDP crisis. In May 2008, the government launched 'Operation Return Home' (*Rudi Nyumbani*), a nationally sponsored IDP resettlement programme. *Rudi Nyumbani* has, however, been heavily criticised by Human Rights groups for a number of reasons: the programme failed to ensure the security of returning IDPs; it was not preceded by reconciliation efforts between communities; it had no provisions for financial compensation to those affected; and it was ill equipped to address the needs of vulnerable groups within the displaced population (including HIV affected groups and children).[35] Most crucially, *Rudi Nyumbani* overlooked how high tensions were in the aftermath of the violence, which made it difficult – and, in some instances, impossible – for some communities to return home. The success of the government's national resettlement programme has therefore been limited.³⁶ According to one estimate 'approximately 200 000 of the 350 000 persons who fled their homes as a result of the post-election violence had not returned.'³⁷

There are strong grounds to question the authenticity of the Government's commitment to resolving the IDP Crisis. Despite fundraising efforts to assist IDPs, most of this compensation has not made its way to those who need it the most. Moreover, up to KSH500 million was reportedly stolen from funds specifically allocated to Kenya's IDPs.³⁸ In some instances, actual names of internally displaced individuals were used to extract the funds. Although corruption scandals have become a fixture of Kenyan politics, this particular scandal constitutes the ultimate betrayal of Kenya's displaced communities.

Despite the continuing displacement crisis, the donor community exerted minimal pressure on the Government to resolve this issue. Throughout the KNDR process and beyond, the issue of IDPs has been viewed predominantly as a matter of humanitarian concern; nevertheless, the issue of resettlement has clear security implications. As Lucy Hannon has observed, 'affected migrant and slum populations are the poorest of the poor, and disenfranchised and dispossessed, among the most likely to turn to violence again in their frustration.'³⁹

Whereas donor governments have been relatively silent on the issue of IDP resettlement, much more pressure has been applied to the Coalition Government in relation to constitutional reform. For the international community, redrafting Kenya's constitution was seen not only as the centrepiece for further reforms, but an essential component in ensuring the country's preparedness for the next General Election.

The birth of the second republic: constitutional reform

The adoption of a new constitution is widely regarded as one of the main achievements of the Government of National Unity. Whereas deep-seated divisions continued to beset the workings of the Coalition Government in nearly all other areas, support for a new constitution was one of the key issues on which the principals presented a united front. From President Kibaki's perspective, 'it was a good legacy to bequeath his country' whereas for Prime Minister Odinga, 'the new constitution would provide a solid platform on which to campaign for the country's highest office.'⁴⁰

As Chapter 1 observed, Kenya's independence era constitution had been cited as one of the key underlying factors for the country's spiral into violence following the 2007 General Election. Through a series of amendments the independence constitution institutionalised the personalised power of presidency, weakened the role of parliament, and created a winner takes all calculus. For two decades, successive attempts were made to reform Kenya's constitution – the most recent attempt occurring under the leadership of President Kibaki in 2005. In the wake of the 2007–08 violence, efforts to reform Kenya's constitution assumed a new sense of urgency. Constitutional reform became a priority area, not only for Kenyans but for international actors as well, who were keen to see the country consolidate the gains of the KNDR process. US President Barack Obama, for instance, described the adoption of a new constitution as 'a singular opportunity to put Kenyan governance on a more solid footing.'[41]

The journey towards adopting a new constitution commenced on February 2009. Kenya's Parliament approved a Committee of Experts (CoE) to review and draft a new constitution. In its initial version, the CoE put forward a draft constitution, which incorporated a hybrid system of government. However, objections to this structure led the CoE to settle upon a harmonised draft that retained a presidential system with checks and balances, a judiciary, a bicameral Parliament (consisting of a National Assembly and a Senate), and regional governments. It also called for at least one-third of MPs to be women. After a process of public consultation and parliamentary approval, the draft constitution was published in May 2010. However, the publication of the document sparked considerable debate, as it was subsequently revealed that a controversial edit had been inserted, which effectively curtailed rights and freedoms for national security purposes. This provision had allegedly been inserted at the Government printers at the request of the National Security Services.[42] While the Government attempted to distance itself from the mysterious edit, the incident was quickly seized upon by those lobbying against the draft constitution.

The drive towards constitutional reform in Kenya took place within a broader context of electoral reform. As noted in the previous chapter, an Independent Review Commission was formed to investigate all aspects of the 2007 election including an account of what went wrong and what lessons could be learned. The final report of IREC (also referred to as the Kriegler report after the Chair of the Commission) made a number of recommendations for improving Kenya's elections. Perhaps the most pertinent recommendation was the call to disband the Electoral Commission of Kenya (ECK). The Interim Independent Electoral Commission (IIEC) replaced the defunct ECK and Parliament approved the appointment of Isaac Hassan as its Chairman. Among the first set of tasks for the IIEC were: to publicise the referendum question; determine the symbols for the campaign; and establish a date for the referendum to be held. The referendum question declared by the IIEC was: 'Do you approve the proposed new Constitution?' with the symbols designated as green for those campaigning in favour of the proposed constitution and red for those campaigning against it.

William Ruto, Minister for Higher Education and Samuel Poghisio, Minister for Information led the 'No' campaign. Their principal objections to the proposed constitution derived from concerns over the incorporation of Kadhi Courts and the failure of the document to condemn abortion. The opposition camp drew strong support from the Christian Church in Kenya and former President Moi who argued that the proposed constitution would lead to disunity. While Kibaki and Odinga came together in support of the proposed constitution, fundamental differences between the PNU and ODM remained, which meant that 'the PNU and ODM did not pull in one direction, even though both supported the draft constitution.'[43] Furthermore, the 'joint secretariat for the Yes campaign, formed by ODM and PNU, was split' and thereby compromised their capacity to 'launch an effective strategy for its adoption.'[44]

The referendum provided an opportunity to test some of the conflict prevention architecture that had been put in place to avoid a repeat of the 2007–08 General Election. The telecommunications industry partnered with the Government to initiate a nation-wide SMS reporting system, which provided a further mechanism to curb incitement. The NCIC also took measures to curb hate speech and incitement, which resulted in charges made against four MPs. In the months prior to the referendum, a group comprising civil society organisations, UNDP, the National Cohesion and Integration Commission (NCIC), and the Government, launched the UWIANO platform (meaning cohesion in Swahili). Operating under the banner of the motto, *Chagua Kenya, Chagua Amani* (Choose Kenya, Choose Peace), UWIANO's activities included a massive civic education programme intended to familiarise Kenyans with the provisions of the constitution and peace rallies held across the country. In the immediate days before the referendum, Kenyans from all walks of life debated the provisions of the constitution, as the Government urged Kenyans to embrace peace – a message that was also conveyed in print and broadcast media.

The lead-up to the referendum was generally peaceful; however, on 13 June 2010, a grenade attack killed five people, including one child at a rally for the No campaign in Uhuru Park. The attack was blamed on Al Shabab militants, yet no one was formally charged for the incident. It served as a stark reminder of just how fragile the security situation remained, and contributed to fears that there may be a repeat of the violence of 2007–08. On 4 August 2010, Kenyans across the country queued in record numbers before the polls opened. Voting day itself was peaceful, as close to 8 000 000 voters (out of 12 400 000) came out to vote (71 per cent of registered voters). The following day, Isaac Hassan announced the results in an overwhelming victory for the yes side with 5 954 767 and 2 687 193 for the no side.

The key features of the new constitution included a more decentralised political system (which involves the devolution of power to local authorities), limiting the power of the president, the creation of a second chamber (the Senate), the creation of a land commission and a judicial commission, and the establishment of a Bill of Rights. With these vital provisions firmly embedded in the architecture of the Kenyan State, the new constitution served as an anchor for further institutional reforms. The Kenyan constitution was now one of the most progressive constitutions on the continent.[45]

On 27 August 2010, Kenyans gathered to celebrate the promulgation of the new constitution. Although it should have been a day reserved for marking the birth of Kenya's Second Republic, the event soon became shrouded in controversy. Among the visiting dignitaries in attendance at this event was Sudanese President Omar al-Bashir, previously indicted by the ICC in connection with the genocide in Darfur.[46] As a state party to the Rome Statute, Kenya was under obligation to arrest al-Bashir. Like so many of its neighbours, Kenya demonstrated that it was unwilling to cooperate with the Court by following through on this obligation. Prime Minister Odinga claimed that ODM was not aware of the invitation for al-Bashir to attend.

On the one hand the controversy over al-Bashir's attendance highlighted further strain within the coalition and differences between the partners in the Government of National Unity. Yet the issues associated with al-Bashir's visit to Kenya ran much deeper. One year prior to the promulgation ceremony, the ICC had begun its own investigations in Kenya. To the extent that Kenya was now a situation country, the obligation to arrest Bashir was much more pressing. Almost immediately the connection to its own ICC investigations was drawn, as commentators contemplated whether the decision to host Bashir might have been intended to send a signal to the ICC. Irrespective of whether it was intended as a signal, the KNCHR, among others, argued that it certainly sent the wrong message to victims of the post-election violence. It was also symptomatic of the challenges facing Kenya's rebirth and the tensions relating to dealing with accountability.

The decision of the ICC to initiate investigations into the post-election violence in Kenya was a direct consequence of the Government's failure to deal with the broader issue of impunity – a key requirement of Agenda Item 4. Not only did the Government prove its unwillingness to carry out fundamental reforms to tackle impunity, there was a deliberate attempt to derail any movement on this issue by frustrating efforts to establish a domestic mechanism for prosecuting perpetrators of the post-election violence. The unwillingness of the Government to punish those bearing responsibility can be attributed to the fact that 'many of them were either instigators or beneficiaries of the violence.'[47] Ironically, as the next section will demonstrate, the evasion of prosecutions and perpetuation of impunity was perhaps the only area in which the Coalition Government demonstrated true bipartisan support.

Prosecuting perpetrators of the post-election violence

As discussed in Chapter 2, the Commission of Inquiry into Post-Election Violence (CIPEV) was one of the main Agenda 4 Commissions established under the rubric of the KNDR process. CIPEV's mandate was threefold:

- to investigate the facts and surrounding circumstances related to acts of violence that followed the 2007 Presidential Election;
- to investigate the actions or omissions of State security agencies during the course of the violence;
- to recommend measures of a legal, political, or administrative nature, as appropriate, including measures with regard to bringing to justice those persons responsible for criminal acts.[48]

The overarching aim of the Commission of Inquiry was, however, 'to prevent any repetition of similar deeds and, in general, to eradicate impunity and promote national reconciliation in Kenya.'[49] In so doing, it was tasked with preparing a final report containing its findings and recommendations. The nominated Chair of the Commission was Justice Philip Waki, supported by a human rights lawyer from the DRC, Pascal Kambale, and former Assistant Commissioner of Police from New Zealand, Gavin McFayden. The Commission was sworn into office on 3 June 2008. Over the course of the next few months, the Commission took evidence in a series of hearings and interviews with a cross-section of the public around the country.

The CIPEV report (also referred to as the Waki report) was presented to the Government on 15 October 2008. Drawing upon the very detailed and heartbreaking testimonials from victims and witnesses, the report recounted the events surrounding the post-election violence. It was a devastating indictment of the government and political leadership of the country, not to mention, a profound statement on the problem of impunity:

> Kenya has an extremely troubled past. Its history of ethnic violence has been papered over for years until it exploded in horror during and after the 2007 elections. The causes of this sort of violence, which began in 1992 with the first multi-party elections, have always been known from official reports of past commissions of inquiry.... However, there has been no serious effort made by any government to punish perpetrators of violence or to address the plight of their victims.[50]

The Report made recommendations of a legal, political, and administrative nature that were required to end the scourge of impunity. For instance, the Report recommended enacting key pieces of legislation, including an International Crimes Act (to allow for incorporating provisions of the Rome Statute within Kenyan Law), a Freedom of Information Bill and the Witness Protection Act. Fundamental reforms to the Administration Police and the Kenya Police Service were also recommended. The key recommendation in the report was, however, the establishment of a Special Tribunal for Kenya (STK), which would 'seek accountability against persons bearing the greatest responsibility for crimes, particularly crimes against humanity, relating to the 2007 general elections in Kenya.'[51] The establishment of a tribunal was to be done within 60 days of the CIPEV report's publication, with the enabling legislation enacted 45 days later.

One of the main controversies that arose from the Commission's work was how to handle some of the sensitive information it had received in relation to the identity of alleged perpetrators. Through gathering evidence and hearing testimonials from witnesses and victims, the names of individuals allegedly involved in the post-election violence – including a number of high profile politicians and businessmen – were brought to the attention of the Commission. This led to a debate among the Commissioners over whether to publish the names of alleged perpetrators in their report. On the one hand, relaying the names of alleged perpetrators seemed to be a logical step in the pursuit of justice for victims of the post-election violence. On the other hand, there were at least three factors that gravitated against the inclusion of alleged perpetrators in the CIPEV Report. First, as the report identified, Kenya's existing witness protection programme was ill-equipped to offer adequate protection to victims and witnesses. Publishing the names of alleged perpetrators could potentially present risks to the safety of victims and witnesses. Second, the nature of the evidence gathered was in a preliminary stage. Should particular criminal incidences relating to the post-election violence move to the trial stage, further investigations would need to be conducted to build upon and substantiate the preliminary evidence that had been gathered. In this regard, there were strong grounds to withhold crucial information and safeguard the evidence that had been gathered thus far. Finally, there was also some concern that publishing the names of suspected perpetrators might result in the Commission's work being subjected to a political cover up. Taken together, these factors provided strong grounds for excluding the names of alleged perpetrators in the CIPEV Report.[52]

Instead of publishing the names of alleged perpetrators, the Commission opted to place the names in a sealed envelope and forward it to the Panel of Eminent African Personalities. This envelope (which became known as the Waki List) was to remain in the custody of the Panel pending the establishment of a tribunal. Given the tendency in Kenya to 'paper over' the issue of impunity, the Commission incorporated a self-implementing mechanism, as the report stated: 'In default of setting up the Tribunal, consideration will be given by the Panel to forwarding the names of alleged perpetrators to the special prosecutor of the International Criminal Court (ICC).'[53] The prosecutor would then 'analyze the seriousness of the information received, with a view to proceeding with an investigation and prosecuting such suspected persons.'[54]

The self-implementing mechanism in the CIPEV report provided a benchmark with which to assess the Government of Kenya's willingness to tackle the problem of impunity. The inclusion of the ICC as fall back was also intended to incentivise the creation of the STK – and therefore, was very much in the spirit of complementarity, which is based on the principle that the ICC can only exercise its jurisdiction where a state is unable or unwilling to prosecute.

On 20 October 2008, a few days after the Waki report was received, Kibaki addressed a crowd of Kenyans at Nyayo Stadium in celebration of Heroes' Day.[55] During the address, Kibaki remarked: 'I am aware that many Kenyans require justice for past injustices, but let us also keep in mind that although the truth will set us free – justice must be tempered with forgiveness for reconciliation to take root.'[56] He continued with remarks that signalled a different avenue to coping with perpetrators of violence: 'Let us prepare as a nation to consider restitution and forgiveness as complementing truth and justice in order to give our nation a fresh start. I want to call upon all Kenyans to forgive one another.'[57] The remarks invited an immediate reaction from observers, including Kofi Annan who emphasised that impunity should not be perpetuated and that perpetrators of the post-election violence should be prosecuted 'even if it would harm the Coalition Government.'[58]

The publication of the CIPEV report became a strong source of division among politicians. Whereas the majority of the PNU had initially demonstrated their support for the report and expressed a willingness to implement its recommendations, the ODM's parliamentary group rejected the findings of the report: 'ODM being part of the coalition government will resist and stop any rendition or surrender of Kenya citizens to a tribunal outside its territory as the national jurisdiction and national systems have not collapsed.'[59] Their position differed from Odinga's initial support for the document and eventually led to major divisions within the ODM.[60] Members of both parties quickly reversed their initial positions as speculation grew over the names on the Waki List. Concerns over the contents of the Waki envelope were heightened following the release of a KNCHR report, which publicly named 219 persons who allegedly participated in the violence. Among those mentioned in the KNCHR report were Deputy Prime Minister, Uhuru Kenyatta, and Minister for Agriculture, William Ruto. Both began legal proceedings to have their names removed from the report.[61]

On 16 December 2008, one day before the first deadline approach, Kibaki and Odinga agreed to implement the report's recommendations, including the establishment of a tribunal. The decision was of particular interest to Kofi Annan, given the Panel's mandate to monitor the implementation of the report. In a brief statement, Annan lauded the Government of Kenya's apparent willingness to implement the CIPEV report:

> The implementation of CIPEV's proposals will go a long way towards ending the culture of impunity and spearheading much-needed institutional reforms in the country. I note that the Parties to the agreement will now prepare and submit to the National Assembly a draft bill for the establishment of the Special Tribunal for Kenya. I trust that the bill will reflect the spirit of CIPEV's proposals and I urge Kenya's leaders to redouble their efforts to implement the CIPEV recommendations and to respect the suggested timeline for action.[62]

Although the CIPEV Report was adopted by Parliament on 27 January 2009, efforts to establish an STK failed on three separate occasions. The first attempt was defeated by Parliament on 12 February 2009. A revised bill was debated and eventually rejected by Cabinet in July 2009. Between 30 July and November 2009, a third and final attempt to establish an STK through a private member's bill was scuttled through a lack of quorum. In all three attempts, the efforts of those seeking to avoid prosecution carried the day. More worrying, however, was the way in which the ICC impacted debates over the creation of an STK. While the inclusion of the ICC as a fall-back option in the CIPEV Report was intended to catalyse a special tribunal, the ICC issue in Kenya soon became subject to political manipulation.

The first attempt: 'Don't be vague, let's go to The Hague'

The first attempt to establish a Special Tribunal consisted of two bills: The Constitution of Kenya (Amendment) Bill was drafted to ensure that the proposed tribunal would be in conformity with the Kenyan Constitution, whereas the second bill, 'The Special Tribunal for Kenya Bill,' proposed the establishment of a tribunal in order to 'seek accountability against persons bearing the greatest responsibility for crimes, particularly crimes against humanity, relating to the 2007 General Elections in Kenya.'[63] In conformity with the recommendations of the Waki Report, the Bill outlined the jurisdiction of the tribunal, including provisions relating to its structure and financing. When it came to the deliberations on the two bills, the first was defeated and thereby rendered the STK bill moot.

The debates in Parliament witnessed the emergence of two distinct groups motivated by rather different concerns. The first group (Group A) included politicians that were either personally involved in orchestrating the violence or had allies they wished to protect. While this group was united in the desire to avoid prosecutions, they differed on the best approach to achieve this. Some members of Group A thought the best way to avoid accountability was to vote down the STK in favor of prosecutions at The Hague, which they considered would be ineffective and slow-moving.[64] Members of this group, such as Lewis Nguyai, coined the phrase 'Don't be Vague, Lets go to The Hague.'[65] Others within Group A put much more stock in the ICC and therefore viewed the STK as preferable to an International Court. John Michuki was among those supporting the STK on the grounds that it could be controlled. 'It is being argued that in the proposed tribunal we shall have some foreigners. Of course they will be there. They will be our employees and we shall control them! We cannot control The Hague!'[66]

From a rather different perspective were those MPs (Group B) who had a sincere interest in the fight against impunity. However, the apparent loopholes in the legislation and the attendant prospect of a domestic mechanism being subject to manipulation led members of Group B to categorically reject the STK in favour of the ICC. Hence, rather ironically, the first attempt to establish an STK was voted down by some members of Group A, who were concerned that a domestic mechanism *would be* effective, and members of Group B who feared that it *would not be*. These alliances went beyond party affiliation and caused intra-party rifts.[67] As the Daily Nation reported on the Parliamentary debate:

> The irony here is that different factions within the coalition were plotting, for different reasons to defeat the Bill. One group, mainly from central Kenya, was concerned that a local tribunal would be open to manipulation, preferring instead The Hague option as the best way to punish the offenders. Another group, mainly from the Rift Valley and concerned that it was the target, was initially virulently opposed to The Hague. But by the time the debate came up in Parliament, it seemed to have had a change of mind, expressing fear that a local tribunal could be used to victimise culprits.[68]

Following the defeat of the bill in Parliament, Annan expressed his concern: 'I believe it is also a blow to efforts aimed at ending the culture of impunity in Kenya, which is a central objective of the Kenya National Dialogue and Reconciliation process.'[69] The Government of Kenya was subsequently granted two extensions for establishing a Special Tribunal.[70]

On 10 July 2009, a Government delegation met with Luis Moreno Ocampo, the ICC Chief Prosecutor, where it agreed to provide him with a report by the end of September 2009. The report would detail progress on investigations and prosecutions, and 'modalities for conducting national investigations and prosecutions of those responsible for the post-election violence by means of a Special Tribunal or another judicial mechanism adopted by Parliament.'[71] The report would also provide information on the steps taken to provide for the safety of victims and witnesses. In the event that a domestic tribunal was not established, the delegation agreed to refer the situation to the Chief Prosecutor in accordance with Article 14 of the Rome Statute.[72] With this agreement in place between the Chief Prosecutor and the Government of Kenya, the grounds for Annan's extension became null and void. Acting on behalf of the Panel, Annan forwarded the Waki envelope to Ocampo on 9 July 2009, with the supporting evidence sent to the Office of the Prosecutor one week later.

The second attempt: cabinet rejects an STK in favour of the TJRC

With trials in The Hague now seemingly more likely, the Government of Kenya made another attempt to establish a Special Tribunal. On 14 July 2009, the Minister of Justice, Mutula Kilonzo, put forward a revised version of the Constitution of Kenya Amendment Bill and the STK Bill. In many respects the revised bills constituted an improvement upon the initial bills presented to Parliament in February. By abolishing presidential immunity and amnesty, removing the powers of the Attorney General and High Court from interfering in the process, the bills represented a tightening up of some of the loopholes that were present in the initial bills. With these improvements to the draft legislation, members of Group B – those with a genuine interest in combating impunity – now preferred setting up a domestic mechanism for prosecuting perpetrators of the post-election violence. Only if an STK could not be established did Group B favour referring the situation to the ICC.

Members of Group A continued to look for ways to avoid prosecution; however, their options were now significantly constrained. The ICC was no longer a distant threat and the proposed STK could no longer be subject to political manipulation. Group A was forced to explore other avenues for avoiding prosecutions. Rather interestingly, William Ruto and Uhuru Kenyatta – who had been on opposing sides during the 2007 elections – jointly proposed a revision of the TJRC Bill to deal with the prosecution of post-election violence suspects.[73]

At its meeting on 30 July, the option of revamping the TJRC became the preferred course, as the Cabinet rejected both the possibility of establishing an STK through the revised Bills as well as the option of referring the situation to the International Criminal Court:

Cabinet today discussed extensively and exhaustively the various options available to it in dealing with the crimes committed during post-election violence.... Cabinet was concerned that while it will not stand for impunity in the pursuit of justice, the country should equally pursue national healing and reconciliation. This does not in any way reduce its desire to punish impunity.

Therefore Cabinet resolved as follows:

i) It reaffirmed its commitment to rule of law, and in particular in its commitment to the international Criminal Court and will cooperate and fulfill its obligations to the Court under the Rome Statute;
ii) It will undertake accelerated and far-reaching reforms in the judiciary, police, and investigative arms of Government to enable them investigate, prosecute and try perpetrators of post-election violence locally;
iii) It will deal with other forms of impunity including extra-judicial killings, corruption, and fraudulent or unlawful acquisition of public land and other public assets; and
iv) It will propose amendments to the Truth Justice and Reconciliation Act that will make the TJRC more representative and effective.[74]

In response to the Cabinet decision, 60 civil society organisations wrote an open letter to the President and the Prime Minister, accusing them of a 'collective conspiracy to protect suspects responsible for the horrendous atrocities of the 2007–08 post-election violence from criminal responsibility'[75] and further reminding them that the TJRC was never intended to be a judicial mechanism. While the TJRC was selected as the preferred mechanism for dealing with the perpetrators of the post-election violence, the TJRC Act was never actually amended or equipped with the requisite powers to prosecute alleged perpetrators. For his part, Mutula Kilonzo who expressed his dissension with the Cabinet decision indicated that he was not prepared to amend the TJRC Act.[76]

The third attempt: scuttled through lack of quorum

The third and final attempt to establish a Special Tribunal was championed by MP Gitobu Imanyara. Through the introduction of a private member's bill, Imanyara sought one final attempt to establish a tribunal. Building on the revised version of the Bills that were brought before Parliament, Imanyara's proposal included a further provision to limit the power of the Executive by furnishing the STK with the capacity to refer cases to the ICC.[77]

Prior to the vote, Imanyara voiced his optimism that he had the necessary support of MPs to pass the bill. To further his confidence in the process, Kibaki and Odinga released a statement in which they proclaimed that 'the Government remains fully committed to discharge its primary responsibility in accordance with the Rome Statute to establish a local judicial mechanism to deal with the perpetrators of the post-election violence.'[78] Notwithstanding this apparent support, the Bill was never debated, as successive attempts between November and December to bring it forward in Parliament failed to achieve the necessary quorum. As Martha Karua stated during one of these sessions: 'It is cowardly of the Executive, ministers and MPs to stay away from the chamber and not come here to declare on which side they are ... whether they are for the local tribunal or not and the reasons thereof.'[79]

During the session on 2 December, Imanyara acknowledged the courage of his colleagues to stand against impunity, even if it was against the advice of their parties 'when the intention to sabotage this Bill was being exhibited most shamelessly.'[80] He also conceded that whereas his efforts had failed, it would not be the last word on the fight against impunity:

> the culture of impunity in Kenya must come to end. Indeed, it will come to an end one day. It may not be today, but let those people out there claiming victory because this Bill has not passed not sleep one more night thinking that the culture of impunity has succeeded, because it has not succeeded! We, therefore, commend the efforts of the international community and, particularly, the International Criminal Court (ICC) for recognizing early enough that there was absolutely no political will on the part of this Government to get a local tribunal established and, therefore, begin the process of bringing justice to those who bear the greatest responsibility for the post-election violence well before the next elections are held.[81]

From Nairobi to The Hague: the ICC in Kenya

When the Government of Kenya failed to meet its deadline for establishing a credible domestic mechanism, as agreed with the Office of the Prosecutor, it requested yet another extension.[82] After the request was rejected, the Government reneged on its commitment to refer the situation to the ICC, with Odinga stating that referrals should be reserved for 'failed states, which Kenya is not.'[83] Following the failure of the Government to refer the case, the Chief Prosecutor moved to request authorisation from the ICC Pre-Trial Chamber to conduct investigations. It was a momentous decision for Kenya, as well as the ICC, as it was the first time in the history of the Court that the Chief Prosecutor launched an investigation *propio motu* (of his own accord).

Rather than viewing the ICC cases as a substitute for other judicial mechanisms, the Chief Prosecutor affirmed that the ICC would constitute one arm of a multi-layered approach to addressing the impunity gap in Kenya. He envisaged a three-pronged approach to justice which would involve the ICC prosecuting those most responsible for the violence; national accountability proceedings for other perpetrators; and mechanisms such as the Truth, Justice and Reconciliation Commission (TJRC) to shed light on the full history of past events and to suggest mechanisms to prevent such crimes in the future. In this regard, the various accountability mechanisms were not seen as *mutually exclusive*, but rather *mutually reinforcing*.[84] While the previous section has demonstrated the difficulties associated with the middle prong of Ocampo's approach, the TJRC process in Kenya encountered similar difficulties.

The truth justice and reconciliation commission

Although a TJRC process had been under consideration in Kenya well before 2007, the post-election violence provided a powerful incentive to revisit this idea. However, the TJRC that was finally delivered in 2008 was the subject of one controversy after another. In terms of substantive issues, there was criticism over the scope of the TJRC's mandate – which encompassed human rights violations, economic crimes, land issues, marginalisation, ethnic violence, and sexual violence between 12 December 1963 and 28 February 2008 – as its remit was much broader than the period following the 2007 elections and its aftermath.

Concerns have also been voiced over the TJRC's approach to amnesty, its lack of financial independence and its system of appointments. Most contentious, however, were the allegations that were brought against the Chair of the Commission, Bethuel Kiplagat, for his alleged involvement in some of the very atrocities that were to be investigated under the remit of the TJRC. There were many calls for Kiplagat to step down.[85] This controversy caused substantial delays to the Commission's work and eventually led two Commissioners to resign.[86] To make matters worse, parts of the report,[87] which was delivered in 2013 were allegedly re-written by the Government so as to shield information from the public.[88]

In the end, the TJRC process lost the confidence of many Kenyans very early on and, therefore, cannot be considered a positive example of truth and reconciliation in a post-conflict setting. Moreover, the countless controversies that plagued the TJRC process tend to vindicate those who expressed concerns with domestic mechanisms in Kenya falling prey to political manipulation.

The court of last resort

In the absence of any legitimate domestic mechanism for prosecuting perpetrators of the 2007–08 post-election violence, the ICC really was the 'Court of Last Resort' in Kenya. From the moment that Ocampo requested permission from the pre-trial chamber to commence investigations in Kenya, there were high expectations in the Court's capacity to effectively prosecute perpetrators of the poll violence. The degree of faith invested in the ICC was in sharp contrast – and can perhaps be attributed to – the complete lack of faith in any national accountability mechanism. Opinion polls conducted by South Consulting revealed that many Kenyans were initially in favour of the ICC process, with over 70 per cent of the respondents expressing confidence in the Court's capacity to effectively prosecute the perpetrators of the post-election violence.[89]

Statements made by the Chief Prosecutor contributed towards elevating expectations among Kenyans, as Ocampo made lofty promises to 'end impunity in Kenya' and assured the public that his cases were strong.[90] The Chief Prosecutor also drew a link between the importance of combating impunity in advance of the next elections.⁹¹ He noted that 'Kenya will show how to manage past violence and how to create a peaceful process for the upcoming elections' and in so doing, 'will be an example to the world.'⁹²

Shortly after the Chief Prosecutor requested an authorisation to initiate investigations, there were attempts to delay the decision of the pre-trial chamber. The International Association of Democratic Lawyers (IADL), an international organisation with links to members of the Cabinet that were allegedly involved in the violence, filed an objection to restrain the ICC from taking action in Kenya. According to Imanyara: 'IADL rushed to file an objection based on "flimsy" grounds to stall the process until after the 2013 General Election at the behest of powerful individuals in the government.'⁹³ A plot also emerged to intimidate potential witnesses, leading some to warn that attempts to delay the pre-trial chamber's decision, 'would subject witnesses to untold suffering and diminish any meaningful trial by the ICC.'⁹⁴

In March 2010, the pre-trial chamber authorised Ocampo to initiate investigations into alleged crimes against humanity that may have been committed in Kenya during the post-election violence. Some Cabinet members expressed their concerns that investigations could inflame tensions during the constitutional referendum process, however, their efforts to lobby for a delay failed to garner the necessary level of support from Cabinet.⁹⁵

On 15 December 2010, Ocampo named six individuals he deemed to bear the greatest responsibility for the post-election violence – three from the ODM and three from the PNU. From the ODM side, he named: Minister for Agriculture, William Ruto; Industrialisation Minister, Henry Kosgey; Journalist, Joshua Arap Sang (Case 1) and from the PNU, he named: Head of the Civil Service, Francis Muthaura; Finance Minister, Uhuru Kenyatta; and Police Commissioner, Mohamed Hussein Ali (Case 2). In a news conference following his presentation of the two cases to ICC judges, Ocampo remarked: 'The post-election period of 2007–2008 was one of the most violent periods of the nation's history. These were not just crimes against innocent Kenyans. They were crimes against humanity as a whole.'⁹⁶

In the summary of the case, Ocampo referred to Mr Ruto, Mr Kosgey and Mr Arap Sang as the 'principal planners and organisers of crimes against PNU supporters.'⁹⁷ He noted how Ruto and Kosgey cultivated perpetrators and Mr Sang used 'his radio programme to collect supporters and provide signals to members of the plan on when and where to attack' which began after the results were announced.

> On 30–31 December 2007, they began attacks in target locations including Turbo town, the greater Eldoret area (Huruma, Kimumu, Langas, and Yamumbi), Kapsabet town, and Nandi Hills town. They approached each location from all directions, burning down PNU supporters' homes and businesses, killing civilians, and systematically driving them from their homes.... On 1 January 2008, the church located on the Kiambaa farm cooperative was attacked and burned with more than hundred people inside.

> At least 17 people died. The brunt of the attacks continued into the first week of January 2008.[98]

The Prosecutor then accused Mr Kenyatta, Mr Muthaura and Major General Ali of planning and executing retaliatory attacks. Muthaura, in his position as Chair of the National Security Advisory Committee, 'authorised the police to use excessive force against ODM supporters and to facilitate attacks against ODM supporters,' which were carried out by Ali as Police Commissioner. Mr Kenyatta was accused of mobilising the Mungiki militia to facilitate attacks against ODM supporters.

> On or about 3 January 2008, Kenyatta, as the focal point between the PNU and the criminal organization the Mungiki, facilitated a meeting with Muthaura, a senior Government of Kenya official, and Mungiki leaders to organize retaliatory attacks against civilian supporters of the ODM. Thereafter, Muthaura, in his capacity as Chairman of the National Security Advisory Committee ('NSAC'), telephoned Ali, his subordinate as head of the Kenya Police, and instructed Ali not to interfere with the movement of pro-PNU youth, including the Mungiki. Kenyatta additionally instructed the Mungiki leaders to attend a second meeting on the same day to finalise logistical and financial arrangements for the retaliatory attacks.[99]

Ocampo further reiterated the importance of prosecuting perpetrators of the post-election violence in advance of the upcoming General Election. 'By breaking the cycle of impunity for massive crimes, victims and their families can have justice. And Kenyans can pave the way to peaceful elections.'[100]

Three of the accused responded immediately to Ocampo's announcement. Muthaura categorically denied the accusations levelled against him: 'The suggestion that I have done anything to warrant criminal investigation is manifest nonsense. It amounts to an unwarranted slur on my reputation and is both unfair and unjustified.'[101] Kenyatta similarly denied the charges: 'My record is clear and it remains very clear that I have never committed any crime.'[102] Ruto confirmed his willingness to cooperate with the Court: 'I am ready, willing and available to face the prosecutor with his witnesses in court as and when I am required to do so.'[103] He insisted further, 'My conscience is clear, I neither participated, organised or had anything to do with the violence.'[104] The pre-trial chamber subsequently issued summonses for the so-called 'Ocampo Six' to appear at The Hague in April 2011.

Conclusion

This chapter has surveyed the performance of the Coalition Government in implementing the reforms agreed to during the KNDR process. Against some of the more pessimistic predictions that followed the peace agreement in 2008, the Coalition Government did hold together throughout the full five-year term.

The government of national impunity 95

Nevertheless, while the task of reforming the country should have been the glue holding the coalition together, 'in practice elite self-interest did so.'[105]

Difficulties within the newly constituted Government of National Unity began to emerge even before the ink had begun to dry on these Agreements. Major disagreements would eventually surface in relation to both substantive and procedural matters. With countless disagreements, often resulting in deadlock, the governance of the country often took a back seat to divisions within the Government. The impact of recurring disputes within the Coalition Government could be most immediately felt in relation to Agenda Item 4. With the rivalling parties caught up in internal disputes and the controversies surrounding power sharing, this left little scope for addressing the underlying causes of the 2007–08 violence. While the Coalition moved at an exceptionally slow pace in addressing Agenda 4, it is also significant that momentum was stifled on some of the earlier Agenda Items relating to insecurity and the resettlement of IDPs.

Whereas deep-seated divisions continued to beset the workings of the Coalition Government in nearly all other areas, the adoption of a new constitution is widely regarded as one of the main achievements of the Government of National Unity. An overwhelming majority of Kenyans voted in favour of the new constitution during the 4 August 2010 referendum. Support for a new constitution was one of the key issues in which the principals presented a united front, even though divisions among their respective parties prevented the PNU and ODM from mounting a joint 'yes' campaign in the lead-up to the referendum. Hence, even in an area where there was widespread agreement, the divisions within the Coalition Government persisted.

The one area in which there was genuine bipartisan support from a cross-section of both the PNU and ODM could be seen in relation to the issue of accountability. The Commission of Inquiry into Post-Election Violence (CIPEV) was one of the main Agenda 4 Commissions established under the rubric of the KNDR process. The overarching aim of the Commission of Inquiry was to eradicate impunity and promote national reconciliation in Kenya. The key recommendation in the report was the establishment of a Special Tribunal for Kenya (STK), which would 'seek accountability against persons bearing the greatest responsibility for crimes, particularly crimes against humanity, relating to the 2007 general elections in Kenya.'[106] Although the CIPEV Report was adopted by Parliament on 27 January 2009, efforts to establish an STK failed on three separate occasions. The first attempt was defeated by Parliament on 12 February 2009. A revised bill was debated and eventually rejected by Cabinet in July 2009. Between 30 July and November 2009, a third and final attempt to establish an STK through a private members bill was scuttled through a lack of quorum. In all three attempts, the efforts of those seeking to avoid prosecution carried the day. Following the three failed attempts to establish an STK, there have been no further attempts to bring perpetrators of the post-election violence to justice,[107] hence earning the Government of National Unity the title of 'Government of National Impunity.' The failure to establish a Special Tribunal eventually paved the way for the International Criminal Court. The next chapter will examine the impact of the ICC's involvement in Kenya, and, in particular, the role of the Court during and after the 2013 General Election.

Notes

1 Bernard Namunane, 'Poll violence: Kibaki hints at amnesty', 20 October 2008, available online at www.nation.co.ke/news/-/1056/482520/-/5fp3g9z/-/index.html (accessed 20 May 2015).
2 Gitobu Imanyara, Hansard, Kenya National Assembly, Official Report, 2 December 2009.
3 Office of the AU Panel of Eminent African Personalities, *Back from the Brink: The 2008 Mediation Process and Reforms in Kenya*, African Union Commission, p. 71, available online at www.knchr.org/Portals/0/GeneralReports/backFromBrink_web.pdf (accessed 20 May 2015).
4 Adam Mynott 'Huge financial cost of Kenya cabinet', *BBC News*, 17 April 2008, available online at http://news.bbc.co.uk/1/hi/world/africa/7352261.stm (accessed 20 May 2015).
5 Ibid.
6 Ibid.
7 Office of the AU Panel of Eminent African Personalities, *Back from the Brink*, p. 73.
8 Ibid., p. 71.
9 Will Ross, 'Two ministers suspended in corruption scandal', *BBC News*, 14 February 2010, available online at http://news.bbc.co.uk/1/hi/world/africa/8515135.stm (accessed 20 May 2015).
10 Interview with David Anderson, African Studies Centre, Oxford, 6 July 2010.
11 Will Ross, 'Two ministers suspended.'
12 Ibid.
13 'Kenya AG faults PM on suspension', *Capital News*, 15 February 2010, available online at www.capitalfm.co.ke/news/2010/02/kenya-ag-faults-pm-on-suspension/ (accessed 20 May 2015).
14 Ibid.
15 Ibid.
16 Barney Jopson, 'Kofi Annan intervenes in Kenya dispute', *Financial Times*, 18 February 2010, available online at www.ft.com/cms/s/0/fb896caa-1c7f-11df-8456-00144feab49a.html#axzz3b65KJ3xV (accessed 20 May 2015).
17 'Statement issued by Mr. Kofi Annan, Chairman of the African Union Panel of Eminent African Personalities 31 January 2011' available online at http://kenyastockholm.com/2011/02/01/impunity-in-kenya-statement-from-kofi-annan/ (accessed 20 May 2015).
18 Office of the AU Panel of Eminent African Personalities, *Back from the Brink*, p. 48.
19 Karen Allen, 'Has Kenya's power-sharing worked', *BBC News*, 3 March 2009, available online at http://news.bbc.co.uk/1/hi/world/africa/7921007.stm (accessed 20 May 2015).
20 Office of the AU Panel of Eminent African Personalities, *Back from the Brink*, p. 72.
21 Ibid.
22 Ibid., p. 79.
23 'Report of the Special Rapporteur on extrajudicial, summary or arbitrary executions', (Alston Report), 26 May 2009, available online at www.extrajudicialexecutions.org/application/media/Kenya%20Mission%202009%20%28A_HRC_11_2_Add.6%29.pdf (accessed 20 May 2015).
24 Statement by Professor Philip Alston, Special Rapporteur on extrajudicial, summary

25 Alston Report, p. 3.
26 'UN Official Calls for Sacking of Ali and Wako February', *Daily Nation*, 25 February 2009, available online at www.nation.co.ke/news/-/1056/534978/-/4ynka9z/-/index.html (accessed 20 May 2015).
27 Xan Rice, 'UN condemns executions carried out by Kenyan police', *Guardian*, 25 February 2009, available online at www.theguardian.com/world/2009/feb/25/un-kenya-executions (accessed 20 May 2015).
28 Alston Report, p. 13.
29 Ibid.
30 Ibid., p. 2; see also 'Alston pushes for protection of witnesses', *Daily Nation*, 28 May 2009, available online at www.nation.co.ke/news/-/1056/604318/-/4hfl3iz/-/index.html (accessed 20 May 2015).
31 'UN Report Alleges Widespread Killing by Kenyan Police', *CNN*, 15 June 2009, available online at http://edition.cnn.com/2009/WORLD/africa/06/05/kenya.united.nations.investigation/ (accessed 20 June 2015).
32 Wako remained in his post until 2011.
33 The Task force was allotted KSH81 million for a period of four years.
34 Internal Displacement Monitoring Centre, 'Kenya IDP figures analysis', available online at www.internal-displacement.org/sub-saharan-africa/kenya/figures-analysis (accessed 20 May 2015).
35 Oliver Mathenge, 'Operation Rudi Nyumbani a flop, says rights agency', *Daily Nation*, 28 October 2008, available online at www.nation.co.ke/News/-/1056/484998/-/tlhtvl/-/ (accessed 20 May 2015).
36 Office of the AU Panel of Eminent African Personalities, *Back from the Brink*, p. 79.
37 Ibid., p. 80.
38 'Audit Reveals Sh500m IDP Cash Loss', *Daily Nation*, 12 January 2012, available online at www.nation.co.ke/News/Audit+reveals+Sh500m+IDP+cash+loss+/-/1056/1304732/-/2kk4cc/-/index.html (accessed 20 June 2015).
39 Lucy Hannon, 'Kenya's displacement crisis', *Humanitarian Access Network*, October 2008, available online at www.odihpn.org/humanitarian-exchange-magazine/issue-40/kenyas-displacement-crisis (accessed 20 May 2015).
40 Office of the AU Panel of Eminent African Personalities, *Back from the Brink*, p. 162.
41 'Remarks by Vice-President Biden in a statement to the press with Kenyan President Mwai Kibaki', 8 June 2010, available online at www.whitehouse.gov/the-press-office/remarks-vice-president-biden-a-statement-press-with-kenyan-president-mwai-kibaki (accessed 20 May 2015).
42 Bernard Namunane, 'No End to Draft Illegal Edit Puzzle', 21 July 2010, available online at www.nation.co.ke/Kenya-Referendum/No-end-to-draft-illegal-edit-puzzle-/-/926046/962444/-/y7pqkpz/-/index.html (accessed 20 May 2015).
43 Office of the AU Panel of Eminent African Personalities, *Back from the Brink*, p. 75.
44 Ibid
45 'Attempts were made to amend the constitution and derail its implementation even before it had been tested' (*Back from the Brink*, p. 180).
46 Xan Rice, 'Omar al-Bashir tarnishes Kenya's landmark day', 27 August 2010, available online at www.theguardian.com/world/2010/aug/27/omar-al-bashir-war-crimes-kenya (accessed 20 May 2015).
47 'With The Hague reality sinking in, leaders are in panic mode', *Daily Nation*, 9 November 2009, available online at www.nation.co.ke/oped/blogs/-/446672/683960/-/1229h2hz/-/index.html (accessed 20 May 2015); see also Xan Rice, 'International Criminal Court to investigate violence after 2007 Kenya election', *Guardian*, 31

March 2010, available online at www.theguardian.com/world/2010/mar/31/international-criminal-court-kenya-violence (accessed 20 May 2015).
48 Kenyan National Dialogue and Reconciliation: Commission of Inquiry on Post-Election Violence, 4 March 2008, available online at www.lcil.cam.ac.uk/sites/default/files/LCIL/documents/transitions/Kenya_14_KNDR_Commission_of_Inquiry.pdf (accessed 20 June 2015).
49 Ibid.
50 *Final Report from Kenya's Commission of Inquiry into Post-Election Violence* ('The Waki Report'), 15 October 2008, available online at https://kenyastockholm.files.wordpress.com/2008/10/the-waki-report.pdf (accessed 20 June 2015), pp. 15–16.
51 Ibid., p. 472.
52 Ibid., pp. 15–18.
53 Ibid., p. 18.
54 Ibid., p. 473.
55 Heroes' Day was previously referred to as Kenyatta Day.
56 Bernard Namunane, 'Poll violence: Kibaki hints at amnesty', 20 October 2008, available online at www.nation.co.ke/news/-/1056/482520/-/5fp3g9z/-/index.html (accessed 20 May 2015).
57 Ibid.
58 Ibid
59 'ODM Parliamentary group meeting rejects Waki Report', *The Standard*, 30 October 2008, available online at www.standardmedia.co.ke/article/1143998194/odm-parliamentary-group-meeting-rejects-waki-report (accessed 20 May 2015).
60 'Waki: row over Ruto threat to quit ODM', *Daily Nation*, 16 November 2008, available online at www.nation.co.ke/news/-/1056/491782/-/view/printVersion/-/nqjvgqz/-/index.html (accessed 20 May 2015).
61 Sam Kiplagat, 'Poll Chaos: Ruto wants court to clear his name', *Daily Nation*, 20 November 2009, available online at www.nation.co.ke/news/politics/-/1064/801576/-/jeuiktz/-/index.html (accessed 20 May 2015).
62 'Statement by HE Kofi Annan on Implementation of CIPEV and IREC' 19 December 2008., available online at http://reliefweb.int/report/kenya/statement-he-kofi-annan-implementation-cipev-and-irec (accessed 20 May 2015).
63 The Special tribunal for Kenya Bill, 2009 'Memorandum of Objects and Reasons' available online at www.kenyalaw.org/Downloads/Bills/2009/The_Special_Tribunal_for_Kenya_Statute_2009.pdf (accessed 20 June 2015).
64 'Why I prefer The Hague Route', *Daily Nation*, 21 February 2009, available online at www.nation.co.ke/news/-/1056/533390/-/4yoe9mz/-/index.html (accessed 20 May 2015); see also 'The Hague Vows to Act Swiftly', *Daily Nation*, 31 March 2009, available online at www.nation.co.ke/News/-/1056/555462/-/u3qj9g/-/' (accessed 20 May 2015).
65 Lewis Nguyai, Hansard, Kenya National Assembly, Official Report, 4 February 2009.
66 John Michuki, Hansard, Kenya National Assembly, Official Report, 4 February 2009.
67 'Puzzling Alliances in fight Against Tribunal Bill', *Daily Nation*, 12 February 2009, available online at www.nation.co.ke/News/politics/-/1064/529716/-/ygqyunz/-/index.html (accessed 20 May 2015).
68 Ibid.
69 Anthony Kariuki, 'Annan to send violence chiefs to The Hague', *Daily Nation*, 13 February 2009, available online at www.nation.co.ke/News/-/1056/529848/-/u1yrxf/-/index.html (accessed 20 May 2015).
70 See 'Kenya PM sees extension to court deadline', *Relief Web*, 18 February 2009, available online at http://reliefweb.int/report/kenya/kenya-pm-sees-extension-local-court-deadline (accessed 20 May 2015).

71 ICC Office of the Prosecutor, 'Agreed Minutes of Meeting Between Prosecutor Moreno-Ocampo and the Delegation of the Government of Kenya', The Hague, 3 July 2009, available online at www.icc-cpi.int/NR/rdonlyres/1CEB4FAD-DFA7-4DC5-B22D-E828322D9764/280560/20090703AgreedMinutesofMeetingProsecutorKenyanDele.pdf (accessed 20 June 2015).
72 Office of the AU Panel of Eminent African Personalities, *Back from the Brink*, p. 107.
73 'Kenya: Cabinet decides on TJRC – Kenya', *Relief Web*, 30 July 2009, available online at http://reliefweb.int/report/kenya/kenya-cabinet-decides-tjrc (accessed 20 May 2015).
74 Ibid.
75 'Open Letter to President Mwai Kibaki and Prime Minister Raila Odinga', 5 August 2009.
76 Anthony Kagiri, 'Mutula backs Imanyara Tribunal Bill', *Capital News*, 10 August 2009, available online at www.capitalfm.co.ke/news/2009/08/mutula-backs-imanyara-tribunal-bill/?wpmp_switcher=mobile (accessed 20 May 2015).
77 'Imanyara: House will nail big fish with proposed bill', *Daily Nation*, 15 August 2009, available online at www.nation.co.ke/news/politics/-/1064/640268/-/kfkl6fz/-/index.html (accessed 20 May 2015).
78 David McKenzie, 'ICC Prosecutor: Suspects in Kenya violence will be tried', *CNN*, 5 November 2009, available online at http://edition.cnn.com/2009/WORLD/africa/11/05/kenya.icc.trials/ (20 May 2015).
79 Laban Wanabisi, 'Kenyan MPs frustrate special court bill again', 2 December 2009, available online at www.capitalfm.co.ke/news/2009/12/kenyan-mps-frustrate-special-courts-bill-again/ (accessed 20 May 2015).
80 Gitobu Imanyara, Hansard, Kenya National Assembly, Official Report, 2 December 2009.
81 Ibid.
82 Macharia Mwangi, 'Tribunal: Kenya to beg Ocampo for more time', *Daily Nation*, 21 September 2009.
83 Caroline Wafula, 'Don't Panic, Raila tells leaders' *Daily Nation*, 18 November 2009, available online at www.nation.co.ke/news/politics/-/1064/688104/-/kcxvyoz/-/index.html (accessed 20 May 2015).
84 'ICC Prosecutor Supports Three-Pronged Approach to Justice in Kenya', 30 September 2009, available online at www.icc-cpi.int/en_menus/icc/situations%20and%20cases/situations/situation%20icc%200109/press%20releases/Pages/pr456.aspx (accessed 20 May 2015).
85 Martin Mutua, 'Eyes on Other Commissioner's as Murungi Resigns', *The Standard*, 20 April 2011, available online at www.standardmedia.co.ke/mobile/?articleID=2000008083&story_title=Eyes%20on%20other%20TJRC%20officials%20as%20Murungi%20resigns (accessed 20 June 2015).
86 Betty Murungi and Ronald Slye were the two Commissioners who resigned.
87 Full Report of the Truth, Justice and Reconciliation Commission (TJRC Report), May 2013, available online at www.kenyamoja.com/tjrc-report/ (accessed 20 May 2015).
88 Christopher Gitari Ndungú, 'Lessons to Be Learned: An Analysis of the Final Report of Kenya's Truth, Justice and Reconciliation Commission', International Centre for Transitional Justice Briefing, 19 May 2014, available online at www.ictj.org/publication/kenya-TJRC-lessons-learned (accessed 20 June 2015).
89 South Consulting, 'The Kenyan National Dialogue and Reconciliation (KNDR) Monitoring Project', Draft Review Report, April 2011, available online at www.iccnow.org/documents/April2011KNDRReport.pdf (accessed 20 June 2015), p. vi.
90 'Ocampo has a strong case in Kenya chaos', *Daily Nation*, 7 November 2009.
91 'ICC Prosecutor: Kenya can be an example to the world', 18 September 2009,

available online at www.icccpi.int/en_menus/icc/situations%20and%20cases/situations/situation%20icc%200109/press%20releases/Pages/pr452.aspx (accessed 20 May 2015).
92 Ibid.
93 Walter Menya, 'Activists protest over bid to delay ICC trial', 8 January 2010, *Daily Nation*, available online at www.nation.co.ke/News/-/1056/838602/-/voss26/-/index.html (accessed 20 May 2015).
94 Ibid.
95 'Ministers push to keep Ocampo probe at bay', *Daily Nation*, 15 April 2010, available online at www.nation.co.ke/News/politics/Ministers%20push%20to%20keep%20Ocampo%20probe%20at%20bay/-/1064/900238/-/lhcdbg/-/index.html (accessed 20 May 2015).
96 Anthony Kariuki and Oliver Mathenge, 'Ocampo names Kenya chaos suspects', 15 December 2010, *Daily Nation*, available online at www.nation.co.ke/news/Ocampo-names-Kenya-chaos-suspects/-/1056/2119320/-/view/printVersion/-/apwycpz/-/index.html (accessed 20 May 2015). See also ICC Office of the Prosecutor, 'Kenya's post-election violence: ICC Prosecutor presents cases against six individuals for crimes against humanity', 15 December 2010, available online at www.icccpi.int/en_menus/icc/press%20and%20media/press%20releases/press%20releases%20%282010%29/Pages/pr615.aspx (accessed 20 May 2015).
97 Ibid.
98 Ibid.
99 Ibid.
100 Ibid
101 Anthony Kariuki and Oliver Mathenge, 'Ocampo Names Kenya chaos suspects.'
102 Ibid.
103 Ibid.
104 Ibid.
105 Office of the AU Panel of Eminent African Personalities, *Back from the Brink*, p. 81.
106 The Waki Report, p. 472.
107 According to a report by the Office of the AU Panel on Eminent Personalities:

> No member of the police had been convicted for such crimes, despite reports of 962 police shootings and evidence that police committed sexual offenses. Only four middle and lower-level perpetrators to date have been taken to court; these cases resulted in two convictions and two acquittals.

> See Office of the AU Panel of Eminent African Personalities, *Back from the Brink*, p. 80.

4 Kenya and the court of last resort
Justice in the hands of the accused

> ... despite assurances of its willingness to cooperate with the Court, the Government of Kenya failed to follow through on those assurances.[1]
> (Fatou Bensouda, Chief Prosecutor of the ICC, 5 December 2014)
>
> As they say, one down, two to go.[2]
> (President Uhuru Kenyatta, 5 December 2014)

Since the KNDR agreements were signed, the Government of Kenya has consistently pledged to deliver justice to the victims of the post-election violence. After the failed attempts to prosecute the perpetrators of the violence through a domestic mechanism yielded to the involvement of the International Criminal Court, the Government maintained that it would fully cooperate with the Court. However, as the two Kenyan cases at the ICC got underway, the Government engaged in efforts to block the cases. Alongside attempts to pull out of the Rome Statute and the initiation of an admissibility challenge against the Court, the Government pursued intense lobbying to have the cases deferred.

In presenting their rationale for the cases to be deferred, the Government of Kenya argued that the ICC's involvement in Kenya risked destabilising the country in the run-up to the 2013 General Election. Nevertheless, during the election, the ICC factor was actually viewed as a stabilising influence that served to deter incidences of hate speech and acts of violence. At the same time, there were a number of unintended consequences associated with the ICC's involvement in Kenya, most notably, provoking an 'alliance of the accused' between Uhuru Kenyatta and his running mate, William Ruto.

Most crucial of all, as a consequence of the 2013 election, the prospect of bringing perpetrators of the post-election violence to justice suffered a critical setback. Given the numerous failed attempts to establish a domestic tribunal under the Coalition Government, the ICC really was the Court of Last Resort; that is, the only remaining option for delivering justice in Kenya. However, in order for the ICC to effectively prosecute the accused, it would require the cooperation of the Kenyan Government. As a consequence of the 2013 election, the Government of Kenya and the accused became one and the same. In this

102 *The responsibility to prosecute*

regard, the last hope for justice in Kenya now ironically resided in the hands of the accused.

This chapter will examine the ICC's involvement in Kenya. It will begin by exploring attempts by the Coalition Government to halt the cases, and the impact of the Court in the lead-up to the 2013 General Election. After considering the way in which the Court was utilised to help the 'alliance of the accused' achieve victory, the remainder of this chapter will explore how the accused used the machinery of the state to shield themselves from prosecutions.

Attempts to block the ICC cases

From the moment the KNDR agreements were signed, the Government of Kenya pledged to deliver justice for the victims of the 2007–08 post-election violence. Even throughout each unsuccessful attempt to establish a Special Tribunal for Kenya, the principals reaffirmed their commitment to ensuring accountability. When the possibility of a domestic mechanism faded – eventually yielding to the Court of Last Resort – the Government of Kenya offered assurances of its intention to fully cooperate with the Court. As the ICC intensified its involvement in the country, the Government's willingness to cooperate with the Court was, however, far from forthcoming. The Chief Prosecutor of the Court, Luis Moreno Ocampo, noted with grave concern how the mood within the Government, and the general approach to the ICC, began to shift once the suspects were named.[3] What followed were multiple attempts to block the ICC's efforts in the wake of Ocampo's identification of the suspected perpetrators.

The first attempt came days after the suspects were named. On 22 December, the Kenyan Parliament passed a non-binding motion requiring the Government to withdraw from the Rome Statute.[4] Parliament's actions drew strong criticism from Kenyan civil society, which regarded it as a futile attempt to evade prosecution for suspected perpetrators. According to the provisions of the Rome Statute, a one-year notice period is required, and, therefore, any attempted withdrawal would have no effect on the cases before the Court. In the aftermath of the Parliamentary motion, the UK High Commissioner, Rob Maccaire, made the following observation:

> You have to ask questions about the motivation of parliamentarians.... These were the very MPs who called for the ICC's involvement, and voted out a local tribunal. Perhaps what they are really saying is that they just want to prevent anyone being held to account for crimes against humanity.[5]

Following the attempted withdrawal from the Rome Statute, the Government of Kenya launched a major diplomatic initiative to have the ICC cases deferred. Under the leadership of then Minister of Foreign Affairs, Kalonzo Musyoka, a group of Cabinet Ministers embarked on a campaign of shuttle diplomacy. The first stage of the initiative was to organise a pan-African protest against the ICC's alleged focus on Africa. After receiving a boost at the IGAD summit in support of the deferral option, Musyoka visited other capitals across the continent in preparation for a forthcoming African Union Summit on 11 January 2011. During the Summit, the Government of Kenya was successful in persuading the African Union to back its request for a deferral. The deferral option was supported on the grounds that Kenya would be in a position to deliver justice to victims of the post-election violence following the continuing process of judicial reform. The AU communiqué further argued that the failure to defer the cases would compromise the 'peace-building and national reconciliation' process in Kenya.[6]

Having secured support for a deferral among their counterparts in Africa, Musyoka's team then proceeded to take their case to the UN Security Council. As highlighted in the introduction, the UN Security Council has the power to not only refer cases to the ICC Chief Prosecutor, but is also equipped with the capacity to defer cases for a period of 12 months (with the possibility of an indefinite renewal). On 8 February 2011, Kenya's permanent mission to the UN forwarded an aid-memoire titled 'Kenya's Reform Agenda and Engagement with the ICC'[7] to all Permanent and Observer Missions at the UN. The aid-memoire presented the Government of Kenya's argument for deferring the cases. On 4 March 2011, the Kenyan Mission wrote to the President of the Security Council requesting that the Council consider a deferral of the cases. Musyoka then proceeded to make his case to the Secretary-General on 8 March 2011. Although the US, UK and France, all Permanent Members of the Security Council made it clear they would not support the request, the Kenyan Mission sent a follow-up letter on 23 March 2011, which requested the Council to reconsider the deferral option on the grounds that the cases could be handled through a domestic mechanism. The diplomatic community in New York maintained its opposition to deferring the Kenyan cases, as did Kenyan expatriates residing in New York who staged a protest outside the United Nations building during Musyoka's visit. Meanwhile, a petition was signed by 800 000 Kenyans in opposition to the deferral option.[8]

In making their request for a deferral of the Kenyan cases, the Government relied on two diverging arguments. The first argument was based on the assertion that the trials would pose a threat to international peace and security.[9] The second argument was based on the claim that the ICC trials could be handled domestically and, therefore, need not involve the Court of Last Resort. In an effort to substantiate the latter claim, Police Spokesperson, Eric Kiraithe, made reference to 6000 post-election violence cases that were pending the establishment of a domestic tribunal.[10] This was accompanied by an order from the Attorney General on 26 April 2011 to commence investigations of the 'Ocampo Six.' These efforts to proceed with domestic prosecutions provided the basis for the Kenyan Government to challenge the admissibility of the cases before the ICC.[11] This request was rejected on 30 May 2011 on the grounds that there was no evidence to support the contention that national proceedings were taking place.[12] The Government filed an appeal to this decision on 20 June, which was also rejected on 30 August 2011.

As the Ocampo Six made their initial appearances before the Court on 7–8 April 2011, the Security Council held informal consultations on the matter and concluded that Kenya's deferral request should be presented to the ICC. Confirmation hearings occurred between September and October 2011, with the chamber eventually confirming charges against four of the accused (Ruto, Sang, Muthaura and Kenyatta).

The Government of Kenya's campaign to block the ICC cases drew sharp criticism from the ICC's Chief Prosecutor. In a statement, Ocampo accused the Government of 'not only sending the wrong signal'[13] but also 'promoting a growing climate of fear that is intimidating potential witnesses and ultimately undermining national and international investigations.'[14] He then provocatively asked: 'My question to the Kenyan Government is this: does the Government of Kenya want justice for the victims? We need an unequivocal answer, an answer that Kenyans and the world could understand.'[15] Further to this, he boldly asked: 'Is the Government of Kenya protecting witnesses or protecting the suspects from investigation? That is the question.'[16] In October 2012, Fatou Bensouda, a Gambian lawyer and former civil servant, succeeded Ocampo as the new Chief Prosecutor of the ICC. Upon assuming the post, Bensouda met with Odinga and Kibaki to express her concerns over delays in responding to requests for information in the two Kenyan cases, and incidences of witness intimidation. In a statement to the media, Bensouda remarked: 'We are working hard every day to address efforts to interfere with our witnesses and our evidence. We are also working to resolve delays in the execution of our requests by the Government of Kenya.'[17]

As the Government of Kenya attempted to derail the ICC cases, there were other politicians who welcomed the presence of the Court insofar as the ICC proved to be a useful tool for eliminating political rivals.[18] An example of this can be seen in the attempt to create an alternate list of suspected perpetrators, which was subsequently forwarded to the Chief Prosecutor.[19] This type of instrumentalisation of the ICC became even more apparent as the 2013 General Election drew closer.

Instrumentalising the ICC

Several of the steps taken by the ICC Chief Prosecutor were intended to ensure that the Court's involvement in Kenya did not become politicised. This is evinced by the fact that the cases actually targeted both sides involved in the 2007–08 clashes; that is, both the PNU and ODM. One-sided trials have been an oft-cited criticism of the Court's involvement in many cases. Apart from investigating and bringing charges against both the PNU and ODM, the Court also took precautions in terms of how it handled the cases. Although the cases were separate, the Court was conscious of the impact its decisions may have on different communities in Kenya. With this in mind, when it came time to announce the confirmation of charges, the Chief Prosecutor took a decision to name the suspects from both cases on the same day. Through these measures the ICC endeavoured to ensure that the process was seen by Kenyans to be fair and legitimate. What the Chief Prosecutor may not have fully appreciated was the fluidity of political parties (and alliances) in Kenya and the extent to which the ICC process would inevitably become politicised, particularly in advance of the next general election.

The announcement of those on the ICC's list was significant for who *was not* included as much as for who *was*. While neither Mwai Kibaki nor Raila Odinga was named, the fact that no single member of Odinga's Luo community was indicted became a critical factor in the political manoeuvring leading to the next General Election. Most notably, the ICC's announcement planted the seeds for a political union between Uhuru Kenyatta and William Ruto. Most observers agreed that the alliance between the two accused was in direct response to their indictments.[20]

There were a number of consequences associated with this 'alliance of the accused.' First and foremost, the merger between Kenyatta (a prominent leader of the Kikuyu community) and Ruto (the undisputed leader of the Kalenjin) significantly reduced the risk of violence in the next election. During the 2007 clashes, the vast majority of the violence occurred between the Kalenjin and Kikuyu communities, particularly in the Rift Valley province. A second consequence of the partnership between Kenyatta and Ruto was the extent to which criticism of the ICC came to feature in their electoral campaign. In the run-up to the election 'both candidates vilified the ICC as a tool of Western neo-colonialism' and turned the election into a referendum on the ICC.[21] In particular, Kenyatta and Ruto drew upon the popular discontent with the Court and therein transformed an apparent 'electoral liability into a major strength.'[22]

Among the issues that Kenyatta and Ruto emphasised in their campaign was the frequently cited criticism of the ICC's focus on Africa. The fact that all of the cases before the Court have been drawn from the African continent has contributed to the perception that the ICC unfairly targets Africa, and is, therefore, a tool of neo-colonialism. This perception of the Court has been unhelpfully bolstered by the actions of the UN Security Council. As noted in the introduction, the Security Council has the power to refer cases to the Chief Prosecutor. To date, the Council has utilised its referral power twice: first in the case of Darfur, and second in Libya. As Louise Arbour has argued, Council referral is an exceptional measure, relevant only in those situations where a country has not actually ratified the Rome Statute. The purpose of the Rome Statute was to establish a consensual system of accountability by encouraging states to ratify and, in this regard, the use of referrals as a political tool goes against these intentions.[23] Moreover, the fact that three of the five permanent members of the Security Council are not signatories to the Rome Statute (yet retain the power to refer cases) exposes a deeply troubling double standard, which compromises the legitimacy of the Court.

While the practice of Security Council referrals is problematic, the narrative of the Court unfairly targeting the African continent fails to take notice of the full range of situations and cases that have been investigated by the Court. The notion of an unfair bias towards Africa also overlooks the fact that most of the cases before the Court were instances of self-referral. In the case of Kenya, the Chief Prosecutor initiated the Court's investigation. While this may be perceived as further evidence of an over-zealous prosecutor intruding in the internal affairs of another African country, in reality the ICC's involvement in Kenya grew directly out of the recommendations of the Kenyan-led Commission of Inquiry into Post-Election violence (CIPEV). Only after several failed attempts to establish a local tribunal did the ICC become involved in Kenya. Moreover, whether or not they were motivated by a genuine interest in accountability, the fact remains that a sizeable number of MPs in Kenya did vote for perpetrators to be prosecuted in The Hague. Nevertheless, Kenyatta and Ruto continued to portray the Court as an unwelcomed attack on Kenyan sovereignty.

> For the international community, we as Kenyans have gone through difficult times but we also have our own solutions ... we have a new constitutional dispensation ... but we demand respect as citizens of this nation. Don't impose your thoughts and ideas on the people of Kenya.[24]

The portrayal of the ICC as an infringement on Kenyan sovereignty served as a useful tool to divert attention from the serious crimes that Kenyatta and Ruto stood accused of.

In the weeks prior to the election, Johnnie Carson, US Assistant Secretary of State, attempted to dissuade Kenyan voters from electing Kenyatta and Ruto by stating that 'choices have consequences.'[25] Carson's statement was intended to warn voters that relations between the outside world and Kenya would not remain the same if they chose to vote for candidates who were suspected of crimes against humanity. Kofi Annan had made a similar appeal to Kenyan voters during his visit to Nairobi in December 2012.[26] These remarks reflected a growing sense of unease among the diplomatic community over the prospect of having to deal with a Head of State facing trial at The Hague. Rather than dissuading voters, their statements emboldened Ruto and Kenyatta and fuelled the narrative of a Western conspiracy working to ensure their defeat at the polls.

The 2013 general election

On Monday 4 March 2013 hundreds of thousands of Kenyans went to the polls in one of the most anticipated elections on the African continent. People began to line the streets before dawn, leading to long queues that spilled over into adjacent streets, with some voters waiting for up to ten hours in the scorching sun to cast their ballots. The election witnessed a voter turnout of 85 per cent – higher than any election in Kenyan history. During the polls, Kenyans voted in six simultaneous elections for candidates at the national and local level (including the presidential ballot, senate, women's representatives, county governors and local county assemblies). It was, of course, the presidential ballot that garnered the most attention, as the son of Jomo Kenyatta, Kenya's first President, was pitted against the son of his greatest political rival, Odinga Odinga.[27] Apart from the legacy of their fathers' rivalry, the 2013 Presidential race was highly anticipated for other reasons.

The candidacy of two suspected masterminds of the 2007–08 post-election violence, both facing prosecution at The Hague, significantly elevated the stakes in this race.

The shadow of 2007–08 loomed large and contributed to a great deal of anxiety in the lead-up to the 2013 General Election. As noted in the previous chapter, while the Coalition Government came together to deliver a new constitutional dispensation, they moved exceptionally slowly on other fundamental reforms. Kenya's internally displaced populations remained unsettled five years after being driven from their homes. Reforms to the security sector had not sufficiently facilitated disarmament and demobilisation efforts, as militia that had been involved in the 2007–08 clashes were still active. Further to this, there was now evidence of new militia forming.[28] Inter-ethnic tensions remained high, given the negligible emphasis placed on healing and reconciliation. Calls for justice and accountability went unanswered – a fact that was painfully reinforced by the candidacies of Kenyatta and Ruto. The ICC process also contributed to a sense of uncertainty leading up to the polls, as the High Court deliberated on the eligibility of Kenyatta and Ruto to stand for office just over two weeks prior to the election.[29]

As Election Day drew closer, signals of a possible repeat of the 2007–08 experience began to emerge.[30] A number of violent inter-communal clashes were reported,[31] exceeding the level of pre-election violence in the lead-up to the 2007 polls.[32] There were also worrying indications that certain groups were actively preparing for violence, while external actors also prepared for the worst by drawing up contingency plans in advance.[33] Given these factors, there was certainly no guarantee that the 2013 polls would be a significant departure from five years earlier. Yet, there was a conscious attempt to break from the past and ensure that peace prevailed in 2013. Messages of peace flooded the airwaves and television stations across the country. On 24 February 2013, the presidential candidates attended a peace prayer at Nairobi's Uhuru Park in a show of solidarity. Moreover, as part of a broader effort to deter incidences of hate speech and incitement, which were rampant in 2007–08, civil society groups embarked on a media monitoring campaign. The NCIC also carefully monitored hate speech throughout the campaign period and during the election. Adama Dieng, the UN Special Adviser on the Prevention of Genocide, visited Nairobi in February 2013 to discuss the responsibility to protect principle with the Kenyan authorities. Further to this, Dieng's office (the UN Office for the Prevention of Genocide and R2P) convened a pre-electoral workshop on the prevention of inter-communal violence.

The Independent Electoral Boundaries Commission (IEBC) (which replaced the IIEC in 2011) led country-wide civic education campaigns. Having the predecessor of the IEBC successfully preside over the constitutional referendum in 2010 boosted public confidence in the IEBC and its Chairman, Isaac Hassan. In an opinion poll conducted in the months preceding the vote, respondents indicated a high level of faith in the capacity of the IEBC to deliver free and fair elections.[34]

On Election Day itself, the national newspapers, the *Daily Nation* and *Standard*, ran the headlines 'Never Again' and 'Let Peace Prevail.' Media outlets had been briefed in advance about the importance of conflict-sensitive reporting. It has, however, been argued that the Kenyan media's efforts to disassociate from the 2007–08 elections became extreme, resulting in unnecessary self-censorship and an atmosphere that stifled democratic debate. For some, the behaviour of the Kenyan media during the polls was a direct consequence of 2007–08 when media outlets stood accused of incitement. The ongoing trial of Joshua Arap Sang, the first journalist to be prosecuted at the ICC, appears to have weighed heavily on the minds of the media. The media's self-censorship became particularly apparent on voting day, as Katherine Bruce-Lockhart observed: 'Incidents such as the confiscation of identity cards by gun-wielding gangs in Mathare and the death of thirteen people in Mombasa ... were under-reported due to fears of sparking panic and further violence.'[35]

As the polls closed and results began to be tallied, the country collectively held its breath and waited for the results. The tallying process was a major point of contention in the 2007 election, therefore Kenyans were urged to remain calm. Television adverts and radio messages reiterated calls for peace in an effort to allay anxiety among the electorate. With the race between Kenyatta and Odinga narrowing, many people began to openly discuss the possibility of a presidential run-off. The increasingly high number of rejected ballots, and questions over whether or not they would be included in the final count, generated considerable confusion.[36] There were also technological difficulties experienced by the transmission of results from the constituency level to the IEBC. Most worrying, however, were the reports of failed BVR (biometric voter registration) machines – the device intended to ensure that the election could not be rigged. Irrespective of these issues, the tallying proceeded and, on 9 March 2013, the IEBC announced that Uhuru Kenyatta had won the Presidential race, capturing 50.07 per cent of the vote to 43.28 per cent for Odinga, avoiding a run-off by 8100 votes.[37]

After the IEBC announced its results, Kenya's reformed institutions faced their most critical challenge to date. In an echo of the election five years prior, Raila Odinga pointed to a series of irregularities during the election and denounced the results as announced by the IEBC. He further indicated his intention to challenge the results through a petition to the Supreme Court. While seemingly reminiscent of the past, the decision to contest the election through the Courts was a powerful indicator of confidence in Kenya's reformed judiciary. Five years prior, a lack of faith in Kenya's judiciary meant that challenges to the poll results played out in the streets, leading to the clashes of 2007–08.

On 30 March 2013, after two weeks of deliberating on the electoral petition, the Supreme Court upheld Uhuru Kenyatta's victory as declared by the IEBC. In a further break with the past, Odinga conceded defeat after the Supreme Court issued its verdict.[38] Uhuru Muigai Kenyatta was sworn in as Kenya's fourth president on 9 April 2013.

The conduct of Kenya's 2013 General Election generated praise from around the world. In particular, the calm demonstrated by voters led to congratulatory statements and commendations. While the outcome of the election put some diplomats in an awkward position, given their attempts to dissuade voters from the Kenyatta–Ruto ticket, they nevertheless praised the Kenyan electorate for their exemplary conduct throughout the process. In spite of some glaring discrepancies, including those referred to above, electoral observers gave the election a seal of approval.[39]

The 2013 elections were widely celebrated within Kenya and around the world as a decisive break from the past. Most notably, the experience of 2013 seemed to be a culmination of the KNDR process that was launched in the wake of the post-election violence. As highlighted in Chapter 2, the African Union sponsored mediation that brought the violence to a standstill was not an end in itself, but the first step in a series of measures designed to prevent a recurrence of violence. The 2013 General Election was, therefore, a litmus test for the long-term issues and solutions that were initiated under Agenda 4 of the KNDR process. A report commissioned by the Global Centre for R2P highlighted the novelty of the Kenyan case in terms of the sustained level of international engagement it elicited:

> While in far too many cases the attention of the world fades in the aftermath of atrocities, in the case of Kenya international support for prevention was sustained from 2007 until the 2013 election. This is shown not only in financial support that was provided to the Kenyan government to undertake wide-ranging reforms, but also in the regular visits to Kenya and messages conveyed by significant international political figures to the Kenyan people.[40]

The outcome of the 2013 election has also been significant from the perspective of the ICC. As noted in the previous chapter, the Government of Kenya based its request for a deferral on the grounds that the ICC trials would destabilise the country in the run-up to the next election. However, one of the consequences – albeit unintended – of the ICC's involvement in Kenya was the alliance it sparked between the Kikuyu and Kalenjin communities. This alliance may have gone a long way towards neutralising a potential source of conflict during the 2013 election. Moreover, there are grounds to believe that politicians were more wary of engaging in hate speech during the 2013 electoral campaign given the watchful eyes of the ICC. In some ways, the outcome of the 2013 elections could be viewed as a vindication of Luis Moreno Ocampo's pledge that the ICC would ensure peace during the next election. In this sense, the 2013 election in Kenya has added to the anecdotal evidence in support of the Court's deterrent function. As the Global Centre for R2P has stated:

> Rather than compromise Kenya's stability, the ICC played a significant, although largely unheralded, deterrent role during the 2013 elections. Those senior political leaders facing charges, namely Kenyatta and Ruto, were all too aware that if they were to incite or aid in the commission of crimes they

would potentially face additional ICC charges. Similarly, other potential perpetrators saw that if powerful Kenyans like Kenyatta and Ruto could be charged at The Hague then surely they could be as well. The danger of being summoned by the NCIC or facing ICC charges also helped reduce the prevalence of hate speech, especially at large public rallies and within the media.[41]

The 2013 election in Kenya could also be perceived as an illustration of R2P and the ICC working in conjunction, and therefore, a genuine illustration of mutual reinforcement between protection and prosecution.

While it is tempting to view the outcome of the 2013 election in a generally positive light, the preceding assessment overlooks a number of crucial factors. First and foremost, the lack of violence during the 2013 election does not necessarily translate into a situation of peace.[42] The alliance between the two leaders of the Kalenjin and Kikuyu communities may have neutralised a potential source of conflict, but this should not be mistaken for genuine reconciliation. According to a report by the US Institute for Peace, 'the 2013 electoral stability was largely achieved by factors that suppressed rather than addressed conflict drivers and potential triggers.'[43] In fact, the 2013 elections demonstrate more of the same in terms of the electorate voting along tribal lines. Most observers would tend to agree that reconciliation was not the true motive behind the Kenyatta–Ruto alliance. The political union was entirely self-serving, designed to protect the political interests of two leaders facing trial at The Hague. Therefore, in all likelihood the alliance will be short lived.

Most crucial of all, the prospect of bringing perpetrators of the post-election violence to justice suffered a critical setback after the 2013 election. Given the numerous failed attempts to establish a domestic tribunal under the Coalition Government, the ICC really was the Court of Last Resort; that is the only remaining option for delivering justice in Kenya. However, in order for the ICC to effectively prosecute the accused, it would require the cooperation of the Kenyan Government. As a consequence of the 2013 elections, the Government of Kenya and the accused were now one and the same. In this regard, the last hope for justice in Kenya now ironically resided in the hands of the accused. As the remainder of this chapter will demonstrate, having secured the highest political office in the country, the accused adopted a strategy whereby they used the machinery of the state to shield themselves from prosecutions. This resulted in significant delays and the eventual collapsing of Case 2, and an uncertain future for Case 1.

Justice in the hands of the accused

Using the state as shield

During his campaign for the presidential bid, Uhuru Kenyatta maintained two crucial assurances in relation to his indictment by the ICC. First and foremost, he emphasised that although he denied the charges against him, he would continue to cooperate with the Court. In this regard, Kenyatta emphasised that he took his obligations before the ICC seriously. Second, Kenyatta referred to the charges before him as a personal challenge given that the crimes he stood accused of committing were alleged to have taken place prior to his assuming office. Therefore, it was understood that he was being charged in an individual capacity. This distinction was crucial to make in order to highlight the point that, should he be successful in the race to State House, it would be him, rather than the Kenyan state that was on trial.

Upon assuming office, Kenyatta began to sharply deviate from both pledges, his commitment to cooperate with the Court and the distinction between himself as an individual and as a Head of State. The first hint of non-cooperation with the Court could be discerned in Kenyatta's inaugural address: 'I assure you again that under my leadership, Kenya will strive to uphold our international obligations, so long as these are founded on the well-established principles of mutual respect and reciprocity.'[44] He continued:

> Central to our continued contribution to the international community, will be the understanding that the world is made up of many countries, cultures, political experiences and world-views. We must remember that no one country or group of countries should have control or monopoly on international institutions or the interpretation of international treaties. While each state has a right to its own view, it must respect the fact that it holds just one view amongst many in the community of nations.[45]

Shortly after their inauguration, Kenyatta and Ruto picked up where the Coalition Government left off in terms of their intense lobbying to block the Kenyan cases. However, whereas the initiative led by Kalonzo Musyoka endeavoured to have the cases deferred, the request was now framed within an expectation that the cases be dropped. The Government toured the African continent to gain support while the Kenyan Ambassador to the UN, Macharia Kamau, wrote a series of letters to the UN Security to seek the termination of the cases.[46]

Putting the issue before his colleagues in the AU, Kenyatta asked them to consider the role of the Court in Africa and its wider implications. As a consequence of his intense lobbying, the AU adopted a position that the continuation of the ICC cases 'undermines the sovereignty of the people of Kenya who expressed their will in 2013, and threatens the process of reconciliation in the country.'[47] At the request of the Kenyan Government, the African Union issued a communiqué during its May Summit threatening an en masse withdrawal from the Rome Statute.[48]

On 12 October 2013, the AU held an extraordinary special session to discuss and, indeed, re-evaluate Africa's relationship with the ICC. During the Summit, President Kenyatta called the court 'a painfully farcical pantomime' and 'a toy of declining imperial powers.'[49] The outcome of the AU summit was a decision to circumscribe the jurisdiction of the ICC, such that 'no charges shall be commenced or continued before any International Court or Tribunal against any serving AU Head of State or Government or anybody acting or entitled to act in such capacity during their term of office.'[50] More specifically, the AU Summit demanded that 'the trials of President Uhuru Kenyatta and Deputy President William Ruto, who are the current serving leaders of the Republic of Kenya, should be suspended until they complete their terms of office.'[51] Several observers expressed concern that the African Union might seek to renegotiate the Rome Statute or pull out of the Court if the cases against Kenyatta and Ruto continued.

Interestingly, the outcome of the AU Summit was in direct contrast to the assurances Kenyatta gave during his campaign, as his position as Head of State was now being cited as grounds for his immunity. Not only did this contradict his initial assurances, it also contravenes Article 27 of the Rome Statute, which highlights the irrelevance of official capacity in determining criminal responsibility:

> This Statute shall apply equally to all persons without any distinction based on official capacity. In particular, official capacity as a Head of State or Government, a member of a Government or parliament, an elected representative or a government official shall in no case exempt a person from criminal responsibility under this Statute, nor shall it, in and of itself, constitute a ground for reduction of sentence.[52]

In conjunction with the ongoing efforts to block the cases through international mechanisms, there have also been persistent attempts to block the cases using domestic legislation. For instance, in September 2013 Parliament voted to repeal the International Crimes Act and withdraw from the ICC. These developments cast doubt on 'the new government's willingness to tackle the culture of impunity for mass atrocity crimes in Kenya.'[53] According to George Kegoro,

> a polarised internal situation has heightened after the new government came to office, with support for justice through the ICC characterised as an act of treachery. President Kenyatta is angry in his speeches and his government has vilified sections of the public that supported the ICC trials. It is clear that President Kenyatta used the Kenyan state as a shield against his personal trial before the ICC, deploying the country's diplomatic and financial resources in that direction. Also, the personal pressure on him resulting from his position as an accused person increased the intolerance of his government, contributing to the shutting of the civil space.[54]

The extent to which civil space has been constrained can be seen in the vilification of civil society in Kenya as 'evil society' and the restriction of funding for NGOs as a punishment for their persistent efforts to promote accountability.[55]

Witness intimidation

Apart from the overt actions of the Government to block the ICC cases were more worrying indications of behind-the-scenes attempts to frustrate the trials through witness intimidation. Key witnesses in the Kenyan cases have 'disappeared', changed their testimony, or refused to give evidence. The Government of Kenya has also been accused of not doing enough to protect victims and witnesses, many of whom have been threatened or strongly dissuaded from testifying.

Kenya has a long-standing history of witness intimidation. The absence of legitimate witness protection and the necessary infrastructure to guarantee the safety and security of witnesses has significantly exacerbated Kenya's culture of impunity. Kenya's history is rife with examples of witness mistreatment ranging from threats, assaults, abduction, torture, and murder. Consequently, prosecutors have frequently struggled to obtain convictions for criminal acts that have been perpetrated in Kenya. In this regard, the limitations of Kenya's witness protection regime go hand and hand with the perpetuation of impunity.

Among the first steps taken to remedy the situation was the establishment of a Witness Protection Programme, which was created through the Witness Protection Act (WPA) in 2006. While the WPA provided a legal framework to protect witnesses, the pace with which the framework became operationalised was incredibly slow – as it took two full years from the Act to the creation of the Witness Protection Unit. In his 2009 report, the UN Special Rapporteur on Extrajudicial Killings was highly critical of Kenya's Witness Protect Programme. As he argued the Programme existed 'on paper only' and had thus far failed to protect a single witness.[56] Among the weaknesses highlighted in his report was the overall lack of funding for the programme, and more critically, the fact that it was located within the Attorney General's Office (the same office responsible for the Kenyan Police Force). As highlighted in the previous chapter, the Special Rapporteur saw first-hand the intimidation of those who provided evidence during his investigations. Alston made an impassioned plea for Kenya to take a crucial first step towards breaking the cycle of impunity by re-committing itself to witness protection.

The quality of Kenya's Witness Protection Programme became increasingly relevant in the context of efforts to prosecute perpetrators of the post-election violence. The Commission of Inquiry on Post-Election Violence also appealed for reforms in this area, as its report maintained, the Witness Protection Act 'must be made to apply to all witnesses to enable them to testify against powerful individuals without fear of retribution.'[57] As the ICC stepped up its involvement in Kenya, the deficiencies in Kenya's Witness Protection regime became even more pronounced. Witnesses who had appeared before the Waki Commission were reportedly receiving death threats. As one group of witnesses confirmed: 'From September last year, we started receiving threatening calls and text messages. We feared to report the matter to the police since we never wanted our identities to be known.'[58] They also reported that politicians and businessmen had been tracing their whereabouts using National Security Intelligence Apparatus, ultimately forcing them to flee.[59] Furthermore, an investigation through one of Kenya's leading newspapers revealed a meeting that had been organised by those allied to a senior Cabinet Minister, demanding that 'witnesses who "betrayed" some leaders from their community to be eliminated.'[60] As one human rights lobby group warned at the time: 'There might be no witnesses when the International Criminal Court (ICC) settles down to try suspected perpetrators of the post-election violence.'[61]

By the time that Ocampo made his first visit to Kenya, a credible witness protection programme was still not in place.[62] On 22 January 2010, Ocampo wrote to Mutula Kilonzo, the Minister for Justice and Constitutional Affairs, to express his concern on the matter:

> I wish to draw your attention to the fact that my office is aware of a growing number of reports suggesting that individuals who previously contributed to the enquiries by Kenya National Human Rights Commission and Waki Commission are perceived as the potential ICC witnesses and had been threatened and intimidated.... As we discussed before our meeting of 3rd of July 2009 in The Hague, following which the Kenyan authority transmitted to my office a report on the operalisation of the witness protection programme, the primary responsibility to protect persons at risk lies first and foremost with Kenyan authority.[63]

The urgency of the situation also prompted Ocampo to write to ICC judges about the matter. As the ICC cases progressed, the threats to witnesses tended to intensify surrounding Ocampo's visits to the country, when tensions were particularly high. Given the limited capacity of the Government's programme to provide protection to witnesses, a handful had been placed under the protection of the KNCHR and the ICC itself.

Pressure continued to mount on the Government of Kenya to make the necessary reforms to its existing programme. On 31 March 2010, 19 European diplomatic missions in Kenya issued a statement expressing their concern with continuing reports of efforts to intimidate witnesses and human rights groups. As the statement indicated: 'The commitment of the Government to proper witness protection will be tested by the financial resources and the effective independence it grants to a future witness protection agency.'[64] In the face of growing pressure, Kenya's Parliament passed the Witness Protection (Amendment) Bill on 7 April 2010. Furthermore, Amos Wako made a request for a Witness Protection expert, Gerhard Van Rooyen, to advise the Government of Kenya on amending its witness protection programme.

Although the ICC welcomed the Witness Protection Amendment bill,[65] there were still challenges to its full implementation. In particular, very little changed with respect to providing security and protection for existing victims and witnesses, as has been noted, 'even as the ICC process begins in earnest, many victims and witnesses of the violence whose participation will be key to ensure justice is done are still living in fear.'⁶⁶ Therefore, irrespective of the key reforms that have been undertaken, the challenge of providing protection for witnesses persisted and would eventually became a major impediment to the cases. The collapse of the case against Francis Muthaura⁶⁷ on 11 March 2013 was, for instance, attributed to a key witness changing their testimony.⁶⁸ Given the continuing difficulties associated with securing witness testimonies, Fatou Bensouda referred to the Kenyan cases as the most challenging the ICC has ever faced.⁶⁹ In October 2013, the ICC issued an arrest warrant against the journalist Walter Barasa for several offences against the administration of justice including, corruptly influencing witnesses in the Kenyan cases. Bensouda continued to highlight the difficulties she faced in prosecuting the Kenyan cases, not only with respect to witnesses intimidation but also in terms of ensuring the cooperation of the Kenyan Government.

'A dark day for international criminal justice'

Whereas the trial of William Ruto and Joshua Arap Sang commenced on 10 September 2013, the Prosecution repeatedly delayed the commencement of Kenyatta's trial. According to the Chief Prosecutor, the grounds for these delays were twofold: persistent difficulties in securing witness testimonies and the lack of cooperation by the Kenyan Government in responding to requests for information. This situation effectively placed Case 2 in a state of deadlock. The standoff between Bensouda and the Government of Kenyatta came to a head in October 2014 when Kenyatta was summoned to the ICC for a Status Conference. The purpose of the Status Conference was to discuss the issue of cooperation between the Prosecution and the Government of Kenya. Prior to the Status Conference a notice from the Prosecution highlighted the tensions at the heart of Case 2: 'The accused person in this case is the head of a government that has so far failed fully to comply with its obligations to the Court, and ... is ultimately responsible for that failure.'⁷⁰

There was considerable speculation over whether or not Kenyatta would attend the hearing; however, much of this speculation was generated from within Kenyatta's inner circle. In the end, Kenyatta travelled to The Hague in his personal capacity, having handed over the reins of the state to his deputy, William Ruto. The Status Conference was held from 7–8 October 2014 before Trial Chamber V(b), which included three judges: Kuniko Ozaki, Robert Fremr and Geoffrey A. Henderson. The hearing was livestreamed through the website of the Court for the benefit of viewers in Kenya and around the world.

During the hearing, the Chief Prosecutor, Fatou Bensouda, highlighted the continuing challenges she faced in her efforts to commence Kenyatta's trial. In particular, she reiterated the difficulties of obtaining the necessary evidence to proceed with the trial. Bensouda conceded that in the absence of the information requested from the Government of Kenya, she would be unable to prove Kenyatta's guilt beyond a reasonable doubt. She drew her remarks to a close by requesting that the judges grant the Prosecution an indefinite adjournment of the trial, pending the Government of Kenya's cooperation in providing the requested information.[71]

The Defence responded to the Prosecution's request with harsh words. Steven Kay, the lead counsel in the Kenyatta case vehemently argued: 'What you heard from the prosecution was a scandalous misrepresentation of the quality of their case as well as the reasons for not pursuing this case.'[72] He continued, 'If the quality of the prosecution evidence was such as it claims to be, why didn't they go to trial? They didn't go to trial because there were fundamental problems throughout that case.'[73] After lambasting the Prosecution for its apparent inadequacy, Kenyatta's defence team filed a petition to have the case terminated on the grounds that an indefinite postponement to the trial breached the rights of the accused:

> We are now in the position that this case has failed, and failed in a way that there is no prospect of it going ahead in the future. If the prosecutor will not withdraw the charges, you [the judges] can act to terminate this case.[74]

Further to this, Kay noted that the judges should render his client 'not guilty' of the charges, as he insisted: 'It would be an affront to justice if my client was not given a verdict of not guilty. If the prosecution had any evidence, we would have a trial. They do not.'[75]

Along with the remarks made by the Prosecution and the Defence teams, Fergal Gaynor, the Legal Representative of the victims in the Kenyatta case was also invited to make a statement. Gaynor was particularly troubled by the incidences of witnesses intimidation in this case, as he pointed out: 'The victims ... are entitled to know who intimidated those witnesses. At whose instigation? And for what purpose?'[76] In response to the Defence's suggestion that the cases be terminated, he argued, 'if this case is terminated, then the [Kenyan] government will see that obstruction of access to evidence is a viable policy.'[77] From the perspective of his clients, Gaynor asked, 'Is it really fair to force them now to pay the price for obstruction of justice by Mr. Kenyatta's government?'[78] However, the issue of utmost concern for Gaynor was the potential implications of the case being terminated, given the fact that no other avenues for delivering justice were available. A termination of this case would effectively amount to a 'complete end for the justice process for the victims in this case.'[79]

After the hearing, Kenyatta was greeted by a swarm of Kenyan MPs who had assembled at the Court in a show of solidarity. As he passed through a crowd of his supporters on the steps of the Court, Kenyatta appeared jubilant: 'God bless the Netherlands, God bless Kenya, God bless the ICC and God bless you!'[80] He then proceeded to make a brief statement in Kiswahili: 'We all know how far we have come. We all know why we are here. We all know where we are going. Everyone can see there is nothing.'[81] The media interviewed several of the MPs that had accompanied the President to The Hague. Many of them joyously predicted that the case would soon fall apart. Kenyatta returned home to a hero's welcome. Although the status hearing had not yet yielded a verdict, the President's return to Nairobi became a moment of celebration for some Kenyans. Thousands lined up to greet the President upon his arrival. A military parade was organised in his honour, as Kenyatta's supporters sang and danced in the streets.[82]

Nearly two months later, Trial Chamber V(b) issued their ruling on the requests made by the Defence and the Prosecution during the Status Conference. On 3 December 2015, the Judges rejected the Defence's request to drop the charges against Kenyatta. At the same time, they also rejected the Prosecution's call for an indefinite adjournment of the trial, which, they determined, would breach the rights of the accused. The Chamber directed the Prosecution to file a notice within one week indicating, 'either (i) its withdrawal of the charges in this case, or (ii) that the evidentiary basis has improved to a degree which would justify proceeding to trial.'[83] On 5 December, Bensouda conceded that she had no option but to drop the charges against Kenyatta.[84] However, she made clear that this did not amount to an exoneration of Kenyatta and reiterated that the charges could be brought against him at any time in the future:

> Despite my persistent efforts and those of my committed Team to advance the course of justice in Kenya, in this instance, those who have sought to obstruct the path of justice have, for now, deprived the people of Kenya of the accountability they deserve.... I wish to say a few words about the failure of the Government of Kenya to cooperate fully and effectively with my investigations in this case ... the material the Government sent us simply did not respond to a significant portion of our Revised Request for Records.... This is despite the fact that ICC Judges clearly confirmed that my Revised Request was valid, and dismissed all of the Government's objections to it. In this situation, the most relevant documentary evidence regarding the post-election violence could only be found in Kenya. Yet, despite assurances of its willingness to cooperate with the Court, the Government of Kenya failed to follow through on those assurances.[85]

In her statement, Bensouda elaborated on the issues her office confronted in trying to move forward with the case, drawing particular attention to three types of challenges:

- several people who may have provided important evidence regarding Mr. Kenyatta's actions, have died, while others were too terrified to testify for the Prosecution;
- key witnesses who provided evidence in this case later withdrew or changed their accounts, in particular, witnesses who subsequently alleged that they had lied to my Office about having been personally present at crucial meetings; and
- the Kenyan Government's non-compliance compromised the Prosecution's ability to thoroughly investigate the charges, as recently confirmed by the Trial Chamber.[86]

118 *The responsibility to prosecute*

Bensouda ended her statement on a very sombre note: 'Today is a dark day for international criminal justice.'[87] Yet she emphasised that the decision would not be 'the last word on justice and accountability for the crimes that were inflicted on the people of Kenya in 2007 and 2008.' Crimes that, in her view 'are still crying out for justice.'[88]

'One down, two to go'

On the day that the charges against him were dropped, Kenyatta was attending a meeting of the Kenyan Private Sector Alliance. The Foreign Affairs Cabinet Secretary, Amina Mohamed, interrupted the meeting to relay the message to Kenyatta. Upon receiving the news Kenyatta appeared to be elated beyond words. Mohamed further intimated that the 'same energy and passion'[89] would be applied to ensuring that the two remaining cases were dropped. In a reference to the trials of his Deputy and Joshua Arap Sang, Kenyatta stated: 'As they say, one down, two to go.'[90] Later that day Kenyatta posted on his Twitter account using the hash tag 'vindicated.'[91]

For some, the collapse of Kenyatta's case was a cause for celebration.[92] A number of African heads of state were similarly jubilant and issued congratulatory statements to Kenyatta.[93] The Government's campaign to have the Kenyan cases dropped had become inextricably linked to a broader discontent with the ICC's activities in Africa. Although 34 African countries have ratified the Rome Statute, the continent has become one of the most vociferous opponents of the Court, given its perceived 'hunting' of Africans. The collapse of Kenyatta's case was therefore received as a victory for critics of the Court. Not all, however, shared in the jubilation surrounding the withdrawal of the charges. The ICC's involvement in Kenya was a last resort, driven by the unwillingness of the Government to establish a local mechanism for prosecuting perpetrators. Having Kenyatta's case collapse at the ICC before reaching the trial stage meant that victims of the post-election violence were doubly let down – first by the Kenyan Government for their failure to prosecute perpetrators, and then by the international community. This outcome has delivered a major blow to the pursuit of justice. Nevertheless, the outcome of the Kenyatta case caught few people by surprise. The decision to withdraw the charges against Kenyatta was the logical end point on an uncertain path towards justice, which had been plagued with obstacles from the start.

The manner in which the case collapsed has led to criticisms over how the Court handled the Kenyan situation. First of all, there has been criticism relating to the way in which the Office of the Prosecutor (OTP) gathered evidence in this case. Some have argued that there was an excessive reliance on existing reports at the expense of the Prosecution conducting its own independent investigations. This approach to gathering evidence, it is argued, ultimately weakened the cases and made them vulnerable to collapse. Moreover, there has also been criticism levelled at OTP for its broader approach to the Kenya situation. As previously mentioned, the expectations surrounding the Kenyan cases were incredibly high, owing in no small part to the statements made by Bensouda's predecessor, Luis Moreno Ocampo. Apart from continuously asserting that he had a strong case in Kenya, Ocampo set his sights on the lofty goal of 'ending impunity in Kenya.' With this in mind, he assured that Kenya would be an example to the world.

Even in the most ideal set of circumstances, the Court would be hard pressed to fulfil such a mission in any situation country. The vigour and certainty with which Ocampo pursued the Kenyan cases facilitated the impression that his quest may have been motivated as much by his desire to score a quick victory for the Court, than his interest in pursuing justice for the victims of the post-election violence. Whatever his intentions were, Ocampo's approach unhelpfully fuelled some of the scepticism towards the Court. Taken together, these factors – combined with the Government's persistent efforts to block the cases – ensured the collapse of Case 2.

By the time Bensouda had inherited the cases from her predecessor, the groundwork had already been set, and in some ways, the fate of the case was already sealed. What did become painfully apparent over time was the Court's reliance on state cooperation. While this was always a factor to contend with, it became exceedingly more complex once the accused in Kenya became the Head of State – effectively placing justice in the hands of the accused. There may, however, be relevant lessons for OTP to draw from this case, as Carla Ferstman, the Director of Redress has argued: 'Prosecuting a President for crimes against humanity and expecting the evidence to come from the government he leads is aspirational, even if it does align with Kenya's obligations under the Statute.'[94] Whatever lessons might be drawn from this experience, there is no doubt that the collapse of Kenyatta's case has cast a shadow of doubt on the Court's capacity to handle future cases.

Just as the commencement of the ICC cases altered Kenya's political landscape, the unravelling of the cases promises to do the same. In particular, the outcome of Kenyatta's case raises important questions for the relationship between the President and his Deputy. As noted, William Ruto and Joshua Arap's Sang trial began in September 2013. While Kenyatta has publicly stated 'one down, two to go,' many doubt whether the Government will go to the same lengths to protect Ruto and Sang. Nevertheless, some have predicted that the cases will unravel on their own given the ongoing difficulties with securing witness testimonies in Case 1.

In the event that the cases do proceed, one to two convictions hardly seems sufficient given the level of violence reached in 2007–08. Moreover, it is highly unlikely that there will be any further attempts to resurrect the idea of a domestic tribunal in the near future. Given that Kenya's long-standing culture of impunity was widely regarded as being at the heart of the post-election violence, the failure to prosecute perpetrators (domestically and internationally) is worrying, as it has left in place the underlying conditions that led to the violence in the first place.

Conclusion

This chapter has assessed the ICC's efforts to prosecute perpetrators of the post-election violence in Kenya. Following the failed attempts to establish a domestic accountability mechanism, the ICC stepped up its involvement in Kenya. Despite assurances from the Kenyan Government that it would fully cooperate with the Court, the Government attempted to do everything in its power to block the cases. Alongside attempts to pull out of the Rome Statute and the initiation of an admissibility challenge against the Court, the Government pursued intense lobbying to have the cases deferred.

In presenting their rationale for the cases to be deferred, the Government of Kenya argued that the ICC's involvement in Kenya risked destabilising the country in the run-up to the 2013 General Election. Nevertheless, during the election, the ICC factor was actually viewed as a stabilising influence that served to deter incidences of hate speech and acts of violence. The conduct of Kenya's 2013 General Election generated praise from around the world. Most notably, the experience of 2013 seemed to be a culmination of the KNDR process that was launched in the wake of the post-election violence. As highlighted in Chapter 2, the African Union sponsored mediation that brought the violence to a standstill was not an end in itself, but the first step in a series of measures designed to prevent a recurrence of violence. The 2013 General Election was, therefore, a litmus test for the long-term issues and solutions that were initiated under Agenda 4 of the KNDR process. Further to this, the 2013 election in Kenya could also be perceived as an illustration of R2P and the ICC working in conjunction, and therefore, a genuine illustration of mutual reinforcement between protection and prosecution.

At the same time, there were a number of unintended consequences associated with the ICC's involvement in Kenya, most notably, provoking an 'alliance of the accused' between Uhuru Kenyatta and his running mate, William Ruto. Moreover, to the extent that Kenyatta and Ruto made critiquing the ICC a central component of their campaign, some have argued that the ICC inadvertently brought them to power. Most crucial of all, as a consequence of the 2013 election, the prospect of bringing perpetrators of the post-election violence to justice suffered a critical setback. Given the numerous failed attempts to establish a domestic tribunal under the Coalition Government, the ICC really was the Court of Last Resort; that is, the only remaining option for delivering justice in Kenya. However, in order for the ICC to effectively prosecute the accused the cooperation of the Kenyan Government would be required. After the 2013 election, the Government of Kenya and the accused were now one and the same. In this regard, the last hope for justice in Kenya was ironically placed in the hands of the accused.

Having secured the highest political office in the country, the accused adopted a strategy whereby they used the machinery of the state to shield themselves from prosecution. In so doing, the Government of Kenya reverted to an approach to sovereignty that both R2P and the ICC were designed to counteract. The Government engaged in overt (as well as covert) actions to block the cases, leading to a showdown with the ICC Prosecutor. Fatou Bensouda was ultimately forced to withdraw the charges against Uhuru Kenyatta. A similar set of difficulties has confronted the cases against William Ruto and Joshua Arap Sang, leading many to predict that Case 1 will similarly unravel.

Although significant steps have been made to address the underlying causes of instability in Kenya (including the adoption of a new constitution in 2010), the failure to hold the perpetrators of the 2007–08 violence accountable for their crimes –domestically and internationally – has been a major setback for the country, as Kofi Annan has argued:

> The 2013 elections avoided widespread conflict, but we should not mistake less violence for peace. The underlying causes of Kenya's crisis are as real as ever and may resurface, since the core reforms that were identified during the mediation have stalled.[95]

Notes

1. ICC Office of the Prosecutor, 'Statement of the Prosecutor of the International Criminal Court, Fatou Bensouda, on the withdrawal of charges against Mr. Uhuru Muigai Kenyatta', 5 December 2015, available online at www.icc-cpi.int/en_menus/icc/press%20and%20media/press%20releases/Pages/otp-statement-05–12–2014–2.aspx (accessed 20 May 2015).
2. 'Uhuru Kenyatta denounces ICC as Kenya charges dropped', *BBC News*, 5 December 2014, available online at www.bbc.co.uk/news/world-africa-30344320 (accessed 20 May 2015).
3. Patrick Mayoyo and AFP, 'Ocampo accuses Kenya of sabotage in chaos probe', *Daily Nation*, 29 May 2011, available online at www.nation.co.ke/news/politics/Ocampo-accuses-Kenya-of-sabotage-in-chaos-probe–/-/1064/1171624/-/r9bq4ez/-/index.html (accessed 20 May 2015).
4. 'Kenya MPs vote to leave ICC over poll violence claims', *BBC News*, 23 December 2010, available online at www.bbc.co.uk/news/world-africa-12066667 (accessed 20 May 2015).
5. 'Parliament move draws criticism', *Daily Nation*, 23 December 2010.
6. Decisions on the Implementation of the Decisions of the International Criminal Court, Doc. Ex.CL/639(XVIII) Assembly/AU/Dec 334 (SVI), 30–31 January 2011.
7. Anyang Nyongo, 'Petition to UN Security Council regarding Kenya cases at the ICC', *Capital FM News*, 14 March 2011, available online at www.capitalfm.co.ke/eblog/2011/03/14/petition-to-un-security-council-regarding-kenyan-cases-at-the-icc/ (accessed 20 May 2015).
8. Peter Atsiaya, 'Pro-ICC groups obtain 800 000 signatures to back trials', *The Standard*, 8 March 2011, available online at www.standardmedia.co.ke/article/2000030707/pro-icc-groups-obtain-800–000-signatures-to-back-trials (accessed 20 May 2015).
9. Hence the invocation of Article 16 of the Rome Statute, which enables the Security Council to use its deferral power in situations that constitute a threat to international peace and security.
10. Fred Mukinda, '6,000 could be charged over Kenya Poll Chaos', *Daily Nation*, March 17, 2011, www.nation.co.ke/News/politics/6000+could+be+charged+over+poll+chaos+/-/1064/1128278/-/91n68/-/index.html (accessed 20 June 2015).
11. 'ICC rejects Kenya's admissibility challenge', *The Hague Justice Portal*, 31 May 2011, available at www.haguejusticeportal.net/index.php?id=12758 (accessed 20 May 2015).
12. Ibid.
13. International Criminal Court, Office of the Prosecutor, 'Statement of the Prosecutor on the situation in Kenya', available online at www.icc-cpi.int/NR/rdonlyres/269744

E4–9F7D-468F-9B24-C2AE74B012D1/283377/StatementICCProsecutoronsituationinKenya1.pdf (accessed 20 May 2015).
14 Ibid.
15 Ibid.
16 Ibid.
17 'The Verbatim Statement of ICC's Bensouda', *The Standard*, 22 October 2012, available online at www.standardmedia.co.ke/article/2000069022/the-verbatim-statement-of-icc-s-bensouda (accessed 20 May 2015).
18 Gakuu Mathenge and Patrick Mathangani, 'Central MPs Split Over Imanyara Bill', *The Standard*, 30 August 2009, available online at www.standardmedia.co.ke/?articleID=1144022767&story_title= (accessed 20 May 2015).
19 'MPs compile new post poll suspects list', *Daily Nation*, 25 July 2009.
20 Simon Allison, 'Kenyan Election Alliance Between Bitter Enemies United By ICC Charges', *Guardian*, 4 December 2012, available online at www.theguardian.com/world/2012/dec/04/kenya-election-alliance-rival (accessed 20 June 2015).
21 Abdullahi Boru Halakhe, 'R2P in Practice: Ethnic Violence, Elections and Atrocity Prevention in Kenya', *Global Centre for the Responsibility to Protect*, Occasional Paper Series, No. 4, December 2013, p. 85.
22 Sam Hawke, 'Kenya's elections in 2013: poverty, ethnicity, and violence', *Social Justice First*, available online at http://socialjusticefirst.com/2013/03/04/kenyas-elections-in-2013-poverty-ethnicity-and-violence/ (accessed 20 May 2015).
23 Louise Arbour, Address to the Stanley Foundation Conference on the Responsibility to Protect, New York, 18 January 2012. Available online at www.r2p10.org (accessed 20 May 2015).
24 Mohamed Adow, 'Kenya's ICC accused unite', *Global Policy Forum*, 3 December 2012, available online at www.globalpolicy.org/international-justice/the-international-criminal-court/icc-investigations/52124-kenyas-icc-accused-unite.html (accessed 20 May 2015).
25 Gabe Joselow, 'US official says Kenya's election have consequences', *Voice of America*, 7 February 2013, available online at www.voanews.com/content/us-official-says-kenya-elections-have-consequences/1599063.html (accessed 20 May 2015).
26 'Kofi Annan Urges Kenyans not to Vote for Indicted Politicians', *BBC News*, 4 December 2012,available online at www.bbc.co.uk/news/world-africa-20602232 (accessed 20 May 2015).
27 The two had been allies in the Kenya African National Union (KANU), as Odinga was appointed as Vice President in 1964. However, in 1966, Odinga split from KANU and formed the Kenya People's Union (KPU). During his time in opposition, Odinga and Kenyatta became bitter rivals. Under Kenyatta's leadership, the KPU was banned and Odinga was imprisoned for 15 months. See Daniel Branch, *Kenya: Between Hope and Despair 1963–2011* (Yale University Press, 2011).
28 Office of the AU Panel of Eminent African Personalities, *Back from the Brink: The 2008 Mediation Process and Reforms in Kenya*, African Union Commission, p. 79, available online at www.knchr.org/Portals/0/GeneralReports/backFromBrink_web.pdf (accessed 20 May 2015).
29 Judie Kaberia, 'Court Dismisses Uhuru, Ruto Eligibility Case', 15 February 2013, available online at www.capitalfm.co.ke/news/2013/02/court-dismisses-uhuru-ruto-eligibility-case/ (accessed 20 June 2015).
30 Simon Allison, 'Kenya elections: reasons to be fearful', *Guardian*, 24 January 2013, available online at www.theguardian.com/world/2013/jan/24/kenya-election-violence-fearful (accessed 20 May 2015).
31 Office of the AU Panel of Eminent African Personalities, *Back from the Brink*, p. 212.
32 Abdullahi Boru Halakhe, 'R2P in Practice', p. 16.

33 Ibid.
34 Bob Tortora and Magali Rheault, 'In Kenya most registered voters lack required voting cards', available online at www.gallup.com/poll/157874/kenya-registered-voters-lack-required-voting-card.aspx (accessed 20 May 2015).
35 Katherine Bruce-Lockhart, 'From incitement to self-censorship: the media in the Kenyan elections of 2007 and 2013', available online at http://freespeechdebate.com/en/discuss/124451/ (accessed 20 May 2015).
36 The Jubilee Alliance accused Christian Turner of trying to deny him an outright victory.
37 Richard Lough, 'Kenya's Odinga to File Supreme Court Election Petition on Friday', *Reuters*, 14 March 2013, available online at www.reuters.com/article/2013/03/14/us-kenya-elections-petition-idUSBRE92D0TJ20130314 (accessed 20 June 2015).
38 Jason Patinkin, 'Uhuru Kenyatta's election victory is upheld by the Supreme Court', *Guardian*, 30 March 2013, available online at www.theguardian.com/world/2013/mar/31/kenya-court-upholds-kenyatta-victory (accessed 20 May 2015).
39 African Union Press Release, Dr. Nkosazana Dlamini Zuma, chairperson of the African Union Commission: 'The African Union Commission salutes the people of Kenya for the successful and peaceful conclusions of the elections', 11 March 2013, available online at http://cpauc.au.int/en/content/statement-dr-nkosazana-dlamini-zuma-chairperson-african-union-commission-announcement-result (accessed 20 May 2015); White House Press Secretary Jay Carney, 'We also congratulate the people of Kenya on the peaceful conduct of the election', 30 March 2013, available online at www.politico.com/politico44/2013/03/wh-urges-peaceful-acceptance-of-kenyan-election-results-160541.html (accessed 20 May 2015).
40 Abdullahi Boru Halakhe, 'R2P in Practice', p. 19.
41 Abdullahi Boru Halakhe, 'R2P in Practice', p. 15.
42 Claire Elder, Susan Stigant and Jonas Claes, 'Elections and violent conflict in Kenya: making prevention stick', *United States Institute for Peace*, 9 November 2014, available online at www.usip.org/publications/elections-and-violent-conflict-in-kenya-making-prevention-stick (accessed 20 May 2015).
43 Ibid., p. 20.
44 'President Kenyatta's inauguration speech', *Capital FM*, 9 April 2013, available online at www.capitalfm.co.ke/eblog/2013/04/09/president-kenyattas-inauguration-speech/ (accessed 20 May 2015).
45 Ibid.
46 Geoffrey Mosoku, 'Questions Raised Over Envoy's Letter to UN', *The Standard*, 13 May 2013, available online at www.standardmedia.co.ke/article/2000083468/queries-raised-over-envoy-s-letter-to-un (accessed 20 June 2015).
47 Solomon Ayele Dersso, ' The AU's Extraordinary Summit decisions on Africa-ICC Relationship', *EJIL Talk*, 28 October 2013, available online at www.ejiltalk.org/the-aus-extraordinary-summit-decisions-on-africa-icc-relationship/ (accessed 20 June 2015).
48 'African Union Accuses ICC of Hunting Africans', *BBC News*, 27 May 2013, available online at www.bbc.co.uk/news/world-africa-22681894 (accessed 20 June 2015).
49 'Could Westgate Deal a Fatal Blow to the ICC', *BBC News*, 17 October 2013, available online at www.bbc.co.uk/news/world-africa-24562337 (accessed 20 June 2015).
50 African Union, Extraordinary Session of the Assembly of the African Union, Addis Ababa, Ethiopia, 12 October 2013, available online at www.au.int/en/content/extraordinary-session-assembly-african-union (accessed 20 June 2015).
51 Alphonce Shiundu, 'Uhuru Kenyatta, William Ruto Failed to Stop The ICC Cases Despite Spirited Fight', *The Standard*, 9 October 2014, available online at www.standardmedia.co.ke/worldcup/?articleID=2000137549&story_title=uhuru-kenyatta-william-ruto-failed-to-stop-the-icc-cases-despite-spirited-fight&pageNo=2 (accessed 20 June 2015).

124 *The responsibility to prosecute*

52 Rome Statute of the International Criminal Court, A/CONF.183/9 of 17 July 1998, Article 27.
53 Abdullahi Boru Halakhe, 'R2P in Practice', p. 18.
54 George Kegoro, 'Uhuru used the State as a shield against his trial', *Daily Nation*, 6 December 2014, available online at www.nation.co.ke/news/Uhuru-used-the-State-as-a-shield-against-his-trial/-/1056/2547530/-/1284714/-/index.html (accessed 20 May 2015).
55 Abdullahi Boru Halakhe, 'R2P in Practice', p. 18.
56 'Report of the Special Rapporteur on extrajudicial, summary or arbitrary executions', (Alston Report), 26 May 2009, available online at www.extrajudicialexecutions.org/application/media/Kenya%20Mission%202009%20%28A_HRC_11_2_Add.6%29.pdf (accessed 20 May 2015).
57 Final Report from Kenya's Commission of Inquiry into Post-election Violence, 15 October 2008 (The Waki Report), p. 17.
58 Jonathan Komen, 'Waki witnesses on the run', 17 October 2009, *Daily Nation*, available online at www.nation.co.ke/News/politics/-/1064/673588/-/xtpqy1z/-/ (accessed 20 May 2015).
59 Ibid.
60 Murithi Mutiga, 'OCampo writes to judges over threats', *Daily Nation*, 30 January 2010, available online at www.nation.co.ke/News/-/1056/852780/-/vpwpw9/-/index.html (accessed 20 May 2015).
61 Denis Odnunga, 'Witnesses at risk, warns lobby', *Daily Nation*, 11 January 2010, available online at www.nation.co.ke/news/politics/-/1064/840302/-/jcf42yz/-/index.html (accessed 20 May 2015).
62 Carol Rwenji, 'Kilonzo says chaos witness threatened', *Daily Nation*, 23 November 2009, available online at www.nation.co.ke/news/-/1056/802518/-/3ebgogz/-/index.html (accessed 20 May 2015).
63 Antony Gitonga and Peter Opiyo, 'Ocampo writes to Mutula over witness threats', 26 January 2010, available online at www.standardmedia.co.ke/business/article/2000001710/ocampo-writes-to-mutula-over-witness-threats (accessed 20 May 2015).
64 'EU asks for proper witness protection', *Daily Nation*, 31 March 2010, available online at www.nation.co.ke/news/EU-asks-for-proper-witness-protection-/-/1056/890784/-/view/printVersion/-/ei4eyaz/-/index.html (accessed 20 May 2015).
65 Oliver Mathenge and Jillo Kadida, '400 Post-poll victims apply to join The Hague trials', 2 September 2010, available online at www.nation.co.ke/news/400-victims-apply-to-join-Hague-trials-/-/1056/1002768/-/131t8rw/-/index.html (accessed 20 May 2015).
66 Patrick Mayoyo, 'Key election chaos witnesses to be flown out', *Daily Nation*, 16 May 2010, available online at www.nation.co.ke/news/Key-election-chaos-witnesses-to-be-flown-out-/-/1056/919788/-/9f2u5d/-/index.html (accessed 20 May 2015).
67 Francis Muthaura was the former Head of the Civil Service and a co-accused with Kenyatta.
68 Robyn Dixon, 'Charges Are Dropped Against Kenyan Suspect', *Los Angeles Times*, 11 March 2011, available online at http://articles.latimes.com/2013/mar/11/world/la-fg-wn-kenya-court-charges-20130311 (accessed 20 June 2015).
69 'Bensouda: Someone Keen to Out Kenya ICC Witnesses', *Daily Nation*, 8 February 2013, www.nation.co.ke/news/Bensouda-Someone-keen-to-out-ICC-Kenya-witnesses/-/1056/1688270/-/ws2s8d/-/index.html (accessed 20 May 2015).
70 ICC Office of the Prosecutor, 'Prosecution notice regarding the provisional trial date', 5 September 2014, available online at www.icc-cpi.int/iccdocs/doc/doc1826503.pdf (accessed 20 May 2015).
71 Felix Olick, 'Kenya: Bensouda Requests Indefinite Adjournment of Uhuru Case Due

to Lack of Evidence', *All Africa*, 5 September 2014, available online at http://allafrica.com/stories/201409080024.html (accessed 20 June 2015).
72 Steven Kay cited in Tom Maliti, 'ICC Prosecutor Asks Court to Decide on Indefinitely Adjourning Kenyatta Case or Terminating it', *International Justice Monitor*, 8 October 2014, available online at www.ijmonitor.org/2014/10/icc-prosecutor-asks-court-to-decide-on-indefinitely-adjourning-kenyatta-case-or-terminating-it/ (accessed 20 June 2015).
73 Ibid.
74 Steven Kay cited in Mike Pflanz, 'Uhuru Kenyatta's ICC Prosecution Close to Collapse as Lawyers Demand Acquittal', *The Telegraph*, 8 October 2014, available online at www.telegraph.co.uk/news/worldnews/africaandindianocean/kenya/11149256/Uhuru-Kenyattas-ICC-prosecution-close-to-collapse-as-lawyers-demand-acquittal.html (accessed 20 June 2015).
75 Ibid.
76 Fergal Gaynor cited in Tom Maliti, 'ICC Prosecutor Asks Court to Decide.'
77 Fergal Gaynor cited in Mike Pflanz, 'As President Kenyatta Faces Accusers, Hague Court Case Nears Collapse', *Christian Science Monitor*, 8 October 2014, available online at www.csmonitor.com/World/Africa/2014/1008/As-President-Kenyatta-faces-accusers-Hague-court-case-nears-collapse-video (accessed 20 June 2015)
78 Fergal Gaynor cited in Tom Maliti, 'ICC Prosecutor Asks Court to Decide.'
79 Fergal Gaynor cited in in Mike Pflanz, 'Uhuru Kenyatta's ICC Prosecution Close to Collapse.'
80 Uhuru Kenyatta cited in Sophie van Leeuwen, 'Kenyatta's Hague Speech: God Bless Kenya, God Bless the ICC', *All Africa*, 11 October 2014, available online at http://allafrica.com/stories/201410131464.html (accessed 20 June 2015).
81 Ibid.
82 'Kenya: A hero's welcome for President Uhuru Kenyatta return from The Hague', *Cameroon Daily Journal*, 9 October 2014, available online at www.cameroonjournal.com/kenya-a-heros-welcome-for-president-uhuru-kenyatta-return-from-the-hague/ (accessed 20 June 2015).
83 ICC Press Release, 'Kenyatta case: ICC Trial Chamber rejects request for further adjournment and directs the Prosecution to indicate either its withdrawal of charges or readiness to proceed to trial', 3 December 2014, available online at www.icc-cpi.int/en_menus/icc/press%20and%20media/press%20releases/Pages/PR1071.aspx (accessed 20 June 2015).
84 Office of the Prosecutor, 'Notice of Withdrawal of Charges Against Uhuru Muigai Kenyatta', 5 December 2014, available online at www.icc-cpi.int/iccdocs/doc/doc1879204.pdf (accessed 20 June 2015).
85 Fatou Bensouda, 'Statement of the Prosecutor of the International Criminal Court, Fatou Bensouda, on the withdrawal of charges against Mr. Uhuru Muigai Kenyatta', Office of the Prosecutor Press Release, 5 December 2014, available online at www.icc-cpi.int/en_menus/icc/press%20and%20media/press%20releases/Pages/otp-statement-05-12-2014-2.aspx (accessed 20 June 2015).
86 Ibid.
87 Ibid.
88 Ibid.
89 'Kenyan President says he is vindicated after ICC drops charges', *Telegraph*, 5 December 2014, available online at www.telegraph.co.uk/news/worldnews/africaandindianocean/kenya/11275616/Kenyan-president-says-he-is-vindicated-after-ICC-drops-charges.html (accessed 20 May 2015).
90 'Uhuru Kenyatta denounces ICC as Kenya charges dropped', *BBC News*, 5 December 2014, available online at www.bbc.co.uk/news/world-africa-30344320 (accessed 20 May 2015).
91 'Kenyan President says he is vindicated after ICC drops charges', *Telegraph*.

92 Fredrick Nzwili, 'Kenyans Rejoice at Collapse of ICC Case Against President Kenyatta', *Christian Science Monitor*, 5 December 2014, available online at www.csmonitor.com/World/Africa/2014/1205/Kenyans-rejoice-at-collapse-of-ICC-case-against-President-Kenyatta-video (accessed 20 June 2015).

93 'IGAD Congratulates President Uhuru Kenyatta on ICC Case Withdrawal', *The Standard*, 8 December 2014, available online at www.standardmedia.co.ke/article/2000143791/igad-congratulates-president-uhuru-kenyatta-on-icc-case-withdrawal (accessed 20 June 2015).

94 Carla Ferstman,'ICC Prosecutor's withdrawal of charges against Kenyatta, a blow to victims of the post-election violence in Kenya', *Redress: Ending Torture, Seeking Justice for Survivors*, 5 December 2014, available online at www.redress.org/downloads/press-release-kenyatta-charges-withdrawal-5-dec-2014.pdf (accessed 20 May 2015).

95 Kofi Annan, 'Justice for Kenya', *New York Times*, 9 September 2013, available online at www.nytimes.com/2013/09/09/opinion/justice-for-kenya.html?_r=0 (accessed on 20 May 2015).

Conclusion

From protection *and* prosecution to protection *from* prosecution

On 26 March 2015, President Uhuru Muigai Kenyatta stood before the Kenyan National Assembly and delivered a momentous State of the Nation Address. In his remarks, Kenyatta formally acknowledged the suffering of Kenyans 'still plagued by painful memories of unresolved murders, the existence of torture chambers and detentions without trial.'[1] He also referred to the Wagalla tragedy, and most notably, the post-election violence that engulfed the country nearly seven years prior.

> Fellow Kenyans ... the time has come to bring closure to this painful past.... To move forward as one nation ... I stand before you today on my own behalf, that of my government and all past governments, to offer the sincere apology of the Government of the Republic of Kenya to all our compatriots for all past wrongs ... I seek your forgiveness.[2]

Kenyatta's statement marked the first time in the country's history that a head of state had issued a formal apology to the people of Kenya and asked for their forgiveness. His remarks echoed an earlier apology delivered by the Chief Justice, Willy Mutunga.[3] Apologies from two high-level officials within a short span of time appeared to signal the Government's internalisation of the Truth Justice and Reconciliation Commission's (TJRC) report and a first step towards implementing its recommendations.[4]

Following his apology, Kenyatta made reference to a number of outstanding criminal cases relating to the post-election violence. More specifically, he discussed the challenges faced by the Director of Public Prosecutions in obtaining convictions for the 6000 reported crimes committed during that period. According to Kenyatta, the challenges derived from a number of issues ranging from 'inadequate evidence, inability to identity perpetrators, witnesses fear of reprisals, and the general lack of technical and forensic capacity at the time.'[5] Given these challenges, Kenyatta recommended that the 6000 outstanding cases be handled through restorative means: 'We must indeed recall our options are not limited to retributive justice. There also exists the promise of restorative justice.'[6] He further added: 'In many ways, Kenyans and humanity overall, have benefited from restorative justice, an approach that is deeply rooted in our cultural and historical realities.'[7]

For many, Kenyatta's apology came too late, as civil society had urged the TJRC report's recommendations to be implemented two years prior. For others, the apology marked a critical step in the country's efforts to move forward. However it was received, the statement was laced with irony. It was, after all, an apology issued by one of the suspected masterminds of the post-election violence – accused of non-cooperation and deliberate obstruction of the ICC cases only four months prior – now extolling the virtues of forgiveness and reconciliation. Through his remarks, Kenyatta effectively closed the door on a seven-year search for justice following one of the darkest moments in Kenya's history. One might question, however, whether the door was ever truly open.

The failure to provide accountability for the crimes committed in Kenya during the 2007–08 post-election violence significantly limits the effectiveness of Kenya's broader reform process. As Kofi Annan has remarked: 'I have continued to follow Kenya's progress, and there is no question that impunity remains one of the greatest sources of underlying tensions.'[8] He further warned: 'If it is not checked, there may yet be future generations of victims in Kenya.'[9]

What is particularly significant is the manner in which impunity has been perpetuated in Kenya. While the principle of R2P was developed to ensure that sovereignty no longer serve as a shield for the commission of atrocities, the Government of Kenya reverted to a traditional understanding of sovereignty that R2P was specifically designed to counteract. In other words, the accused used the machinery of the state to shield themselves from accountability. In this regard, a case that commenced with the intention of delivering both protection and prosecution swiftly developed into the opposite – protection *from* prosecution for the suspected perpetrators.

Reflecting on the situation in Kenya, the former UN Special Adviser on the Prevention of Genocide, Francis Deng, has observed the following:

> We keep saying rhetorically that there is no conflict between justice and peace, and that the two are complementary. In reality when you have a situation where the people who are to be held accountable are in positions of power, it's not easy.[10]

Interestingly, Deng made these comments in 2010 – three years prior to the General Election which saw Uhuru Kenyatta elected to the top office in the country. While the outcome of the 2013 election did deliver a blow to the prospects for justice, the pursuit of justice in Kenya was dealt its first significant setback five years prior, during the Kenyan National Dialogue and Reconciliation (KNDR) process.

The KNDR process is widely credited for bringing an end to the eight weeks of bloodshed that nearly brought Kenya to the brink of civil war. Nevertheless, the overwhelmingly positive evaluation of the Kenyan case tends to overlook some of the striking compromises within the KNDR agreements. Although the KNDR process did effectively bring about an end to the crisis, it simultaneously entrenched some of the suspected perpetrators of the violence within the Government of National Unity, while also tasking them with reforming the country. Hence, there was a tension between the ultimate aims of the KNDR process – which included ending the problem of impunity – and the vehicle for achieving this – the Coalition Government.[11] In this regard, it would appear that the measures designed to protect the population in the Kenyan case have undermined the efforts to prosecute perpetrators. The application of R2P and the ICC in Kenya were, however, intended to function in a complementary manner, such that the initiation of the ICC cases would reinforce the initial success of the R2P-inspired mediation process. A key lesson from this case could therefore be the need to ensure a greater degree of coherence between the responsibility to protect and the responsibility to protect.

Nevertheless, by focusing exclusively on the implications for the R2P–ICC relationship, we tend to overlook a much more fundamental lesson that can be drawn from this case. Irrespective of how R2P and the ICC are applied – whether they are utilised concurrently, sequentially or completely independently of one another – the most significant challenges associated with applying the two will by no means hinge on the precise relationship *between* R2P and the ICC. A prior, and arguably much more compelling, challenge derives from the tension *within* each instrument by virtue of the fact that each fundamentally seeks to reinterpret how sovereignty is understood, while at the same time being utterly dependent on the cooperation of sovereign states. In this regard, the tension that manifested in the Kenyan case – endeavouring to hold the Government accountable while simultaneously relying on the Government's support – is mirrored within both R2P and the ICC.

The necessity of securing state cooperation has profoundly influenced the evolution of both the responsibility to protect and the International Criminal Court, such that crucial stages in the development of each have been marked by significant compromises. The R2P provisions within the 2005 World Summit Outcome Document have, for instance, been heavily criticised for bargaining away the original formulation of R2P. According to Simon Chesterman:

> [B]y the time RtoP was endorsed by the World Summit in 2005, its normative content had been emasculated to the point where it essentially provided that the Security Council could authorize, on a case by-case basis, things that it had been authorizing for more than a decade[12]

As such, appeals to R2P were restricted to circumstances 'not when humanity needed it, but selectively, when the Security Council powers saw it fit.'[13]

The ICC has similarly been forced to balance two opposing inclinations: curbing the power of states and relying on their cooperation. This has become particularly apparent in the relationship between the ICC and the UN Security Council. The Rome Statute's provisions on Security Council referral power effectively 'tethers the apparently impartial and independent Court to the partial and political Council.'[14] As Mark Kersten has observed:

130 Conclusion

> Both R2P and the ICC were inspired by the limitations of the UNSC to appropriately and effectively intervene – judicially and militarily. Yet, rather than provide any real challenge to the functioning of the Council, both R2P and the ICC affirmed the Council's power, authority and legitimacy in international law and politics.[15]

Consequently, it is argued that R2P and ICC 'share a tendency to gravitate towards the very power that they are supposed to constrain'[16] and consequently 'reinforce that which they claim to transcend, sovereign states.'[17]

While the extent of compromise that R2P and the ICC have had to accommodate may appear contrary to the intentions of their original architects, it is more than likely that both would have remained on a theoretical plane in the absence of such compromise. A high degree of compromise can, therefore, be viewed as a logical consequence of translating the ideals of the responsibility to protect and the responsibility to prosecute into practice.

Navigating through the tension that resides at the heart of R2P and the ICC will, however, continue to present challenges in the application of both instruments. Although this tension cannot be easily overcome, it can perhaps be better managed. Among the many factors that will determine the effectiveness of R2P and the ICC in specific cases is the issue of perception, and more specifically, the extent to which they are viewed as consensual and locally driven rather than externally imposed. The issue of perception certainly influenced the relative effectiveness of these instruments in the case of Kenya.

In spite of the high level of concerted, behind-the-scenes support, the AU led mediation process in Kenya was viewed as a locally owned process. This went a long way towards enhancing the legitimacy of the Panel's efforts, boosting domestic support for the process, and ultimately contributing towards its broader success. By contrast, it is certainly no accident that those who had an interest in undermining the ICC process in Kenya improved their efforts by portraying the trials as an externally driven process. In so doing, opponents of the Court consciously severed the links between the ICC cases and the failure to establish a credible domestic mechanism, while also downplaying the fact that several Kenyan MPs voted in favour of The Hague option.

A further factor that will influence the effectiveness of R2P and the ICC in specific situations are the expectations that are placed upon each. Despite the fact that R2P and the ICC have been in existence for over a decade, both are relatively novel instruments. In this sense, there are limits to what each can be reasonably expected to achieve. Whereas the ICC cases in Kenya were initiated with the weight of elevated expectations, and the lofty goal of 'ending impunity in Kenya,' the association between the AU mediation and the responsibility to protect principle was much more subdued throughout the crisis. Although Annan clearly viewed the post-election crisis in Kenya through the prism of R2P, he refrained from inflating expectations by explicitly invoking the principle. As this case highlights, by elevating expectations we do a disservice not only to the architects of R2P and the ICC, but more crucially, to the affected populations who may come to rely on these instruments.

Notwithstanding that the perpetrators of the post-election violence have not been held to account, the international response to this crisis has had a profound impact in Kenya. Since the country's independence, countless investigations have been conducted and reports have been written on a number of subjects ranging from human rights violations, grand corruption, atrocity crimes, and impunity. The one thing that all preceding reports and investigations have had in common is the dust they have gathered on the shelves following their publication. The CIPEV report, unlike all preceding reports, actually became a subject of debate among the political elite in Kenya and for some, a matter of real concern. Although the provisions for establishing a Special Tribunal were defeated on three separate occasions, the issue was seriously debated.

Moreover, the image of Kenya's political leaders at The Hague, being forced to account for their actions, was unprecedented. As a report by the Global Centre for R2P observed: 'Those who were once deemed beyond the law were forced to engage with international mechanisms of justice.'[18] While it may not be possible to fully attribute the calm of the 2013 elections to the ICC process in Kenya, particularly given the associated complexities and unintended consequences of the Court's role in the country, the presence of the ICC did give Kenya's political leaders a reason to carefully consider their actions and temper their language in the run-up to the polls.

As the country continues to come to grips with the legacy of the 2007–08 post-election violence, the path towards responsible sovereignty still appears far in the distance. Forward momentum along this path seems to be invariably accompanied by backward steps. Nevertheless, the shift in consciousness that has emerged as a result of applying the responsibility to protect and the responsibility prosecute in Kenya is irreversible. On this basis alone there is much hope that the experience of 2007–08 will never again be repeated, and that those who have suffered through Kenya's darkest moment will not have suffered in vain.

Notes

1 President Uhuru Kenyatta State of the Nation Address, 27 March 2014, available online at www.kenya-today.com/news/read-president-uhuru-kenyatta-state-union-address-full-speech (accessed 20 May 2015).
2 Ibid.
3 'CJ Apologises for Biased Past Judicial System', *Daily Nation*, 25 March 2015, available online at www.nation.co.ke/news/Chief-Justice-Willy-Mutunga-Western-Kenya-Tour-Judiciary/-/1056/2665738/-/ub3dosz/-/index.html (accessed 20 June 2015).
4 Christopher Gitari Ndungú, 'Lessons to Be Learned: An Analysis of the Final Report of Kenya's Truth, Justice and Reconciliation Commission', International Centre for Transitional Justice Briefing, 19 May 2014, available online at www.ictj.org/publication/kenya-TJRC-lessons-learned (accessed 20 June 2015).
5 President Uhuru Kenyatta State of the Nation Address.
6 Ibid.
7 Ibid.

8 Kofi Annan, 'Justice for Kenya', *New York Times*, 9 September 2013, available online at www.nytimes.com/2013/09/09/opinion/justice-for-kenya.html?_r=0 (accessed on 20 May 2015).
9 Ibid.
10 Interview with Francis Deng, United Nations, New York, 13 July 2010.
11 In other words, the political arrangement that was considered necessary for ending the violence planted the seeds for perpetuating impunity. However, with the stability of the country at stake, this compromise was perhaps unavoidable.
12 Simon Chesterman, 'Leading from Behind: The Responsibility to Protect, the Obama Doctrine, and Humanitarian Intervention in Libya', *Ethics & International Affairs*, 25.3 (2011), pp. 279–85.
13 Ibid.
14 Mark Kersten, 'A Fatal Attraction: The UN Security Council and the Relationship Between R2P and the International Criminal Court', 27 February 2013, available online at http://justiceinconflict.org/2013/02/27/a-fatal-attraction-the-un-security-council-and-the-relationship-between-r2p-and-the-international-criminal-court/ (accessed on 20 May 2015), p. 12.
15 Ibid., p. 9.
16 Ibid.
17 Ibid.
18 Abdullahi Boru Halakhe, 'R2P in Practice: Ethnic Violence, Elections and Atrocity Prevention in Kenya', *Global Centre for the Responsibility to Protect*, Occasional Paper Series, No. 4, December 2013, p. 18.

Bibliography

Adow, M., 'Kenya's ICC accused unite', *Global Policy Forum*, 3 December 2012, available online at www.globalpolicy.org/international-justice/the-international-criminal-court/icc-investigations/52124-kenyas-icc-accused-unite.html (accessed 20 May 2015).

Africa Review of Business and Technology, 'Post-election Violence Causes Regional Fallout: Post-election Violence in Kenya Has Already Left its Mark on East African Business', April 2008, available online at www.entrepreneur.com/tradejournals/article/179048794.html (accessed 20 May 2015).

African Peer Review Mechanism, 'Country Review Report of the Republic of Kenya', 2006.

African Union Press Release, Dr. Nkosazana Dlamini Zuma, chairperson of the African Union Commission: "The African Union Commission salutes the people of Kenya for the successful and peaceful conclusions of the elections', 11 March 2013, available online at http://cpauc.au.int/en/content/statement-dr-nkosazana-dlamini-zuma-chairperson-african-union-commission-announcement-result (accessed 20 May 2015).

African Union, Decisions on the Implementation of the Decisions of the International Criminal Court, Doc. Ex.CL/639(XVIII) Assembly/AU/Dec 334 (SVI), 30–31 January 2011.

African Union, Extraordinary Session of the Assembly of the African Union, Addis Ababa, Ethiopia, 12 October 2013, available online at www.au.int/en/content/extraordinary-session-assembly-african-union (accessed 20 June 2015).

Agreement on the Principles of Partnership of the Coalition Government, 28 February, 2008.

Ainley, K., 'The Responsibility to Protect and the International Criminal Court', *International Affairs*, 19.1 (2015), pp. 37–54.

Al Jazeera, 'African Leaders Accuse ICC of "Race Hunt"', 28 May 2013, available online at www.aljazeera.com/news/africa/2013/05/201352722331270466.html (accessed 20 June 2015).

Albright, M.K. and Williamson, R.S., 'The United States and R2P: From Words to Actions', Report of the Working Group on R2P, 2013, available online at www.usip.org/sites/default/files/PW-UnitedStates-And-R2P-Words-To-Action.pdf (accessed 20 May 2015).

All Africa, 'Kenyans Unite for Peace Prayers' 24 February 2013, available online at http://allafrica.com/view/group/main/main/id/00023074.html (accessed 20 June 2015).

Allen, K., 'Has Kenya's power-sharing worked', *BBC News*, 3 March 2009, available online at http://news.bbc.co.uk/1/hi/world/africa/7921007.stm (accessed 20 May 2015).

Bibliography

Allison, S., 'Kenyan Election Alliance Between Bitter Enemies United By ICC Charges', *Guardian*, 4 December 2012, available online at www.theguardian.com/world/2012/dec/04/kenya-election-alliance-rival (accessed 20 June 2015).

Allison, S., 'Kenya elections: reasons to be fearful', *Guardian*, 24 January 2013, available at 'www.theguardian.com/world/2013/jan/24/kenya-election-violence-fearful (accessed 20 May 2015).

Alston, P., 'Report of the Special Rapporteur on extrajudicial, summary or arbitrary executions', (Alston Report), 26 May 2009, available online at www.extrajudicial executions.org/application/media/Kenya%20Mission%202009%20%28A_HRC_11_2_Add.6%29.pdf (accessed 20 May 2015).

Alston, P., 'Statement by Professor Philip Alston, Special Rapporteur on extrajudicial, summary or arbitrary executions, United Nations Human Rights Council', Geneva 3 June 2009, available online at www.un.org/webcast/unhrc/11th/statements/Alston_STMT.pdf (accessed 20 May 2015).

Amani Forum, Regional Parliamentarians Fact Finding Mission to Kenya on the Post Election Violence, 13–21 January 2008, The Great Lakes Parliamentary Forum on Peace, available online at www.responsibilitytoprotect.org/files/Fact-Finding%20Mission%20Report%20by%20Great%20Lakes%20Parliamentarians%20on%20Kenyan%20Post-Election%20Violence.pdf (accessed 20 May 2015).

Anderson, A., *Histories of the Hanged: Britain's Dirty War in Kenya and the End of Empire* (Weidenfeld and Nicolson, 2005).

Anderson, D., 'Majimboism: The Troubled History of an Idea', in Daniel Branch, Nic Cheeseman, and Leigh Gardner (eds), *Our Turn to Eat: Politics in Kenya Since 1950* (Lit Verlag, 2010), pp. 23–52.

Annan, K.A., 'Justice for Kenya', *New York Times*, 9 September 2013, available online at www.nytimes.com/2013/09/09/opinion/justice-for-kenya.html?_r=0 (accessed on 20 May 2015).

Annan, K.A., Press Conference Serena Hotel Nairobi, 26 January 2008.

Annan, K.A., 'Statement by HE Kofi Annan on Implementation of CIPEV and IREC' 19 December 2008, available online at http://reliefweb.int/report/kenya/statement-he-kofi-annan-implementation-cipev-and-irec (accessed 20 May 2015).

Annan, K.A., 'Statement issued by Mr. Kofi Annan, Chairman of the African Union Panel of Eminent African Personalities 31 January 2011, available online at http://kenyastockholm.com/2011/02/01/impunity-in-kenya-statement-from-kofi-annan/ (accessed 20 May 2015).

Arbour, L., Address to the Stanley Foundation Conference on the Responsibility to Protect, New York, 18 January 2012, available online at www.r2p10.org (accessed 20 June 2013).

Asia Pacific Centre for the Responsibility to Protect, 'Research in Focus in 2012', available online at www.r2pasiapacific.org/docs/R2P%20Fund/Research%20in%20Focus%20Booklet%202012.pdf (accessed 20 June 2015).

Atsiaya, P., 'Pro-ICC groups obtain 800 000 signatures to back trials', *The Standard*, 8 March 2011, available online at www.standardmedia.co.ke/article/2000030707/pro-icc-groups-obtain-800-000-signatures-to-back-trials (accessed 20 May 2015).

Babbitt, E., 'Mediation and the Prevention of Mass Atrocities', in Monica Serrano and Thomas G. Weiss (eds), *The International Politics of Human Rights: Rallying to the R2P Cause?* (Routledge, 2014), pp. 29–47.

Ban Ki-Moon, *Implementing the Responsibility to Protect; Report of the Secretary-General*, UN doc. A/63/677, 12 January 2009.

Barkan, J., 'Hearing on the immediate and underlying causes and consequences of flawed democracy in Africa', prepared for the of Senate Foreign Relations Committee's Subcommittee on African Affairs, 7 February 2008, available online at http://csis.org/files/media/csis/congress/ts080212barkan.pdf (accessed 20 May 2015).

BBC News, 'New Kenya leader promises reform', 30 December 2002, available online at http://news.bbc.co.uk/1/hi/world/africa/2614963.stm (accessed 20 May 2015).

BBC News, 'Kenyans reject new constitution', 22 November 2005, available online at http://news.bbc.co.uk/1/hi/world/africa/4455538.stm (accessed 20 May 2015).

BBC News, 'Profile: Kenya's Secretive Mungiki Sect', 24 May 2007, available online at http://news.bbc.co.uk/1/hi/world/africa/6685393.stm (accessed 30 June 2015).

BBC News, 'Chaos Mars Kenya Party Primaries', 20 November 2007, available online at http://news.bbc.co.uk/1/hi/world/africa/7103746.stm (accessed 20 May 2015).

BBC News, 'Kibaki and Moi Speech Excerpts', 30 December 2007, available online at http://news.bbc.co.uk/1/hi/not_in_website/syndication/monitoring/media_reports/2615369.stm (accessed 20 May 2015).

BBC News, 'Kibaki named victor in Kenya vote', 30 December 2007, available online at http://news.bbc.co.uk/1/hi/world/africa/7164890.stm (accessed 20 May 2015).

BBC News, 'Odinga rejects Kenya poll result', 31 December 2007, available online at http://news.bbc.co.uk/1/hi/7165406.stm accessed 20 May 2015).

BBC News, 'Kenyan Violence Hits Fuel Supply', 4 January 2008, available online at http://news.bbc.co.uk/2/hi/7171439.stm (accessed 20 May 2015).

BBC News, 'Kenya's dubious election', 8 January 2008, available online at http://news.bbc.co.uk/1/hi/world/africa/7175694.stm (accessed 20 May 2015).

BBC News, 'Annan hits out at Kenya abuses', 26 January 2008, available online at http://news.bbc.co.uk/1/hi/world/africa/7210419.stm (accessed 20 May 2015).

BBC News, 'Progress at Kenya Peace Talks', 8 February 2008, available online at http://news.bbc.co.uk/1/hi/world/africa/7235038.stm (accessed 20 June 2015).

BBC News, 'Bush urges Kenya power-sharing', 16 February 2008, available online at http://news.bbc.co.uk/1/hi/world/americas/7248271.stm (accessed 20 May 2015).

BBC News, 'Kenya Poll Crisis Talks Suspended', 26 February 2008, available online at http://news.bbc.co.uk/1/hi/world/africa/7265234.stm (accessed 20 June 2015).

BBC News, 'Kenya MPs vote to leave ICC over poll violence claims', 23 December 2010, available online at www.bbc.co.uk/news/world-africa-12066667 (accessed 20 May 2015).

BBC News, 'Kenya: Wagalla Massacre Survivors Testify', 18 April 2011, available online at www.bbc.co.uk/news/world-africa-13123813 (accessed 20 June 2015).

BBC News, 'Kofi Annan Urges Kenyans not to Vote for Indicted Politicians', 4 December 2012, available online at www.bbc.co.uk/news/world-africa-20602232 (accessed 20 May 2015).

BBC News, 'ICC rejects Kenya bid to halt election violence probe', 30 May 2011, available online at www.bbc.co.uk/news/world-africa-13593469 (accessed 20 May 2015).

BBC News, 'African Union Accuses ICC of Hunting Africans', 27 May 2013, available online at www.bbc.co.uk/news/world-africa-22681894 (accessed 20 June 2015).

BBC News, 'Could Westgate Deal a Fatal Blow to the ICC', 17 October 2013, available online at www.bbc.co.uk/news/world-africa-24562337 (accessed 20 June 2015).

BBC News, 'Uhuru Kenyatta denounces ICC as Kenya charges dropped', 5 December 2014, available online at www.bbc.co.uk/news/world-africa-30344320 (accessed 20 May 2015).

Bellamy, A.J., *The Responsibility to Protect* (Polity Press, 2009).

Bellamy, A.J., 'The Responsibility to Protect: Five Years On', *Ethics and International Affairs*, 24.2 (2010), pp. 143–69.

Bellamy, A.J., *Global Politics and the Responsibility to Protect* (Routledge, 2011).

Bellamy, A.J., et al. (eds), The *Responsibility to Protect and International Law* (Martinus Nijhoff/Brill, 2011).

Bensouda, F., Address to the Stanley Foundation Conference on Responsibility to Protect, New York, 18 January 2012, available online at www.stanleyfoundation.org/r2p.cfm (accessed 20 May 2015).

Bensouda, F., 'Statement of the Prosecutor of the International Criminal Court, Fatou Bensouda, on the withdrawal of charges against Mr. Uhuru Muigai Kenyatta', Office of the Prosecutor Press Release, 5 December 2014, available online at www.icccpi. int/en_menus/icc/press%20and%20media/press%20releases/Pages/otp-statement-05-12-2014-2.aspx (accessed 20 June 2015).

Biden, J., 'Remarks by Vice-President Biden in a statement to the press with Kenyan President Mwai Kibaki', 8 June 2010, available online at www.whitehouse.gov/the-press-office/remarks-vice-president-biden-a-statement-press-with-kenyan-president-mwai-kibaki (accessed 20 May 2015).

Branch, D., *Defeating Mau Mau, Creating Kenya: Counterinsurgency, Civil War and Decolonization* (Cambridge University Press, 2009).

Branch, D., *Kenya: Between Hope and Despair 1963–2011* (Yale University Press, 2011).

Brown, S., 'Donor Responses to the 2008 Crisis in Kenya: Finally Getting it Right?' *Journal of Contemporary African Studies*, 27.3 (2009), pp. 389–406.

Brown, S., 'Quiet Diplomacy and Recurring "Ethnic Clashes" in Kenya', in Chandra Lekha Sriram and Karin Wermester (eds), *From Promise to Practice: Strengthening UN Capacities for the Prevention of Violent Conflict* (Lynne Rienner, 2003), pp. 69–100.

Bruce-Lockhart, K., 'From incitement to self-censorship: the media in the Kenyan elections of 2007 and 2013', available online at http://freespeechdebate.com/en/discuss/124451/ (accessed 20 May 2015).

Byers, M., 'High Ground Lost on UN's Responsibility to Protect', *Winnipeg Free Press*, 18 September 2005, available online at www.ligi.ubc.ca/?p2=/modules/liu/news/view.jsp&id=142 (accessed 20 May 2015).

Cameroon Daily Journal, 'Kenya: A hero's welcome for President Uhuru Kenyatta return from The Hague', 9 October 2014, available online at www.cameroonjournal.com/kenya-a-heros-welcome-for-president-uhuru-kenyatta-return-from-the-hague/ (accessed 20 June 2015).

Capital FM, President Kenyatta's inauguration speech', 9 April 2013, available online at www.capitalfm.co.ke/eblog/2013/04/09/president-kenyattas-inauguration-speech/ (accessed 20 May 2015).

Capital News, 'Kenya AG faults PM on suspension', 15 February 2010, available online at www.capitalfm.co.ke/news/2010/02/kenya-ag-faults-pm-on-suspension/ (accessed 20 May 2015).

Carney, J., White House Press Secretary, 'We also congratulate the people of Kenya on the peaceful conduct of the election', 30 March 2013, available online at www.politico.com/politico44/2013/03/wh-urges-peaceful-acceptance-of-kenyan-election-results-160541.html (accessed 20 May 2015).

Carter Centre, *Observing Kenya's March 2013 National Elections*, Final Report, available online at www.cartercenter.org/resources/pdfs/news/peace_publications/election_reports/kenya-final-101613.pdf (accessed 30 June 2015).

Cassese, A., *International Criminal Law*, 3rd edn (Oxford University Press, 2013)
Chatterjee, D.K. and Scheid, D.E. (eds), *Ethics and Foreign Intervention* (Cambridge University Press, 2003).
Chesterman, S., 'Leading from Behind: The Responsibility to Protect, the Obama Doctrine, and Humanitarian Intervention in Libya', *Ethics & International Affairs*, 25.3 (2011), pp. 279–85.
Cohen, R., 'How Kofi Annan Rescued Kenya', *New York Review of Books* 55.2, 14 August 2008, available online at www.nybooks.com/articles/archives/2008/aug/14/how-kofi-annan-rescued-kenya/ (accessed 20 May 2015).
CNN, 'UN Report Alleges Widespread Killing by Kenyan Police', 15 June 2009, available online at http://edition.cnn.com/2009/WORLD/africa/06/05/kenya.united.nations.investigation/ (accessed 20 June 2015).
Commission of Human Rights, 'Report of the Independent Expert to Update the Set of Principles to Combat Impunity', 8 February 2005, E/CN.4/2005/102/Add.1.
Commission of Inquiry into Post-election Violence, Final Report, 15 October 2008
Committee to Protect Journalists, 'Attacks on the Press in Kenya: 2008', available online at https://cpj.org/2009/02/attacks-on-the-press-in-2008-kenya.php (accessed 20 May 2015).
Cooper, R.H. and Voïnov-Kohler, J. (eds), *Responsibility to Protect: The Global Moral Compact for the 21st Century* (Palgrave, 2008).
Daily Nation, 'EU Might Cut Aid Over Poll Results Crisis', 16 January 2008.
Daily Nation, 'Solve Crisis or Suffer Aid Cuts, Warn Donors', 17 January 2008.
Daily Nation, 'Europeans Vote to Freeze Aid', 18 January 2008.
Daily Nation, 'Your Role is Vital and We Can't Afford to Fail, Annan Tells MPs', 13 February 2008, available online at www.ogiek.org/news-4/news-post-08-02-417.htm (accessed 20 May 2015).
Daily Nation, 'Annan's Team Strikes Half-Way Deal in Talks', 14 February 2008.
Daily Nation, 'Raising Funds to arm gangs for revenge poison delicate peace', 27 February 2008.
Daily Nation, 'Talks Suspended as US Threatens to Act', 27 February 2008.
Daily Nation, 'Pressure Mounts to End Crisis', 28 February 2008.
Daily Nation, 'Waki: row over Ruto threat to quit ODM', 16 November 2008, available online at www.nation.co.ke/news/-/1056/491782/-/view/printVersion/-/nqjvgqz/-/index.html (accessed 20 May 2015).
Daily Nation, 'UN Official Calls for Sacking of Ali and Wako February', 25 February 2009, available online at www.nation.co.ke/news/-/1056/534978/-/4ynka9z/-/index.html (accessed 20 May 2015).
Daily Nation, 'Puzzling Alliances in fight Against Tribunal Bill', 12 February 2009, available online at www.nation.co.ke/News/politics/-/1064/529716/-/ygqyunz/-/index.html (accessed 20 May 2015).
Daily Nation, 'Why I prefer The Hague Route', 21 February 2009, available online at www.nation.co.ke/news/-/1056/533390/-/4yoe9mz/-/index.html (accessed 20 May 2015).
Daily Nation, 'The Hague Vows to Act Swiftly', 31 March 2009, available online at www.nation.co.ke/News/-/1056/555462/-/u3qj9g/-/index.html (accessed 20 May 2015).
Daily Nation, 'Alston pushes for protection of witnesses', 28 May 2009, available online at www.nation.co.ke/news/-/1056/604318/-/4hfl3iz/-/index.html (accessed 20 May 2015).

138 Bibliography

Daily Nation, 'MPs compile new post poll suspects list', 25 July 2009.
Daily Nation, 'Imanyara: House will nail big fish with proposed bill', 15 August 2009, available online at www.nation.co.ke/news/politics/-/1064/640268/-/kfkl6fz/-/index.html (accessed 20 May 2015).
Daily Nation, 'Ocampo has a strong case in Kenya chaos', 7 November 2009.
Daily Nation, 'With The Hague reality sinking in, leaders are in panic mode', 9 November 2009, available online at www.nation.co.ke/oped/blogs/-/446672/683960/-/1229h2hz/-/index.html (accessed 20 May 2015).
Daily Nation, 'EU asks for proper witness protection', 31 March 2010, available online at www.nation.co.ke/news/EU-asks-for-proper-witness-protection-/-/1056/890784/-/view/printVersion/-/ei4eyaz/-/index.html (accessed 20 May 2015).
Daily Nation, 'Ministers push to keep Ocampo probe at bay', 15 April 2010, available at www.nation.co.ke/News/politics/Ministers%20push%20to%20keep%20Ocampo%20probe%20at%20bay/-/1064/900238/-/lhcdbg/-/index.html (accessed 20 May 2015).
Daily Nation, 'Parliament Move Draws Criticism', 23 December 2010.
Daily Nation, 'Audit Reveals Sh500m IDP Cash Loss', 12 January 2012, available online at www.nation.co.ke/News/Audit+reveals+Sh500m+IDP+cash+loss+/-/1056/1304732/-/2kk4cc/-/index.html (accessed 20 June 2015).
Daily Nation, 'Bensouda: Someone Keen to Out Kenya ICC Witnesses', 8 February 2013, www.nation.co.ke/news/Bensouda-Someone-keen-to-out-ICC-Kenya-witnesses/-/1056/1688270/-/ws2s8d/-/index.html (accessed 20 May 2015).
Daily Nation, 'CJ Apologises for Biased Past Judicial System', 25 March 2015, available online at www.nation.co.ke/news/Chief-Justice-Willy-Mutunga-Western-Kenya-Tour-Judiciary/-/1056/2665738/-/ub3dosz/-/index.html (accessed 20 June 2015).
Dersso, S.A., 'The AU's Extraordinary Summit decisions on Africa-ICC Relationship', *EJIL Talk*, 28 October 2013, available online at www.ejiltalk.org/the-aus-extraordinary-summit-decisions-on-africa-icc-relationship/ (accessed 20 June 2015).
Dixon, R., 'Charges Are Dropped Against Kenyan Suspect', *Los Angeles Times*, 11 March 2011, available online at http://articles.latimes.com/2013/mar/11/world/la-fg-wn-kenya-court-charges-20130311 (accessed 20 June 2015).
Doyle, M., Human Rights, Sovereignty and Military Intervention: A Dialogue with JS Mill Institute for Ethics Law and Armed Conflict Seminar Series, 9 February 2010.
Drumbl, M., *Atrocity, Punishment and International Law* (Cambridge University Press, 2007).
Elder, C., et al., 'Elections and violent conflict in Kenya: making prevention stick', *United States Institute for Peace*, 9 November 2014, available online at www.usip.org/publications/elections-and-violent-conflict-in-kenya-making-prevention-stick (accessed 20 May 2015).
European Union Election Observation Mission (EUEOM), Kenya 2007, 'Preliminary Statement', Nairobi January 1, 2008.
Evans, G., 'Response to Reviews by Michael Barnett, Chris Brown and Robert Jackson', *Global Responsibility to Protect* 2.3 (2010), pp. 320–7.
Evans, G., 'The Responsibility to Protect: Meeting the Challenges', lecture to the 10th Asia Pacific Programme for Senior Military Officers, S. Rajaratnam School of International Studies, Singapore, 5 August 2008, available online at www.crisisgroup.org/en/publication-type/speeches/2008/the-responsibility-to-protect-meeting-the-challenges.aspx (accessed 20 October 2014);
Evans, G., *The Responsibility to Protect: Ending Mass Atrocity Crimes Once and For All* (Brookings Institution, 2009).

Evans, G., Address to the Stanley Foundation Conference on Responsibility to Protect, 18 January 2012, available online at www.stanleyfoundation.org/r2p.cfm (accessed 20 May 2015).

Ferstman, C., 'ICC Prosecutor's withdrawal of charges against Kenyatta, a blow to victims of the post-election violence in Kenya', Redress: Ending Torture, Seeking Justice for Survivors, 5 December 2014, available online at www.redress.org/downloads/press-release-kenyatta-charges-withdrawal-5-dec-2014.pdf (accessed 20 May 2015).

Financial Times, 'Kibaki re-elected as President of Kenya', 30 December 2007, available online at www.ft.com/cms/s/0/7aacfdd6-b6f1-11dc-aa38-0000779fd2ac.html#axzz3awmaGFXo (accessed 20 May 2015).

Genser, J. and Cotler, I., *The Responsibility to Protect: The Promise of Stopping Mass Atrocities in Our Time* (Oxford University Press, 2011).

Gettleman, J., 'Disputed Vote Plunges Kenya into Bloodshed', *New York Times*, 31 December 2007, available online at www.nytimes.com/2007/12/31/world/africa/31kenya.html?pagewanted=all&_r=0 (accessed 20 May 2015).

Gettleman, J., 'Signs in Kenya that the killings were planned', *New York Times*, 21 January 2008, available online at www.nytimes.com/2008/01/21/world/africa/21kenya.html?pagewanted=all&_r=0 (accessed 20 May 2015).

Gettleman, J., 'Kenya's Political Rivals Meet', *New York Times*, 25 January 2008, Available at: www.nytimes.com/2008/01/25/world/africa/25kenya.html?_r=0 (accessed 20 May 2015).

Gitonga, A. and Opiyo, P., 'Ocampo writes to Mutula over witness threats', 26 January 2010, available online at www.standardmedia.co.ke/business/article/2000001710/ocampo-writes-to-mutula-over-witness-threats (accessed 20 May 2015).

Global Centre for the Responsibility to Protect, 'Our Work: R2P Focal Points', available online at www.globalr2p.org/our_work/r2p_focal_points (accessed 20 June 2015).

Global Centre for the Responsibility to Protect, 'UN Security Council Resolutions Referencing R2P', 23 April 2013, available online at www.globalr2p.org/resources/335 (accessed 20 June 2015).

Griffiths, M., 'The Prisoner of Peace: An Interview with Kofi A. Annan', Geneva: Centre for Humanitarian Dialogue, 9 May 2008, 18, available online at http://reliefweb.int/sites/reliefweb.int/files/resources/6F9DC0AD3921DFA7C12575890033E862-Full_Report.pdf (accessed 20 May 2015).

Halakhe, A.B., 'R2P in Practice: Ethnic Violence, Elections and Atrocity Prevention in Kenya', *Global Centre for the Responsibility to Protect*, Occasional Paper Series, No. 4, December 2013.

Hannon, L., 'Minister Forces Kenya to Hold Torture Inquiry', *Mail and Guardian*, 17 April 1998, available online at http://mg.co.za/article/1998-04-17-minister-forces-kenya-to-hold-torture-inquiry (accessed 20 June 2015).

Hannon, L., 'Kenya's displacement crisis', *Humanitarian Access Network*, October 2008, available online at www.odihpn.org/humanitarian-exchange-magazine/issue-40/kenyas-displacement-crisis (accessed 20 May 2015).

Hawke, S., 'Kenya's elections in 2013: poverty, ethnicity, and violence', *Social Justice First*, available online at http://socialjusticefirst.com/2013/03/04/kenyas-elections-in-2013-poverty-ethnicity-and-violence/ (accessed 20 May 2015).

Hehir, A., *The Responsibility to Protect: Rhetoric, Reality and the Future of Humanitarian Intervention* (Palgrave Macmillan, 2011).

Human Rights House Network, 'Kenyan Government Lifts Ban on Live Broadcasts',

5 February 2008, available online at http://humanrightshouse.org/Articles/892.html (accessed 20 June 2015).

Human Rights House, 'I acted under pressure – says Electoral Commission Chairman, Kivuitu', 2 January 2008, available online at http://humanrightshouse.org/noop/page.php?p=Articles/8420.html&d=1 (accessed 20 May 2015).

Human Rights Watch, *Ballots to Bullets. Organized Political Violence and Kenya's Crisis of Governance*, 2.1(A), March 2008, available online at www.hrw.org/sites/default/files/reports/kenya0308web.pdf (accessed on 20 May 2015).

Hunt, K., 'Violence Threatens Kenya's Economy', *BBC News*, 2 January 2008, available online at http://news.bbc.co.uk/2/hi/business/7168060.stm (accessed 20 May 2015).

ICC Office of the Prosecutor, 'OTP Statement in relation to events in Kenya', 5 February 2008, available online at www.icc-cpi.int/NR/rdonlyres/1BB89202-16AE-4D95-ABBB4597C416045D/0/ICCOTPST20080205ENG.pdf (accessed on 20 May 2015).

ICC Office of the Prosecutor, 'Agreed Minutes of Meeting Between Prosecutor Moreno-Ocampo and the Delegation of the Government of Kenya', The Hague, 3 July 2009, available online at www.icc-cpi.int/NR/rdonlyres/1CEB4FAD-DFA7-4DC5-B22D-E828322D9764/280560/20090703AgreedMinutesofMeetingProsecutorKenyanDele.pdf (accessed 20 June 2015).

ICC Office of the Prosecutor, 'ICC Prosecutor: Kenya can be an example to the world', 18 September 2009, available online at www.icccpi.int/en_menus/icc/situations%20and%20cases/situations/situation%20icc%200109/press%20releases/Pages/pr452.aspx (accessed 20 May 2015).

ICC Office of the Prosecutor, 'ICC Prosecutor Supports Three-Pronged Approach to Justice in Kenya', 30 September 2009, available online at www.icc-cpi.int/en_menus/icc/situations%20and%20cases/situations/situation%20icc%200109/press%20releases/Pages/pr456.aspx (accessed 20 May 2015).

ICC Office of the Prosecutor, 'Kenya's post-election violence: ICC Prosecutor presents cases against six individuals for crimes against humanity', 15 December 2010, available online at www.icccpi.int/en_menus/icc/press%20and%20media/press%20releases/press%20releases%20%282010%29/Pages/pr615.aspx (accessed 20 May 2015).

ICC Office of the Prosecutor, 'Prosecution notice regarding the provisional trial date', 5 September 2014, available online at www.icc-cpi.int/iccdocs/doc/doc1826503.pdf (accessed 20 May 2015).

ICC Office of the Prosecutor, 'Statement of the Prosecutor of the International Criminal Court, Fatou Bensouda, on the withdrawal of charges against Mr. Uhuru Muigai Kenyatta', 5 December 2015, available online at www.icc-cpi.int/en_menus/icc/press%20and%20media/press%20releases/Pages/otp-statement-05-12-2014-2.aspx (accessed 20 May 2015).

ICC Press Release, 'Kenyatta case: ICC Trial Chamber rejects request for further adjournment and directs the Prosecution to indicate either its withdrawal of charges or readiness to proceed to trial', 3 December 2014, available online at www.icc-cpi.int/en_menus/icc/press%20and%20media/press%20releases/pages/pr1071.aspx (accessed 20 June 2015).

Imanyara, G., Hansard, Kenya National Assembly, Official Report, 2 December 2009.

Internal Displacement Monitoring Centre, 'Kenya IDP figures analysis', available online at www.internal-displacement.org/sub-saharan-africa/kenya/figures-analysis (accessed 20 May 2015).

International Coalition for the Responsibility to Protect, 'The International Criminal Court and the Responsibility to Protect', available online at http://responsibilitytopro

tect.org/index.php/about-rtop/related-themes/2416-icc-and-rtop (accessed 20 May 2015).
International Commission on Intervention and State Sovereignty, *The Responsibility to Protect* (International Development Research Centre, 2001).
International Criminal Court, 'State Parties to the Rome Statute', available online at www.icc-cpi.int/en_menus/asp/states%20parties/Pages/the%20states%20parties%20to%20the%20rome%20statute.aspx (accessed 20 May 2015).
International Criminal Court, 'The ICC at a Glance', available online at www.icc-cpi.int/iccdocs/PIDS/publications/ICCAtAGlanceEng.pdf (accessed 20 May 2015).
International Criminal Court, Office of the Prosecutor, 'Statement of the Prosecutor on the situation in Kenya', available online at www.icc-cpi.int/NR/rdonlyres/269744E4-9F7D-468F-9B24-C2AE74B012D1/283377/StatementICCProsecutoronsituationinKenya1.pdf (accessed 20 May 2015).
International Crisis Group, 'Kenya in Crisis', *Africa Report* 137, 21 February 2008, p.i, available online at www.crisisgroup.org/~/media/Files/africa/horn-of-africa/kenya/137_kenya_in_crisis_web.pdf (accessed 20 May 2015).
International Peace Institute, 'Conflict Prevention and the Responsibility to Protect', *IPI Blue Paper* No. 7, Task Forces on Strengthening Multilateral Security Capacity, (New York, 2009).
Interview with David Anderson, African Studies Centre, Oxford, 6 July 2010.
Interview with Edward Luck, International Peace Institute, New York, 14 July 2010.
Interview with Francis Deng, United Nations, New York, 13 July 2010.
Interview with John Githongo, Inuka Trust, Nairobi, 13 August 2010.
Interview with Michela Wrong, UK, 19 March 2010.
IREC, 'Report of the Independent Review Commission on the General Elections Held in Kenya on 27 December 2007', 17 September 2008, available online at http://aceproject.org/regions-en/countries-and-territories/KE/reports/independent-review-commission-on-the-general (accessed 20 June 2015).
IRIN News, 'Kenya: Spreading the word of hate', January 22, 2008, available online at www.irinnews.org/report/76346/kenya-spreading-the-word-of-hate (accessed 20 May 2015).
Jopson, B., 'Kofi Annan intervenes in Kenya dispute', *Financial Times*, 18 February 2010, available online at www.ft.com/cms/s/0/fb896caa-1c7f-11df-8456-00144feab49a.html#axzz3b65KJ3xV (accessed 20 May 2015).
Joselow, G., 'US official says Kenya's elections have consequences', *Voice of America*, 7 February 2013, available online at www.voanews.com/content/us-official-says-kenya-elections-have-consequences/1599063.html (accessed 20 May 2015).
Juma, M.K., 'African Mediation of the Kenyan Post-2007 Election Crisis', *Journal of Contemporary African Studies*, 27.3 (2009), pp. 407–30.
Kaberia, J., 'Court Dismisses Uhuru, Ruto Eligibility Case', 15 February 2013, available online at www.capitalfm.co.ke/news/2013/02/court-dismisses-uhuru-ruto-eligibility-case/ (accessed 20 June 2015).
Kagiri, A., 'Mutula backs Imanyara Tribunal Bill', *Capital News*, 10 August 2009, available online at www.capitalfm.co.ke/news/2009/08/mutula-backs-imanyara-tribunal-bill/?wpmp_switcher=mobile (accessed 20 May 2015).
Kagwanja, P. and Southall, R., 'Introduction: Kenya – A Democracy in Retreat?' *Journal of Contemporary African Studies* 27.3, (2009), pp. 259–77.
Kariuki, A., 'Annan to send violence chiefs to The Hague', *Daily Nation*, 13 February 2009, available online at www.nation.co.ke/News/-/1056/529848/-/u1yrxf/-/index.html (accessed 20 May 2015).

Bibliography

Kariuki, A. and Mathenge, O., 'Ocampo Names Kenya chaos suspects', 15 December 2010, *Daily Nation*, available online at www.nation.co.ke/news/Ocampo-names-Kenya-chaos-suspects/-/1056/2119320/-/view/printVersion/-/apwycpz/-/index.html (accessed 20 May 2015).

Kegoro, G., 'Uhuru used the State as a shield against his trial', *Daily Nation*, 6 December 2014, available online at www.nation.co.ke/news/Uhuru-used-the-State-as-a-shield-against-his-trial/-/1056/2547530/-/1284714/-/index.html (accessed 20 May 2015).

Kenya National Commission on Human Rights, *On the Brink of the Precipice: A Human Rights Account of Kenya's Post-Election Violence*, Kenyan National Commission on Human Rights, August 2008, available online at http://fidakenya.org/sites/default/files/khrc-report...on-the-blink.pdf (accessed 20 May 2015).

Kenyan National Commission for Human Rights, 'Still Behaving Badly', Second Periodic Report of the Election Monitoring Project, December 2007, available online at www.rwi.lu.se/NHRIDB/Africa/Kenya/Kenya_KNCHR_Election_Report_2007.pdf (accessed 20 May 2015).

Kenyan National Dialogue and Reconciliation: Commission of Inquiry on Post-Election Violence, 4 March 2008, available online at www.lcil.cam.ac.uk/sites/default/files/LCIL/documents/transitions/Kenya_14_KNDR_Commission_of_Inquiry.pdf (accessed 20 June 2015).

Kenyans for Peace, Truth and Justice, 'Countdown to Deception: 30 Hours that Destroyed Kenya', 18 January 2008, available online at www.africog.org/reports/KPTJ-%20Countdown%20to%20Deception.pdf (accessed 20 May 2015).

Kenyatta, U., 'President Uhuru Kenyatta State of the Nation Address', 27 March 2014, available online at www.kenya-today.com/news/read-president-uhuru-kenyatta-state-union-address-full-speech (accessed 20 May 2015).

Kersten, M., 'A Fatal Attraction: The UN Security Council and the Relationship Between R2P and the International Criminal Court', 27 February 2013, available online at http://justiceinconflict.org/2013/02/27/a-fatal-attraction-the-un-security-council-and-the-relationship-between-r2p-and-the-international-criminal-court/ (accessed on 20 May 2015).

Kiai., M., 'Statement to US House of Representatives', 6 February 2008, available online at https://kenyanemergency.wordpress.com/2008/02/06/maina-kiais-statement-to-us-house-of-representatives/ (accessed 20 May 2015).

Kikoler, N., 'Responsibility to Protect', Keynote paper at the International Conference 'Protecting People in Conflict and Crisis: Responding to the Challenges of a Changing World', Oxford, September 2009, available online at www.rsc.ox.ac.uk/publications/responsibility-to-protect (accessed 20 October 2014).

Kikoler, N., 'Guinea: An Overlooked Case of the Responsibility to Prevent in Practice', in Serena K. Sharma and Jennifer M. Welsh (eds), *The Responsibility to Prevent: Overcoming the Challenges of Atrocity Prevention* (Oxford University Press, 2015), pp. 304–23.

Kimani, M., 'East Africa Feels Blows of Kenyan Crisis', *Africa Renewal* 22.1, 1 April 2008, p. 3, available online at www.un.org/ecosocdev/geninfo/afrec/vol. 22no1/221-kenyan-crisis.html (accessed 20 May 2015).

Kiplagat, S., 'Poll Chaos: Ruto wants court to clear his name', *Daily Nation*, 20 November 2009, available online at www.nation.co.ke/news/politics/-/1064/801576/-/jeuiktz/-/index.html (accessed 20 May 2015).

Klopp, J.M., 'Pilfering the Public: The Problem of Land Grabbing in Contemporary Kenya', *Africa Today*, 47.1 (2000), pp. 7–26.

Knight, A. and Egerton, E., *Routledge Handbook of the Responsibility to Protect* (Routledge, 2012).

Komen, J., 'Waki witnesses on the run', 17 October 2009, *Daily Nation*, available online at www.nation.co.ke/News/politics/-/1064/673588/-/xtpqy1z/-/ (accessed 20 May 2015).

Kouchner, B., 'Statement on Violence in Kenya', 31 January 2008, available online at www.ambafrance-ke.org/Statement-by-Bernard-Kouchner-on (accessed 20 October 2014).

Leonard, D.K., et al., The Political and Institutional Context of the 2007 Kenyan Elections and Reforms Needed for the Future, *Journal of African Elections*, 8.1 (2009), pp. 71–107.

Lindberg, T., 'Protect the People', *Washington Times*, 26 September 2005, available online at www.washingtontimes.com/news/2005/sep/26/20050926-092835-2083r/ (accessed 20 May 2015).

Lindenmayer, E. and Kaye, J.L., 'A Choice for Peace: The Story of 41-days of Mediation in Kenya', *International Peace Institute*, August 2009, available online at http://responsibilitytoprotect.org/kenyamediation_epub.pdf (accessed 20 May 2015).

Lough, R., 'Kenya's Odinga to File Supreme Court Election Petition on Friday', *Reuters*, 14 March 2013, available online at www.reuters.com/article/2013/03/14/us-kenya-elections-petition-idUSBRE92D0TJ20130314 (accessed 20 June 2015).

Luck, E., 'The Responsibility to Protect: Growing Pains or Early Promise', *Ethics and International Affairs*, 24.2 (2010), pp. 349–65.

Maathai, W., 'Statement on the Unrest and Violence in Kenya', 1 January 2008 available online at http://greenbeltmovement.org.s126284.gridserver.com/a.php?id=270 (accessed 20 May 2015).

Maliti, T., 'Kenya: The Long Dark Night for Business', *Africa Report*, November 21, 2008, available online at www.theafricareport.com/archives2/business/3278865-kenya-the-long-dark-night-for-business.html (accessed 20 May 2015).

Maliti, T., 'ICC Prosecutor Asks Court to Decide on Indefinitely Adjourning Kenyatta Case or Terminating it', *International Justice Monitor*, 8 October 2014, available online at www.ijmonitor.org/2014/10/icc-prosecutor-asks-court-to-decide-on-indefinitely-adjourning-kenyatta-case-or-terminating-it/ (accessed 20 June 2015).

Manby, B., 'Was the APRM Process in Kenya a Waste of Time: Lessons that Should be Learned for the Future', *Open Society Institute*, April 2008, available online at www.afrimap.org/english/images/paper/Manby_APRM-Kenya.pdf (accessed 20 May 2015).

Mango, C. and Savula, A., 'Kenya: Foreign Powers Will Not Dictate to the Government', *CCM*, 17 February 2008, available online at https://chamachamwananchi.wordpress.com/2008/02/17/kenya-foreign-powers-will-not-dictate-to-the-government-warns-government/ (accessed 10 April 2013).

Mathenge, G. and Mathangani, P., 'Central MPs Split Over Imanyara Bill' *The Standard*, 30 August 2009, available online at www.standardmedia.co.ke/?articleID=1144022767&story_title= (accessed 20 May 2015).

Mathenge, O., 'Operation Rudi Nyumbani a flop, says rights agency', *Daily Nation*, 28 October 2008, available online at www.nation.co.ke/News/-/1056/484998/-/tlhtvl/-/ (accessed 20 May 2015).

Mathenge, O. and Kadida, J., '400 Post-poll victims apply to join The Hague trials', 2 September 2010, available online at www.nation.co.ke/news/400-victims-apply-to-join-Hague-trials-/-/1056/1002768/-/131t8rw/-/index.html (accessed 20 May 2015).

144 Bibliography

Mathews, K. and Coogan, W.H., 'Kenya and the Rule of Law: The Perspective of Two Volunteers', *Maine Law Review* 60 (2008).

Mayoyo, P., 'Key election chaos witnesses to be flown out', *Daily Nation*, 16 May 2010, available online at www.nation.co.ke/news/Key-election-chaos-witnesses-to-be-flown-out-/-/1056/919788/-/9f2u5d/-/index.html (accessed 20 May 2015).

Mayoyo, P. and AFP, 'Ocampo accuses Kenya of sabotage in chaos probe', *Daily Nation*, 29 May 2011, available online at www.nation.co.ke/news/politics/Ocampo-accuses-Kenya-of-sabotage-in-chaos-probe-/-/1064/1171624/-/r9bq4ez/-/index.html (accessed 20 May 2015).

McKenzie, D., 'ICC Prosecutor: Suspects in Kenya violence will be tried', *CNN*, 5 November 2009, available online at http://edition.cnn.com/2009/WORLD/africa/11/05/kenya.icc.trials/ (20 May 2015).

McVeigh, T., 'Dozens Die in Kenyan Riots', *Guardian*, 27 January 2008, available online at www.theguardian.com/world/2008/jan/27/kenya.tracymcveigh (20 June 2015).

Megret, F., 'ICC, R2P and the International Community's Evolving Interventionist Toolkit', 23 December 2010, available online at http://papers.ssrn.com/sol3/papers.cfm?abstract_id=1933111 (accessed 20 May 2015).

Mennecke, M., 'The International Criminal Court', in Monica Serrano and Thomas G. Weiss (eds), *The International Politics of Human Rights: Rallying to the R2P Cause?* (Routledge, 2014), pp. 87–104.

Menya, W., 'Activists protest over bid to delay ICC trial', 8 January 2010, *Daily Nation*, available online at www.nation.co.ke/News/-/1056/838602/-/voss26/-/index.html (accessed 20 May 2015).

Michuki, J., Hansard, Kenya National Assembly, Official Report, 4 February 2009.

Mills, K., The Responsibility to Protect and the International Criminal Court: Competing or Complementary' *AP R2P Brief* 4.2 (2014), available online at www.r2pasiapacific.org/docs/R2P%20Ideas%20in%20Brief/R2P%20and%20the%20ICC%20Vol%204%20No%202%202014.pdf (accessed 20 May 2015).

MOD, The British Army Overseas Deployments, 'The British Army in Africa', available online at www.army.mod.uk/operations-deployments/22724.aspx (accessed 20 May 2015).

Mosoku, G., 'Questions Raised Over Envoy's Letter to UN', *The Standard*, 13 May 2013, available online at www.standardmedia.co.ke/article/2000083468/queries-raised-over-envoy-s-letter-to-un (accessed 20 June 2015).

Mueller, S., 'The Political Economy of Kenya's Crisis', *Journal of Eastern African Studies*, 2.2 (2008), pp. 185–210.

Mukinda, F., '6,000 could be charged over Kenya Poll Chaos', *Daily Nation*, March 17, 2011, www.nation.co.ke/News/politics/6000+could+be+charged+over+poll+chaos+//1064/1128278/-/91n68/-/index.html (accessed 20 June 2015).

Mutiga, M., 'Ocampo writes to judges over threats', *Daily Nation*, 30 January 2010, available online at www.nation.co.ke/News/-/1056/852780/-/vpwpw9/-/index.html (accessed 20 May 2015).

Mutua, M., 'Eyes on Other Commissioner's as Murungi Resigns', *The Standard*, 20 April 2011, available online at www.standardmedia.co.ke/mobile/?articleID=2000008083&story_title=Eyes%20on%20other%20TJRC%20officials%20as%20Murungi%20resigns (accessed 20 June 2015).

Mwagiru, M., *The Water's Edge: Mediation of Violent Electoral Conflict in Kenya* (Institute of Diplomacy and International Studies, 2008).

Mwangi, M., 'Tribunal: Kenya to beg Ocampo for more time', *Daily Nation*, 21 September 2009.

Mynott, A., 'Huge financial cost of Kenya cabinet', *BBC News*, 17 April 2008, available online at http://news.bbc.co.uk/1/hi/world/africa/7352261.stm (accessed 20 May 2015).
Nairobi Star, 'Kenya Donors Have Few Options in Crisis', 19 January 2008.
Namunane, B., 'Poll violence: Kibaki Hints at Amnesty', 20 October 2008, available online at www.nation.co.ke/news/-/1056/482520/-/5fp3g9z/-/index.html (accessed 20 May 2015).
Namunane, B., 'No End to Draft Illegal Edit Puzzle', 21 July 2010, *Daily Nation* available online at www.nation.co.ke/Kenya-Referendum/No-end-to-draft-illegal-edit-puzzle-/-/926046/962444/-/y7pqkpz/-/index.html (accessed 20 May 2015).
National Assembly, 'The Report by the Parliamentary Select Committee to Investigate Ethnic Clashes in Western and other parts of Kenya', 1992.
Ndungú, C.G., 'Lessons to Be Learned: An Analysis of the Final Report of Kenya's Truth, Justice and Reconciliation Commission', International Centre for Transitional Justice Briefing, 19 May 2014, available online at www.ictj.org/publication/kenya-TJRC-lessons-learned (accessed 20 June 2015).
New York Times, 'Rice in Kenya to press talks to end crisis', 18 February 2008, available online at www.nytimes.com/2008/02/18/world/africa/18iht-kenya.1.10135967.html?_r=0 (accessed 20 May 2015).
Nguyai, L., Hansard, Kenya National Assembly, Official Report, 4 February 2009.
Nguyen, K. and Hull, C., 'Kenyan minister criticizes crisis mediator Annan', *Reuters*, 12 February 2008, available online at http://uk.reuters.com/article/2008/02/12/uk-kenya-crisis-idUKL1264995120080212 (accessed 20 May 2015).
Njeri, J., 'Kibaki: Dream or Nightmare', *BBC News*, 2 January 2008, available online at http://news.bbc.co.uk/1/hi/world/africa/7079210.stm (accessed 20 May 2015).
Nyongo, A.',Petition to UN Security Council regarding Kenya cases at the ICC', *Capital FM News*, 14 March 2011, available online at www.capitalfm.co.ke/eblog/2011/03/14/petition-to-un-security-council-regarding-kenyan-cases-at-the-icc/ (accessed 20 May 2015).
Nzwili, F., 'Kenyans Rejoice at Collapse of ICC Case Against President Kenyatta', *Christian Science Monitor*, 5 December 2014, available online at www.csmonitor.com/World/Africa/2014/1205/Kenyans-rejoice-at-collapse-of-ICC-case-against-President-Kenyatta-video (accessed 20 June 2015).
Odnunga, D., 'Witnesses at risk, warns lobby', *Daily Nation*, 11 January 2010, available online at www.nation.co.ke/news/politics/-/1064/840302/-/jcf42yz/-/index.html (accessed 20 May 2015).
Office of the AU Panel of Eminent African Personalities, *Back from the Brink: The 2008 Mediation Process and Reforms in Kenya*, African Union Commission, available online at www.knchr.org/Portals/0/GeneralReports/backFromBrink_web.pdf (accessed 20 May 2015).
Office of the Prosecutor, 'Notice of Withdrawal of Charges Against Uhuru Muigai Kenyatta', 5 December 2014, available online at www.icc-cpi.int/iccdocs/doc/doc1879204.pdf (accessed 20 June 2015).
Ogemba, P., 'Pattni Cleared in Goldenberg Scam', *Daily Nation*, 19 April 2013, available online at www.nation.co.ke/News/politics/Pattni-cleared-in-Goldenberg-scam/-/1064/1753240/-/146dhe5z/-/index.html (accessed 20 June 2015).
OHCHR, 'Fact-Finding Mission to Kenya', 6–28 February 2008, available online at http://responsibilitytoprotect.org/OHCHR%20Kenya%20Report.pdf (accessed 20 May 2010).
Olick, F., 'Kenya: Bensouda Requests Indefinite Adjournment of Uhuru Case Due to

146 Bibliography

Lack of Evidence', *All Africa*, 5 September 2014, available online at http://allafrica.com/stories/201409080024.html (accessed 20 June 2015).

Opiyo, P., 'Kivuitu Wins Jurist Award', *All Africa Stories*, 13 December 2007.

Orford, A., *International Authority and the Responsibility to Protect* (Cambridge University Press, 2011).

Pallister, D., 'Scandals Cast Shadow Over Kenya's Government', *Guardian*, 6 July 2004, available online at www.theguardian.com/world/2004/jul/06/kenya.davidpallister (accessed 20 June 2015).

Panapress, 'Kagame calls for military intervention in Kenya crisis', 31 January 2008, available online at www.panapress.com/Kagame-calls-for-military-intervention-in-Kenyan-crisis-13-511451-17-lang1-index.html (accessed 20 May 2015).

Patinkin, J., 'Uhuru Kenyatta's election victory is upheld by the Supreme Court', *Guardian*, 30 March 2013, available online at www.theguardian.com/world/2013/mar/31/kenya-court-upholds-kenyatta-victory (accessed 20 May 2015).

Pattison, J., *Humanitarian Intervention and the Responsibility to Protect: Who Should Intervene?* (Oxford University Press, 2010).

Permanent Mission of Brazil to the United Nations, 'Responsibility While Protecting', UN Doc. A/66/551-S/2011/701, 11 November 2011.

Pflanz, M., 'As President Kenyatta Faces Accusers, Hague Court Case Nears Collapse', *Christian Science Monitor*, 8 October 2014, available online at www.csmonitor.com/World/Africa/2014/1008/As-President-Kenyatta-faces-accusers-Hague-court-case-nears-collapse-video (accessed 20 June 2015)

Pflanz, M., 'Uhuru Kenyatta's ICC Prosecution Close to Collapse as Lawyers Demand Acquittal', *Telegraph*, 8 October 2014, available online at www.telegraph.co.uk/news/worldnews/africaandindianocean/kenya/11149256/Uhuru-Kenyattas-ICC-prosecution-close-to-collapse-as-lawyers-demand-acquittal.html (accessed 20 June 2015).

Ping., J., 'The Responsibility to Protect in Africa', Addis Ababa, 23 October 2008, available online at www.responsibilitytoprotect.org/index.php/component/content/article/129-africa/1910-african-unions-commission-on-r2pkeynote-speech-by-chairperson-jean-ping (accessed 20 June 2015).

Preamble to the Agreement on the Principles of Partnership of the Coalition Government, 28 February 2008.

Public Radio International, 'America Abroad', reported and hosted by Deborah Amos, 7 March 2009; 'International Community Coming to Realize "The Responsibility to Protect"', *UCLA Today*, 15 April 2009, available online at http://today.ucla.edu/portal/ut/international-community-coming-88897.aspx (accessed 22 April 2010).

Relief Web, 'Kenya PM sees extension to court deadline', 18 February 2009, available online at http://reliefweb.int/report/kenya/kenya-pm-sees-extension-local-court-deadline (accessed 20 May 2015).

Relief Web, 'Kenya: Cabinet decides on TJRC – Kenya', 30 July 2009, available online at http://reliefweb.int/report/kenya/kenya-cabinet-decides-tjrc (accessed 20 May 2015).

Remarks by Ambassador Susan E. Rice, U.S. Permanent Representative to the United Nations, on the UN Security Council and the Responsibility to Protect, at the International Peace Institute Vienna Seminar (15 June 2009).

Report of the Judicial Commission Appointed to Inquire into Tribal Clashes in Kenya, 1999.

Reuters, 'EU Condemns Pre-election Violence in Kenya', 21 December 2007, available online at www.reuters.com/article/2007/12/21/us-kenya-election-idUSL2120415120071221 (accessed 20 May 2015).

Reynolds, P., 'Diplomacy Falters as Kenya Burns', *BBC News*, 4 January 2008, http://news.bbc.co.uk/1/hi/world/africa/7170600.stm (accessed 20 May 2015).

Rice, X., 'Riots and vote-rigging claims as Kenyan polls go to the wire', *Guardian*, 30 December 2007, available online at www.theguardian.com/world/2007/dec/30/kenya.xanrice (accessed 20 May 2015).

Rice, X., 'Fury as Kenyan leader names ministers', *The Guardian*, 8 January 2008, available online at www.theguardian.com/world/2008/jan/08/kenya.xanrice (accessed 20 May 2015).

Rice, X., 'MoD Threatens to Halt Training of Kenyan Military over Claims of Rights Abuses', *Guardian*, 29 July 2008, available online at www.guardian.co.uk/world/2008/jul/29/kenya.military (accessed 20 May 2015).

Rice, X., 'UN condemns executions carried out by Kenyan police', *Guardian*, 25 February 2009, available online at www.theguardian.com/world/2009/feb/25/un-kenya-executions (accessed 20 May 2015).

Rice, X., 'International Criminal Court to investigate violence after 2007 Kenya Election', *Guardian*, 31 March 2010, available online at www.theguardian.com/world/2010/mar/31/international-criminal-court-kenya-violence (accessed 20 May 2015).

Rice, X., 'Omar al-Bashir tarnishes Kenya's landmark day', *Guardian* 27 August 2010, available online at www.theguardian.com/world/2010/aug/27/omar-al-bashir-war-crimes-kenya (accessed 20 May 2015).

Rieff, D., 'R2P, R.I.P', *New York Times*, 7 November 2011.

Rome Statute of the International Criminal Court, A/CONF.183/9 of 17 July 1998.

Ross, W., 'Two ministers suspended in corruption scandal', *BBC News*, 14 February 2010, available online at http://news.bbc.co.uk/1/hi/world/africa/8515135.stm (accessed 20 May 2015).

Rwenji, C., 'Kilonzo says chaos witness threatened', *Daily Nation*, 23 November 2009, available online at www.nation.co.ke/news/-/1056/802518/-/3ebgogz/-/index.html (accessed 20 May 2015).

Sahnoun, M., 'Uphold Continent's Contribution to Human Rights, Urges Top Diplomat', *All Africa*, 21 July 2009, available online at http://allafrica.com/stories/200907210549.html (accessed 20 May 2015).

Saxon, D., 'The International Criminal Court and the Prevention of Crimes' in Serena K. Sharma and Jennifer M. Welsh (eds), *The Responsibility to Prevent: Overcoming the Challenges of Atrocity Prevention* (Oxford University Press, 2015), pp. 119–59.

Schabas, W., *Introduction to the International Criminal Court*, 4th edn (Cambridge University Press, 2011).

Sharma, S.K. and Welsh, J.M. (eds), *The Responsibility to Prevent: Overcoming the Challenges of Atrocity Prevention* (Oxford University Press, 2015).

Shiundu, A., 'Uhuru Kenyatta, William Ruto Failed to Stop The ICC Cases Despite Spirited Fight, *The Standard*, 9 October 2014, available online at www.standardmedia.co.ke/worldcup/?articleID=2000137549&story_title=uhuru-kenyatta-william-ruto-failed-to-stop-the-icc-cases-despite-spirited-fight&pageNo=2 (accessed 20 June 2015).

Sihanya, B. and Okello, D., 'Mediating Kenya's Post-Election Crisis: The Politics and Limits of Power Sharing Agreement', in Karuti Kanyinga and Duncan Okello (eds), *Tensions and Reversals in Democratic Transitions: The Kenya 2007 General Elections* (Society for International Development: Nairobi, 2010).

Smith, A.M., 'The Emergence of International Justice as Coercive Diplomacy: Challenges and Prospects', *HRP Research Working Paper Series* (Cambridge, MA: Harvard Law School, 2012)

148 Bibliography

Sneider, M., 'Implementing the Responsibility to Protect in Kenya and Beyond', address to the World Affairs Council of Oregon, Portland State University, Portland, Oregon, 5 March 2010, available online at www.crisisgroup.org/en/publication-type/speeches/2010/implementing-the-responsibility-to-protect-in-kenya-and-beyond.aspx (accessed 20 October 2014);

Snyder, J. and Vinjamuri, L., 'Trials and Errors: Principle and Pragmatism in Strategies of International Justice', *International Security*, 8, 3 (2003/4), pp. 5–44.

South Consulting, 'KNDR Review Reports' available online at www.south.co.ke/index.php/projects-and-reports/kndr-project/2-uncategorised/11-review-reports (accessed 20 June 2015).

South Consulting, 'The Kenyan National Dialogue and Reconciliation (KNDR) Monitoring Project', Draft Review Report, April 2011, available online at www.iccnow.org/documents/April2011KNDRReport.pdf (accessed 20 June 2015).

Steinberg, D., 'Responsibility to Protect: Coming of Age?' *Global Responsibility to Protect*, 1.4 (2009), pp. 432–41.

Stubb, A., 'Keynote address at Hanforum', 28 August 2009, available online at http://formin.finland.fi/public/default.aspx?contentid=169644&nodeid=15149&contentlan=2&culture=en-US (accessed 22 April 2010);

Sunday Nation, 'Britain Does Not Recognise Kibaki', 20 January 2008.

Sydney Morning Herald, 'Annan Hopes for Kenyan Deal Next Week', 9 February 2008, available online at www.smh.com.au/world/annan-hopes-for-kenyan-deal-next-week-20080208-1r5z.html (accessed 20 June 2015).

Thavis, J., 'Pope appeals for immediate end to ethnic violence in Kenya', Catholic News Service, 7 January 2008, available online at www.catholicnews.com/data/stories/cns/0800088.htm (accessed 20 May 2015).

The East African Standard, 'Steadman releases its last poll before election',19 December 2007.

The Economist, 'The Responsibility to Protect: An Idea Whose Time Has Come – And Gone?' 23 July 2009, available online at www.economist.com/node/14087788 (accessed 20 June 2015).

The Guardian, 'Uhuru Kenyatta's election victory upheld by Supreme Court', 30 March 2013, available online at www.theguardian.com/world/2013/mar/31/kenya-court-upholdskenyatta-victory (accessed 20 May 2015).

The Hague Justice Portal, 'ICC rejects Kenya's admissibility challenge', 31 May 2011, available online at www.haguejusticeportal.net/index.php?id=12758 (accessed 20 May 2015).

The Independent International Commission on Kosovo, *The Kosovo Report: Conflict, International Response, Lessons Learned* (Oxford University Press, 2001).

The International Republican Institute, 'Kenya Presidential, Parliamentary and Local Elections, December 2007: Election Observation Mission Final Report', available online at www.iri.org/sites/default/files/Kenya%27s%202007%20Presidental,%20Parliamentary%20and%20Local%20Elections.pdf (accessed 20 May 2015).

The Special Tribunal for Kenya Bill, 2009 'Memorandum of Objects and Reasons' available online at www.kenyalaw.org/Downloads/Bills/2009/The_Special_Tribunal_for_Kenya_Statute_2009.pdf (accessed 20 June 2015).

The Standard, 'EU Adds Pressure on Leaders', 14 January 2008.

The Standard, 'Ranneberger Explains US Stance on Crisis', 5 February 2008.

The Standard, 'US, Canada Ban Threat as Talks Register Gains', 5 February 2008.

The Standard, 'Agree or Else...', 8 February 2008.

The Standard, 'ODM Parliamentary group meeting rejects Waki Report', 30 October 2008, available online at www.standardmedia.co.ke/article/1143998194/odm-parliamentary-group-meeting-rejects-waki-report (accessed 20 May 2015).

The Standard, 'The Verbatim Statement of ICC's Bensouda', 22 October 2012, available online at www.standardmedia.co.ke/article/2000069022/the-verbatim-statement-of-iccs-bensouda (accessed 20 May 2015).

The Standard, 'IGAD Congratulates President Uhuru Kenyatta on ICC Case Withdrawal', 8 December 2014, available online at www.standardmedia.co.ke/article/2000143791/igad-congratulates-president-uhuru-kenyatta-on-icc-case-withdrawal (accessed 20 June 2015).

The Telegraph, 'Kenyan President says he is vindicated after ICC drops charges', 5 December 2014, available online at www.telegraph.co.uk/news/worldnews/africaandindianocean/kenya/11275616/Kenyan-president-says-he-is-vindicated-after-ICC-drops-charges.html (accessed 20 May 2015).

The White House, Office of the Press Secretary, 'Fact Sheet: A Comprehensive Strategy and New Tools to Prevent and Respond to Atrocities', 23 April 2012, available online at www.whitehouse.gov/the-press-office/2012/04/23/fact-sheet-comprehensive-strategy-and-new-tools-prevent-and-respond-atro (accessed 20 June 2015).

TJRC, Full Report of the Truth, Justice and Reconciliation Commission (TJRC Report), May 2013, available online at www.kenyamoja.com/tjrc-report/ (accessed 20 May 2015).

Tortora, B. and Rheault, M., 'In Kenya most registered voters lack required voting cards', available online at www.gallup.com/poll/157874/kenya-registered-voters-lack-required-voting-card.aspx (accessed 20 May 2015).

Tutu, D., 'Responsibility to Protect', *International Herald Tribune*, 20 February 2008.

UN Security Council, 'Statement by the President of the Security Council', S/PRST/2008/4, 6 February 2008.

United Nations General Assembly, '2005 World Summit Outcome', A/60/L.1, 20 September 2005, paragraphs 138 and 139.

United Nations News Centre, 'Secretary-General calls for restraint from all Kenyans in post-election violence', 31 December 2007, available online at www.un.org/apps/news/story.asp?NewsID=25189&Cr=kenya&Cr1#.VWB6OqZ95FU (accessed 20 May 2015).

United Nations News Centre, 'UN Genocide Adviser Urges End to Violence, Sends Staffers There', January 2008, available online at www.un.org/apps/news/story.asp?NewsID=25425&Cr=kenya&Cr1 (accessed 25 March 2010).

United Nations News Centre, 'Ban Ki-moon calls on Kenyans to "wake up" and halt the violence', 1 February 2008, available online at www.un.org/apps/news/story.asp?NewsID=25477#.VWFdraZ95FU (accessed May 2015).

United Nations, 'Press conference by United Nations Emergency Relief Coordinator to Update Humanitarian Situation in Kenya, 9 January 2008', available online at www.un.org/press/en/2008/080109_Holmes.doc.htm (accessed 20 May 2015).

United Nations, 'Press conference to seek flash appeal seeking more than $40 million in humanitarian, early recovery aid for 500 000 Kenyans', 16 January 2008, available online at www.un.org/press/en/2008/080116_Holmes.doc.htm (accessed 20 May 2015).

United Nations, Department of Public Information, 'Secretary-General Troubled by Escalating Kenyan Tensions, Violence', SG/SM/11356-AFR/1641, 2 January 2008, available online at www.un.org/press/en/2008/sgsm11356.doc.htm (accessed 20 May 2015).

US Sub-Committee on Africa and Global Health, 'The Political Crisis in Kenya: A Call for Justice and Peaceful Resolution', 6 February 2008.

Van Leeuwen, S., 'Kenyatta's Hague Speech: God Bless Kenya, God Bless the ICC', *All Africa*, 11 October 2014, available online at http://allafrica.com/stories/201410131464.html (accessed 20 June 2015).

Volman, D., 'U.S. Military Activities in Kenya, African Security Research Project', January 2008, available online at http://concernedafricascholars.org/african-security-research-project/?p=3 (accessed 20 May 2015).

Wachira, G., *Citizens in Action: Making Peace in the Post-Election Crisis in Kenya – 2008* (NPI-Africa, 2010).

Wafula, C., 'Don't Panic, Raila tells leaders', *Daily Nation*, 18 November 2009, available online at www.nation.co.ke/news/politics/-/1064/688104/-/kcxvyoz/-/index.html (accessed 20 May 2015).

Wamai, N. 'The International Criminal Court and the Kenyan Election', *The Huffington Post*, 7 May 2013, available online at www.huffingtonpost.co.uk/gates-cambridge-scholars/kenya-election_b_3206562.html (accessed 20 June 2015).

Wanabisi, L., 'Kenyan MPs frustrate special court bill again', 2 December 2009, available online at www.capitalfm.co.ke/news/2009/12/kenyan-mps-frustrate-special-courts-bill-again/ (accessed 20 May 2015).

Weiss, T., 'Halting Atrocities in Kenya', Great Decisions 2010, available online at www.globalr2p.org/media/files/kenya-fpa-weiss.pdf (accessed 20 May 2015).

Welsh, J.M. (ed.), *Humanitarian Intervention and International Relations* (Oxford University Press, 2006).

Welsh, J.M., 'Responsibility to Protect and the Language of Crimes: Collective Action and Individual Culpability', in Don Scheid (ed.), *Armed Humanitarian Intervention* (Cambridge University Press, 2014).

Wheeler, N.J., *Saving Strangers* (Oxford University Press, 2000).

Wrong, M., *It's Our Turn to Eat: The Story of a Kenyan Whistleblower* (Harper Collins, 2009).

Index

accountability *see* impunity
Adeniji, Oluyemi 61
African Peer Review Mechanism 34–5
African Union: and ICC cases 103, 111–12; importance of role in mediation 56–60; and KNDR process 45–60
African Union Summit 103
Agenda Item 4 61–5, 76, 77, 78, 84
Akiwumi Commission 33
Ali, Mohammed Hussein 22, 37, 79, 80, 93, 94
All Africa Conference of Churches (AACC) 47, 48
Alston, Philip 79–80, 113
Anderson, David 77
Annan, Kofi: abilities of 57–8; and CIPEV report 87; and friction within Coalition 76–7, 78; and General Election (2013) 106, 121; and ICC 11; and impunity 11, 62, 86, 87, 89, 128; and KNDR process 11, 45, 48–50, 52, 53, 54–5, 57–8, 61, 62, 75, 76–7, 78; and Kosovo 2–3; and Responsibility to Protect 45, 56, 130; and Special Tribunal 89
Arbour, Louise 47, 105
armed militia 31–2
Atrocity Prevention Board 4–5
Australia 58

Ban Ki-Moon 46, 47, 52
Barasa, Walter 115
Barkan, Joel 52
al-Bashir, Omar 83–4
Bensouda, Fatou 101, 104, 115–16, 117–18
biometric voter registration (BVR) 108
Brown, Stephen 38
Bruce, Colin 48
Bruce-Lockhart, Katherine 108

Cabinet: and constitutional referendum 20–2, 93; of Grand Coalition 76–8; and Special Tribunal 89–90
campaigning: election 24, 36, 37, 105, 107, 109; referendum 82–3
Canada 2, 58
Carson, Johnnie 106
Central Province 25–6
Centre for International Conflict Resolution 57
Chesterman, Simon 129–30
CIPEV 13, 62, 64, 76, 84–7, 113, 131
civil society: and impunity 90, 112; and KNDR 51; and referendum 83; and Responsibility to Protect (R2P) 5
Coalition Government *see* Government of National Unity
Cohen, Roger 56
collective responsibility 4
Columbia University 57
Commission of Inquiry into Post-Election Violence (CIPEV) 13, 62, 64, 76, 84–7, 113, 131
Concerned Citizens for Peace (CCP) 51
constitution: referendum 20–1, 63, 82–3, 95; reform to 31, 34, 62–3, 76, 81–4, 95
Constitution of Kenya (Amendment) Bill 88, 89
Constitutional Review Committee 62–3
Coordination and Liaison Office (CLO) 63–4
Corell, Hans 53–4
corruption 33, 77, 81

Daily Nation 88
deferral of court cases 101–4
democracy in Kenya 31, 34–5
demonstrations, banning of 24
Deng, Francis 47, 128

Index

deterrence, and ICC 6–7, 101, 109–10
Dieng, Adama 107
displacement 27–8, 32, 80–1
dispute resolution mechanism 78
donor agencies/governments 29, 35, 37–8, 58, 81

economic impact of violence 28, 29
electoral campaigns 24, 36, 37, 105, 107, 109
Electoral Commission of Kenya (ECK) 21, 22, 35–6, 61, 82
Erler, Gernot 53–4
escalation prevention 60
ethnicity issues 32, 36, 107
European Union 22, 36, 37, 58, 114
European Union Observer Mission 36, 37
Evans, Gareth 10, 56

Ferstman, Carla 119
Focal Points 5
Forum of Former African Heads of States 48
France 47, 103
Frazer, Jendayi 48

Gaynor, Fergal 116
General Election (2002) 20, 34
General Election (2007): calm voting 21; campaign of 36; election day 21, 108; and Electoral Commission of Kenya 35–6; forensic audit of 52–3; immediate aftermath of 19–23; impact of violence 27–30; and Independent Review Commission 61; independent reviews of 53; irregularities 21–2; and the media 107, 108; possible re-run 52–3; pre-poll preparedness 37–8; pre-poll violence 37; predictability of violence 34–8; results 21–2, 108; rigging 22–3, 64; turnout 21; underlying causes of violence 30–4; violence unfolds 22–7; world watches 46–9; *see also* violence, post-election
General Election (2013) 1–2, 101–2, 106–10; and ICC 109–15; and KNDR process 109; lack of true reconciliation 110; positive outcome of 108–10; pre-election violence 107; and shadow of 2007 election 107; tallying process 108; and underlying issues 121; voting patterns 32
Gettleman, Jeffrey 24–5
Githongo, John 38, 64
Global Centre for R2P 109–10, 131

Global Focal Points Network 5
governance crisis 31
Government of Kenya (2013): election of 106–10; and ICC 110–19; and witness intimidation 113–15
Government of National Unity: arguments over Cabinet 76–7; and constitutional reform 81–4, 95; continuing insecurity 79–80; discord within 76–81; and displacement crisis 80–1; and ICC 89, 91–6, 101–4; and impunity 84–91; and ministerial suspensions 77–8; and perpetrators of violence 84–91, 129; power struggles 77; public view of 78; and reforms 78–9, 107; and Special Tribunal 88–91; and UN Special Rapporteur 80; *see also* KNDR process

Hannon, Lucy 81
Hassan, Isaac 82
hate speech 36, 83, 107
Holmes, John 29
human rights activists 79
Human Rights Watch 24, 26, 27, 56, 60, 65
humanitarian activities/aid 28–30

ICC *see* International Criminal Court (ICC)
ICISS 2, 3, 4, 8, 56, 60
IDP situation 27–8, 32, 80–1
Imanyara, Gitobu 75, 90–1, 93
Implementing the Responsibility to Protect 4, 9, 60
impunity: and CIPEV report 62, 85–7; continuing problem 128; and domestic prosecution of perpetrators of violence 84–91; and ICC 91–4, 101–21; and international actors 38; and mediation 129; and sovereignty 9; and Special Tribunal 88–91; and Truth, Justice and Reconciliation Commission 91–2; and UN Special Rapporteur 79; as underlying cause of violence 32–4; and witness intimidation 113–15
incitement 36, 83, 107, 108
Independent Electoral and Boundaries Commission (IEBC) 1, 63, 107, 108
Independent Review Commission (IREC) 61, 64, 82
Intergovernmental Authority on Development (IGAD) summit 51, 102–3
Interim Independent Electoral Commission 82

Index   153

Internally Displaced Persons (IDP) 27–8, 32, 80–1
International Association of Democratic Lawyers 93
International Coalition for R2P 8
International Commission of Jurists 35–6
International Commission on Intervention and State Sovereignty (ICISS) 2, 3, 4, 8, 56, 60
International Committee for the Red Cross 29
International Criminal Court (ICC): African bias 105–6, 118; and African Union 103, 111–12; aim of 6; attempts to block 110–13; and al-Bashir, Omar 83–4; challenges facing 7, 117–18; collapse of cases 115, 117–19; compromises within 129; considering information 46; conviction rate 7; as court of last resort 92–4, 101–21; criticisms of 7, 105–6, 118–19; and deferral of cases 102–4; deterrent function 6–7, 8, 109–10; and enforcement 7; and evidence gathering 118; evolution of 5–7, 129–30; expectations of 130–1; and General Election (2013) 109–10; and Government of Kenya (2013) 110–19; and Government of National Unity 89, 91–6, 101–4; and impunity 86, 91–4, 101–21; instrumentalising of 104–6; jurisdiction of 7; justice in the hands of the accused 110–15; Kenya to withdraw from 112; and Kenyatta, Uhuru 13, 89, 93, 94, 101, 105–6, 109–12, 115–20; launches investigation 91, 93; legitimacy of 7, 11; naming of suspects 93–4, 102, 104–5; and Ocampo, Luis Moreno 89, 92, 93–4, 102, 104, 114, 119; opening an investigation 7, 11; perception of 130; pre-trial chamber 93; and public expectation 92; relationship with R2P 8–10, 11–12, 129; and Rome Statute 105; and Ruto, William 94, 101, 104, 105–6, 109–10, 111, 112, 115, 119; and Special Tribunal 89, 90; and state cooperation 129; Status Conference 115–17; tensions within 129–30; threshold for intervention 9–10; and UN Security Council 129–30; and witness intimidation 113–15
International Crisis Group (ICG) 22–3
international impact of crisis 28–9
International Peace Institute 59

international response 37–8, 46–9, 131

Juma, Dan 24
Juma, Monica 28–9

Kagame, Paul 30
Kalenjin communities 23, 24, 25–6, 32, 105, 109, 110
Kamau, Macharia 111
Karua, Martha 50, 53, 59, 90–1
Kay, Steven 116
Kaye, Josie 53, 54, 55
Kegoro, George 112
Kenyan African National Unity (KANU) 20
Kenyan Association of Manufacturers 51
Kenyan Elections Observers Log 21
Kenyan Human Rights Commission (KHRC) 24
Kenyan National Commission for Human Rights (KNCHR) 23–4, 35, 37, 84, 87
Kenyan National Dialogue and Reconciliation process *see* KNDR
Kenyan Private Sector Alliance 28, 51
Kenyan Red Cross 29, 50, 51, 80
Kenyans for Peace, Truth and Justice (KPTJ) 51
Kenyatta International Conference Centre (KICC) 21, 22, 23
Kenyatta, Jomo 31, 32
Kenyatta, Uhuru: 'alliance of the accused' 13, 101, 105–6; apologises to the people of Kenya 127–8; case collapses 117–19; and CIPEV report 87; and General Election (2013) 1, 106, 107, 108, 109–10; and ICC 13, 89, 93, 94, 101, 105–6, 109–12, 115–20; inaugural address 111; and outstanding criminal cases 127–8; and post-election violence 93, 94; and State of the Nation Address 127; trial delayed 115–17
Kersten, Mark 129–30
Kiai, Maina 35, 64
Kiambaa massacre 25, 93–4
Kibaki, Mwai: and CIPEV report 86, 87; and Coalition 55–6, 64, 76–8; and constitutional reform 34, 81, 82; and Electoral Commission of Kenya 35; and General Election (2002) 20–1; and General Election (2007) 20, 22–4, 30, 35, 38; and ICC 104, 105; and impunity 33, 86; inauguration of in 2002 20; and KNDR process 45, 47–8, 49–50, 51–2, 58; meets with Condaleeza Rice 55; and

Kibaki, Mwai *continued*
  ministerial suspensions 77–8; and nominations 78; and past injustices 75, 86; and post-election violence 23–4, 33, 51; and Special Tribunal 87, 90; sworn in 22; *see also* Party of National Unity (PNU)
Kibera 27
Kikuyu communities 23–6, 28, 31, 32, 36, 105, 109, 110
Kikwete, Jakaya 55
Kilaguni Lodge, Tsavo National Park 53–4
Kilonzo, Mutula 50, 89, 90, 114
Kiplagat, Bethuel 92
Kiraithe, Eric 103
Kisumu 26
Kivuitu, Samuel 21, 22, 35–6
KNDR process: Agenda of 51; and Agenda Item 4 61–5; and Annan, Kofi 11, 45, 48–50, 52, 53, 54–5, 57–8, 61, 62, 75, 76–7, 78; as atrocity prevention tool 57; best practice analysis 57; and civil society input 51; compromises within 128–9; discord after the accord 76–81; early interventions 47–8; effectiveness of 57–60; and far-reaching reforms 63–5; formal negotiations begin 50–2; and General Election (2013) 109; impediments to 48; importance of African Union role 56–60; and impunity 129; and Kibaki, Mwai 45, 47–8, 49–50, 51–2, 58; as model of R2P 10–11, 56–60; negotiations drag on 54–6; and Odinga, Raila 45, 47–8, 49–50, 55–6; and ODM 48, 50, 51–2, 53–6; outside input 51; overcoming the political crisis 52–4; Panel of Eminent Africans 48–56; and PNU 48, 50, 51–4, 58–9; and power-sharing 53–6; press briefings 50–1; and pressure from external actors 58–9; as preventive action 60, 61–3; road map for negotiations 51; set-backs 51–2; suspension of peace talks 55
Kosgey, Henry 93–4
Kosovo 2
Kouchner, Bernard 47
Kriegler report 82
Kufour, John 48

Lambsdorff, Alexander 22
land disputes 32
Lindenmayer, Elisabeth 53, 54, 55
live broadcast ban 24, 52
Luck, Edward 10, 46–7, 57, 59, 60

Luhya communities 23, 25–6
Luo communities 23, 24, 25–6, 36, 105

Maccaire, Rob 102
Mathai, Wangari 30
Mathare 27
Mbalambala 33
media 1, 24, 25, 36, 50–1, 52, 107, 108
mediation *see* KNDR process
Megret, Frederic 8
Mennecke, Martin 9
Michuki, John 88
militia, armed 31
Mills, Kurt 6–7, 10
Mkapa, Benjamin 48, 50
Mohamed, Amina 118
Moi, Daniel Arap 31, 32, 82
Mudavadi, Musalia 22, 50
Mueller, Suzanne 31
Mungiki 26, 31, 94
Museveni, Yoweri 48, 49
Musyoka, Kalonzo 30, 48, 102–3
Muthaura, Francis 93, 94, 115
Mutunga, Willy 127
Mwagiru, Makumi 27, 34, 59
Mynott, Adam 77

National Accord and Reconciliation Act 54, 55
National Alliance Rainbow Coalition (NARC) 20–1, 31, 34
National Cohesion and Integration Commission (NCIC) 32, 83, 107
National Focal Points 5
NATO 2
Nguyai, Lewis 88
Nyanza 26

Obama, Barack 82
Ocampo Six 103–4
Ocampo, Luis Moreno 89, 92, 93–4, 102, 104, 114, 119
Odinga, Raila: and CIPEV report 87; and Coalition 55–6, 64, 76–7; and constitutional reform 20, 21, 81, 82; and General Election (2002) 20; and General Election (2007) 20, 21, 22, 23, 30; and General Election (2013) 1, 108; and ICC 91, 104, 105; and KNDR process 45, 47–8, 49–50, 55–6; meets with Condaleeza Rice 55; and ministerial suspensions 77–8; and nominations 78; and Special Tribunal 90; *see also* Orange Democratic Movement (ODM)

Office of the High Commissioner for
  Human Rights (OHCHR) 25, 27, 32, 37
Okello, Duncan 38
Ongeri, Samuel 50, 77
Operation Return Home 80–1
Orange Democratic Movement (ODM):
  and Cabinet suspensions 78; and CIPEV
  report 87; and constitutional reform
  82–3; and election campaign 36; and
  General Election (2007) 20, 21, 22–3,
  30; and ICC 93–4, 104; and KNDR
  process 48, 50, 51–2, 53–6; and post-
  election violence 23–5, 26–7, 28, 93–4;
  and power-sharing 53–6

Panel of Eminent Africans: and cabinet
  problem 77, 78; formal negotiations
  begin 50–2; importance of in mediation
  process 56–60; and KNDR process
  48–60; members of 48, 53–4, 55; and
  Waki List 86
Party of National Unity (PNU): and
  CIPEV report 87; and constitutional
  reform 82–3, 95; and election campaign
  36; and General Election (2007) 20, 21,
  22, 23, 30, 52; and ICC 93–4, 104; and
  KNDR process 48, 50, 51–4, 58–9; and
  post-election violence 23–4, 25–6, 93–4;
  and power-sharing 53–6
party primaries 36
Pillar III 10, 60
police: Ali, Mohammed Hussein 22, 37,
  79, 80, 93, 94; and CIPEV report 85;
  and continuing insecurity 79–80;
  corruption 33; partiality of 27; and post-
  election violence 26–7; 94; and pre-
  election violence 37; reform 80
post-election violence *see* violence, post-
  election
pre-poll preparedness 37–8
prevention of atrocities 3, 4–5, 6, 8, 60;
  Agenda Item 4 61–5, 76, 77, 78, 84; *see
  also* Responsibility to Protect (R2P)
Principles of Partnership of the Coalition
  Government 55–6, 61
privatisation of violence 31–2
public gatherings ban 23, 24, 52

R2P *see* Responsibility to Protect (R2P)
radio broadcasts 25, 36, 93, 108
Ranneberger, Michael 58
Red Cross 27, 29, 50, 51, 80
referendum, constitutional 20–1, 63, 82–3,
  95

Regional Parliamentarians of the Great
  Lakes 29
reprisal attacks 25–6
Responsibility to Protect (R2P): as
  academic subject 5; compromises within
  129–30; conceptual development of 46;
  criticisms of 5, 56–7; evolution of 2–5,
  129; expectations of 130–1; Kenya as
  model for 10–11, 56–60; perception of
  130; relationship with ICC 8–10, 11–12,
  129; and state cooperation 129; tensions
  within 129–30; three protection
  responsibilities 3, 9–10; threshold for
  intervention 4; and UN Security Council
  130; UN Special Adviser 46; *see also*
  KNDR process
Responsibility to Protect Working Group 8
Responsibility While Protecting 5
Rice, Condaleeza 55
Rice, Susan 47
Rift Valley province 24–5, 32
rigging 22–3, 64
Rome Statute 5–6, 7, 8–9, 89, 102, 105,
  111, 112
Rudi Nyumbani 80–1
Ruto, William: 'alliance of the accused'
  105–6, 110; and constitutional
  referendum 82; and General Election
  (2013) 1, 105–6, 107, 109–10; and ICC
  94, 101, 104, 105–6, 109–10; 111, 112,
  115, 119; and KNDR 50; and post-
  election violence 87, 89, 93–4;
  suspension of 77; trial of 112, 115, 119
Rwanda 2, 6, 30, 39

Sahnoun, Mohamed 3, 60
Sang, Joshua Arap 25, 93–4, 108, 115,
  118, 119
security services 24, 26–7, 37, 79–80
self-defence 25–6
Sihanya, Ben 38
Song, Sang-Hyun 6
South Consulting 64, 92
sovereignty issues 2–3, 12, 13, 56–7, 106,
  111, 120, 128, 129
Special Tribunal for Kenya (STK) 76, 85,
  87–91
Special Tribunal for Kenya Bill 88–9
Status Conference for Kenyatta 115–17
Sudan 83–4
Supreme Court, Kenyan 1, 108
suspension of ministers 77–8

tallying process 21, 22–3, 35, 52–3, 108

Tanzania 48, 55
taxonomy of interests 38
tourism 28
transport links 28
Truth, Justice and Reconciliation Commission (TJRC) 62, 89–90, 91–2
Tutu, Desmond 47, 48

Uganda 27, 28, 48, 49
Ugandan Red Cross 27
UN Department of Political Affairs 52
UN Development Programme 49, 51
UN High Commissioner for Human Rights 47
UN Human Rights Council 33, 79
UN Secretary General 46, 47, 52
UN Security Council 2, 4, 7, 47, 103–4, 105, 129–30
UN Special Advisor on the Prevention of Genocide 46, 47, 59, 107, 128
UN Special Advisor on R2P 10
UN Special Rapporteur on Extra-judicial Killings 79–80, 113
United Kingdom 29, 58, 102, 103
United Nations: and background to R2P 2–4; headquarters in Kenya 28–9; humanitarian aid to Kenya 29; and ICC 7, 9–10; and impunity 33; World Summit (2005) 3–4, 8–9, 10, 129
United States 4–5, 29, 35, 38, 47, 48, 52, 58, 64, 103, 106, 110
UWIANO 83

violence, post-election: and Coalition 79; and Commission of Inquiry into Post-Election Violence (CIPEV) 13, 62, 64, 76, 84–7, 113, 131; and domestic prosecution 103; economic impact of 28, 29; ethnic dimension to 23; excessive police force 26–7; Government response to 37; and ICC 101–21; impact of 27–30; and international actors 37–8, 131; international impact of 28–9; and Kenyatta, Uhuru 93, 94, 127–8; and Kibaki, Mwai 23–4, 33, 51; and ODM 23–5, 26–7, 28, 93–4; organised violence 24–5; and outstanding criminal cases 127–8; patterns of 23–7; and PNU 23–4, 25–6, 93–4; pre-poll 37; predictability of 34–8; and preventing recurrence of violence 61–3; privatisation of 31–2; prosecution of perpetrators 84–91, 101–6, 110–21; reprisal attacks 25–6; and Ruto, William 87, 89, 93–4; spontaneous 23–4; underlying causes of 30–4, 61–3; unfolding of 23–7

Wachira, George 30
Wagalla massacre (1984) 33
Waki List 86, 87, 89
Waki, Philip 85
Waki Commission/Report (CIPEV report) 84–7, 88, 113–14
Wako, Amos 77–8, 79, 114
Wetangula, Moses 58–9
witness intimidation 104, 113–15, 116, 117
Witness Protection Act 2006 113
Witness Protection (Amendment) Bill 2010 114–15
witness protection programme 79, 86, 113
World Summit (2005) 3–4, 8–9, 10, 129